Re-envisioning Landscape /Architecture

Catherine Spellman, ed.

G000061201

Actar

In memory of Enric Miralles and Peter Smithson

It is impossible to deny the urban condition: it is the setting for most of our loves and hates, it underscores our language of reference for our daily actions, and it is so often present in this book. Only a few weeks ago, when I was at last persuaded to scratch around in the deeper Californian desert, I was always conscious of the minutiae that referred to each other as fragments of human interaction: tracks, markers, remnants, cuttings, foldings—shadows even. Indeed, I was reassured by them, being the creature that I am: nurtured in damp valleys that have been overlaid twenty or a hundred times by wind, husbandry, battles, greed, or the occasional good idea and riddled by lost codes of association or interdependence over which poets become lyrical and economists become ever-so-slightly silly. To a North European, the level of indulgence that was encouraged by Simon Schama's *Landscape and Memory* (published seven years ago) sustained one's creative cynicism with all its tales of strange doings in the forest and reminders of the general hocus-pocus that serves as history in an overlaid and over-ripe culture. It suggested a love-hate relationship towards nature and whatever lurked over the dark and fragmented horizon. It even revealed a despotic instinct in the bosom of the most modest lupine grower.

But here, with her re-envisionaries, Catherine Spellman has found a pre-dominantly American collection of sensitive observers. Fortunately without the opportunity of our indulgence, without the fallback upon all those layers—so they read to me as "fresh." Dare I even say as "innocent?" As if, stripped of that old-world laziness, they can contemplate the first (or at most, second) coming of tracks, shelters, plantations onto virgin soil as an adventure. Their eyes are pleased with the simple lines of demarcation or of the horizon line; they are delighted with the first ambiguities between town or turf. In the process they may have rediscovered architecture.

The new architecture celebrates the fold-over of contrived surface with grasped surface. The new sensibility is toward terrain rather than patches or pockets. There is even a search for peace without escape—difficult for one to imagine amongst the chatter of an old city.

So I think that I may have caught the sniff of the book: they're *Romantics* these academics and designers who purport to explain significant motives and syndromes (as academics must) or references and inspirations (as designers seem to think they should). Assuming that landscape is too tricky a concept to act purely as an escape-territory from that of the city, it seems more interesting to involve it as a carrier for a series of notions about intervention.

For me, it becomes even more intriguing if we pull the vegetal towards the artificial and the fertile towards the urban but in the end, to find in Will Bruder's words "the magic of a place discovered": now *that's* architecture.

An image that captures several relationships that *Re-envisioning Landscape/ Architecture* suggests might be evoked by the montage of a hand and a mitten. The hand is photographed, the mitten is real. One or the other could be thought of as architecture or landscape. The relationship is one of shaking hands. The hand presumably would fit into the mitten; as it is shown, it is holding on to or perhaps being held by the mitten. The background is black and white paper. The hand emerges from the white; the mitten submerges into the black. They come together at the line that divides the montage into half, with the mitten crossing the boundary between the white and the black. We know from association and experience that the mitten has a function, that it is made by the hand and serves to warm the hand. We know that the mitten fulfills its function if it fits the size and shape of the hand and if the air surrounding it is cool. We can also read how the montage is made. The paper is cut and the mitten is slipped in-between the folds. In this fit with the hand, the mitten is given a new meaning. Here the author of the montage is using the mitten to convey an idea about the relationship between an object and its context (it could be said between an architecture and its landscape), the way we perceive that relationship, the method with which it is made, and the technology used to make it.

To envision is to imagine something that is not in existence by forming a picture of it in your mind. *Re-envisioning Landscape/Architecture* suggests that the relationship between landscape and architecture might be imagined over and over again, in such a way that each is defined less as a quantifiable object and more as an idea, a way of seeing, act of making, and way of engaging culture and society. Within the *Re-envisioning Landscape/Architecture* project, the terms *landscape* and *architecture* are used in a number of multifaceted and interwoven ways. For example, landscape sometimes recalls images of a pastoral scene, the arrangement of natural features to allow for a particular type of habitation or a particular phenomenal quality that gives identity to place. Architecture infers the organization of material to create form, the making of structures to house human activities, or the interpretation of place through a particular body of ideas. Certainly the meaning of these terms can be found to overlap, and the relationship between them can most often be described as complex, challenging, or changing. At specific times, in distinct places, and under different circumstances this relationship will take different forms. For example, sometimes a harmonic balance may be sought between the shape of the landscape and that of architecture; or a critical manipulation of the ephemeral qualities of the landscape, such as the light, air, or time, may unite an architecture to its landscape; or the two may be placed in a strong contrast to one another, uniting landscape and architecture through the tension of juxtaposition. In any case, the landscape/architecture relationship is one that offers a multitude of possibilities and is constantly shifting, developing, and transforming. *Re-envisioning Landscape/Architecture* attempts to imagine this relationship in its many forms and it seeks to give it definition without exactly defining it.

Re-envisioning Landscape/Architecture began in a discussion with my colleague from the School of Landscape Architecture and Planning, Laurel McSherry. We found that we shared a concern for the integration of landscape into design, a desire to bridge the gap between our respective disciplines, and the opinion that within practice and education we needed to profoundly rethink our relationship to what could be considered Nature. At one time our respective disciplines —landscape and architecture—were considered one and the same. The architect's responsibility continued beyond the building envelope to include the site, the neighborhood, and the city that it was a part of. Today, these responsibilities are separated into distinct disciplines that often do not consider the other in their design process or in their pedagogical pursuits. Our hope was that through a series of projects entitled *Re-envisioning Landscape/Architecture*, we could inspire a resurgence of communication between the disciplines through a sharing of ideas, projects, and pedagogics that make connections between the two.

The initial Re-envisioning project was a symposium held in the fall of 1998. Funding for the symposium was made possible with a grant from the Graham Foundation for Advanced Studies in the Fine Arts, funds from the Schools of Architecture and Planning and Landscape Architecture and the Herberger Center for Design Excellence at Arizona State University. The symposium intended to expand on and contribute to current knowledge in architecture and landscape architectural design education; offer new models for collaboration among academics, practitioners, and the public; and cultivate intelligent public awareness and participation in design and planning processes. Eight speakers were invited to the symposium: Christine Boyer, Will Bruder, David Heymann, Richard Haag, Linda Jewell, Charles Menefee, Götz Stöckmann, and Peter Waldman. Together they represented positions in design education, practice, history, theory, and criticism. Essays by these authors in the *Re-envisioning Landscape/Architecture* book are revised versions of the presentations made at this symposium.

In considering the book as a project separate from the symposium, I felt that it was appropriate to broaden the base of the collection, expanding views and opinions on the subject. A second source of essays for the book comes from the lecture series that the School of Architecture at Arizona State University sponsors each academic year. The series "In Response to Context," "Directing Architecture," and "Re-envisioning Landscape/Architecture," have each in their own way touched on issues relevant to discussions between landscape and architecture. From these series an additional sixteen authors were invited to rework their original lectures into essays for the collection in this book. They are Nan Ellin, Coy Howard, Alberto Kalach, Mark Klett, Martha LaGess, Bruce

Lindsey, Darren Petrucci, Alessandra Ponte, Albert Pope, Mary-Ann Ray and Robert Mangurian, Laurel McSherry, Michael Rotondi, Peter Smithson, Achim Wollscheid, and myself.

The essays in this book are intentionally varied and various, offering a diverse assortment of perceptions, thoughts, examples, comments, histories, and innovations about the relationship between landscape and architecture. The authors offer many perspectives on and definitions for these two disciplines, sometimes they are explicit and in other instances they are more obscure and open to interpretation and creative reading. A close coordination of ideas between the authors was not attempted; rather I wanted the book to be a collection of individual *re-envisionings* around the subject. The essays are organized in such a way to emphasize difference and variety. Having said this, there are several threads that run through them.

One may be summarized as a focus on the way people think about, understand, rationalize, or form mental relationships between landscape and architecture. Processes of knowing and perceiving space, place, and thought underline several of the essays in this collection. This thread, for example, is laid out in Christine Boyer's essay "Cognitive Landscapes," which introduces landscape/architecture to the cognitive sciences by focusing on how computers, and consequently people, extract and evoke meaning while looking, reading, writing, and talking. The essay argues that landscape/architecture attribute subjective meanings, perceptions, and memory to the natural environment; it also questions how meaning is interpreted and translated by design. Coy Howard's essay "The Messy Middle" discusses the conceptual and philosophical attributes of pairing, coupling, and being in the position between oppositional forces. He makes an argument for diversity, embracing inclusion and addressing the cultural concerns of the public. The essay "Topographic Memory," by Bruce Lindsey considers topography remembered as a form of knowledge. "This kind of knowing," Lindsey suggests, "is generally felt before it is thought and sets the context for our models of mind which structure our imaginations." The essay "Objects of Attention" by Laurel McSherry suggests how place is made meaningful through experience and time. In a poetic narrative McSherry questions how landscapes hold and give up memory, how they are similar and different from architecture, and how they inspire us to make connection to place. Charles Menefee's piece "Constructed Intention: An Architecture of Place" proposes that there is no conceptual distinction that readily separates the realms of architecture and landscape. The essay explores a series of issues that unite the two through a glimpse at the Bendons Alley house in Charleston, South Carolina.

The development of strategies for looking at, interpreting, and making place unite a second grouping of essays, which mostly use actual projects to illustrate their thoughts and methods. For example in the essay "It's All One Thing," Michael Rotondi explains the process of working with the Lakota Indians to plan their new campus for Sinte Gleska University. Traditionally the Lakota knew all aspects of their landscape, where everything in it and on it existed in a dynamic balance based on reciprocity and respect. Peter Smithson's essay "Empooling" explains how the formation of buildings can carry with it an "empooling of space-between," similar to ocean tidal pools where what is within that space-between seems extraordinarily vivid. Behind this parallel lies the realization that the focus of attention has shifted from the building as object to its action on the special shaping of the territory. The essay uses the Smithsons' work at the Tecta Factory in Lauenforde, Germany, to illustrate the idea of empoolment. My own essay "Reveries with Water" discusses issues of context in reference to a specific site and series of design interventions that explore the relationship between oneiric and material phenomena in the making of architecture. Mary-Ann Ray and Robert Mangurian's essay "City Proposals: 29 Drawings for East West Hollywood" is a series of speculative interventions for east West Hollywood, relaying some thoughts on the physical situation and possible future of the city. Martha LaGess's essay "Themes of the Architectural Meta-Project" looks at questions of representation in architecture through a study of the construction document. The essay argues that representation was once viewed as an entirely passive carrier of information about the world and today it has an active role in constructing people's view of the world. Peter Waldman's essay "Semper Fidelis: On Numbers in the Night" looks at his project Parcel X in North Garden, Virginia, to consider a process of design that starts with reading site as a first resource in the most visceral of terms. The essay "Projects and Interpretations: Architectural Strategies of Enric Miralles" defines several themes developed by Miralles in his work. The essay combines commentary taken from several contemporary authors , my memories of conversations with him, and my own impressions of the work.

The third thread discusses the inherent connections existing between nature and urbanism. These essays weave together ideas that are varied in scale and scope.

For example, Albert Pope's essay "Last Horizon" offers a comprehensive and insightful review of the shifting relationship between the urban and the natural. The essay looks at how the urban and the natural, integrated in their meaning, are mirrored by an extraordinary transformation of urbanism in the 1950s. The essay shows how the radical fragmentations at work in both the urban and the natural describe a singular continuum or "world" in formation at the leading edge of urban construction. With a focused discussion of a single project, David Heymann in his essay "Terrors and Pleasures of the (New) Automaton" examines strategies for making nature in the public realm. The essay uses the Cockrell Butterfly Center (1994), a glass-enclosed rain forest at Houston's Museum of Natural Science, to question the authenticity of what we consider natural. Underlying the essay is an interest in the broad shift toward a phenomenal definition of nature that has occurred in the "after" Modern. Darren Petrucci's essay "Stripscape," develops a series of strategies and tactics for urban renewal that offer an innovative and inspired reading of the difficulties of unsightly commercial corridors. At the scale of urban planning, Alberto Kalach's essay "The Return to a Lacustrian City" looks at the problems of unchecked urban growth that ignore the natural environment, in particular the water environment of Mexico City. The essay explains a hydrological rescue plan that considers the city's ecological, economic, and social benefits.

The fourth thread that runs through several of the essays addresses issues of history and culture in respect to the relationship between landscape and architecture. How we live and how that is transmitted from one generation to the next underlines the intentions in many of these essays. For example, Nan Ellin's essay "A Vulnerable Urbanism," emphasizes process over product in the planning of urban environments. The essay eloquently defines vulnerability as "an openness towards and acceptance of our human qualities along with a certain relinquishing of control, an embracing of our shadows, and recognizing change as the only constant." Alessandra Ponte's photo essay "Testing Homes for America," illustrates through vivid example, how culture is inextricably connected to place and, therefore, unites landscape, architecture, and culture. These provoking images show how collective thought influences place. Linda Jewell's essay "The American Outdoor Theater: A Voice for the Landscape in the Collaboration of Site and Structure" introduces culture through a historical survey of the American outdoor theater. These theaters provide inspirational models for how structures can more convincingly connect with the earth, sky, and surrounding landscape to demonstrate that human culture and nature can enhance each other. "The Magic of a Place Discovered" by Will Bruder surveys examples of architecture from modernism that draw on and contribute to the making of an integrated landscape/architecture. In addition to the work of Wright, Aalto, Goff, Scarpa, and Soleri, Bruder reviews several of his own projects that bring landscape and architecture together with thought and intention. Mark Klett's essay, "The Third View Project" documents changes in the American Western landscape through photography and electronic media. The rephotographs of the existing images show how changes in culture affect landscape. The "Environment Shifted" by Götz Stöckmann and Achim Wollscheid records a conversation between architect and artist that revolves around interpretations of meaning in the environment, context, and the place of history in landscape.

To conclude, the essays collected here offer many interpretations and possibilities for the relationship between architecture and landscape. What they hold in common is an assumption that this relationship should be considered at every stage in the design process, at every negotiation between realms of thought, and whenever culture and place are to be incorporated with understanding and meaning. The collection is based in a belief that the landscape/architecture relationship is at the center of all inspired design, therefore, in one way or another each essay addresses how this relationship is created, nurtured, and maintained to ensure the making of integrated design work. Together these essays infer the importance of time, experience, and process in the forming of a solid landscape/architecture relationship. All the authors, directly or indirectly, imply that the landscape/architecture relationship emphasizes the importance of projects over objects, experience and involvement over disengaged observation. Ultimately, the collection suggests that how we think, act, make, remember, or convey our experiences with landscape and architecture together will determine how we are able to re-envision its form and meaning in our own work. The book claims that the process of uniting landscape and architecture is layered and inclusive. It is about imagining and allowing experience to influence design.

Catherine Spellman, editor

Cognitive Landscapes
M. Christine Boyer

The "/" between "landscape/architecture" in the title generates awareness that there will be a border metaphor at the core of these discussions. How to bridge the gap—a gap that never seems to be closed—between architecture and landscape? How to frame anew or re-envision a set of crucial interactions: landscape/cityscape, nature/technology, subject/object, meaning/nonmeaning. In order to address this crossing, attention is shifted momentarily away from the boundary between landscape/architecture to another boundary between landscape architecture and the cognitive sciences [fig.1]. There is little awareness of the cognitive sciences among architects, landscape architects, or urbanists, for they seldom question how computers and subsequently people think, extract, and evoke meaning while looking, reading, writing, and talking. And yet landscape architecture, it is argued here, is all about cognition. Even though landscape architects seldom address the subject directly, they nevertheless attribute subjective meanings, perceptions, and memory to the natural environment. Yet questions abound with respect to the meaning of these attributions.

For example, how are romantic and nostalgic feelings engendered by a landscape view? Is nature always to be a place of escape, a return to the garden of Eden, or a restorative place full of salvation? How does a garden tell stories? How do landscapes communicate values of harmony, repose, equilibrium, and orientation? How are memory and gardens or landscapes structured alike? Indeed why is memory—or the concept of remembrance—even related to nature? Surely it goes far beyond the placement of memorials in parks and the traditional association of death with the natural environment. Must the spectator be immersed in nature for it to communicate its message? Can the viewer also relate to the environment through photography, the cinema, and

[Fig.1] Magritte, *The Human Condition*, (1934). In this painting the viewer sees an easel standing in front of a window on which rests a painting depicting part of the landscape which is blocked from view by both the easel and the painting. Magritte is suggesting that whatever we perceive to be reality, or landscape in this case, is already framed by preconceived structures such as windows, doors, mirrors.
© Rene Magritte, VEGAP, Barcelona 2003

written texts? And might these representational forms reflect back on the manner in which landscapes are designed and experienced [fig.2]?

This paper explores answers to some of these questions by focusing on four different examples of cognition and landscape architecture. First, it explores frame-like modes of perception by juxtaposing Marvin Minsky's "A Framework of Representing Knowledge" (1974) against theories of the picturesque landscape. Second, it explores the issue of associative memory and the surrealist investigation of Parc Buttes-Chaumont in Aragon's *Paris Peasant* (1924). Third, it discusses cognition and the centrality of symbols in Gygory Kepes' *The New Landscape in Art and Science* (1954) and Kevin Lynch's *The Image of the City* (1960). Finally, the effect of computers on the production of new forms of visual knowledge is examined and explored in the proposal of Rem Koolhaas and OMA for Parc de la Villette, Paris (1983) as it is represented in Rem Koolhaas and Bruce Mau's *S,M,L,XL* (1995).

1 Models of cognition: the symbolic paradigm and connectionist mode

Recognizing the explosive growth of information and research and how it affected knowledge and memory, Vanevar Bush in 1945 was concerned that our ability to process information had limitations. Although the human processor was likened to that of an information machine or computer, Bush noted, the human mind works by associations, not alphabetically.

"With one item in its grasp, it snaps instantly to the next that is suggested by the association of thoughts, in accordance with some intricate web of trails carried by the cells of the brain. It has other characteristics, of course; trails that are not frequently followed are prone to fade, items are not fully permanent, memory is transitory. Yet the speed of action, the intricacy of trails, the detail of mental pictures, is awe-inspiring beyond all else in nature."[1]

The classical art of memory gives us some insight into Vanevar Bush's associative structures of information. It also involves a process of visualization based on the storage and retrieval of symbols. The ancient Greeks developed a system of artificial memory by manipulating a set of places and icons in the mind. Thinking of the rooms of a house as a mental picture or template, the rooms formed a series to be remembered in a particular order. Striking images or beautiful icons were associated with things that needed to be remembered

[Fig.2] Peter Walker, *Burnett Park* taken from *Peter Walker: Experiments in Gesture, Seriality and Flatness,* Linda Jewell, editor, Rizzoli Publications, New York, 1990, page 23.
© Peter Walker, VEGAP, Barcelona 2003.

and these stored in different rooms of the house. A mental stroll through the sequentially ordered places enabled the user to recall the images and icons stored in each place, and these in turn acted as prompts to remember what they represented. The storage and retrievable of symbols from memory and their transformation according to an established set of rules gave rise in the cognitive sciences to the symbolic paradigm.[2]

But there is also another form of memory: the combinatorial art of Raymond Lull. He believed that there were certain basic principles of knowledge, and that by exhausting every combinatorial arrangement, the mind could eventually explore all this terrain. He used various geometrical figures to explain his ideas: words arranged in a circle and lines connecting each word to all the others. Or he developed a series of concentric circles that rotated about a central axis—various permutations of the concepts stored around the circles would stimulate the mind to make innumerable associations. Meditating on these bizarre combinations enabled the mind to wander off in curious directions. While still based on the manipulation of symbols, this model of memory stressed the network of linkages, or how items are connected to each other, and gives rise to connectionist modes of cognition.

Thus these two models of memory represent two different models of cognition. Conventional models take cognition to be the manipulation of symbols in accordance with pre-existing combinatorial rules like the classical art of memory. They assume that cognitive information flows in a linear and sequential manner and that all new knowledge is stored according to the arrangements determined by a program stored in memory. Computers are based on these conventional models—the rules that govern operations are written in propositional forms that manipulate symbols. These are stored inside a computer memory and hence the distinctions between software/hardware and processor/memory. The computer inputs the symbols into memory, combines and reorganizes them into symbolic structures, erases them, outputs them, compares patterns of symbols for similarities or difference, and branches on the outcome of such tests.

Connections models, on the other hand, spread cognitive activities across networks of interconnected units like Lull's combinatorial model of memory. The connections, rather than the units per se, hold the pivotal role in the functioning of the network. In this case information flows synchronically and diachronically across a series of connections in the network. Cognitive processes are assumed to be distributed and parallel, not linear and causal. Information is not locatable but stored in the connections or links between units and distributed across the network. Memory in this case becomes the effect of relationships or differences between connections. Thus connections models move away from a model of memory that locates symbols in specific storage spaces: it does not look for memory traces that are stored in specific locations and retrieved from those locations.

Having established a link between the arts of memory, models of cognition, and computers, the questions arises of how this is related to the disjunction between landscape/architecture and the crossing of borders between the two?

2 Frame-like modes of perception

Marvin Minsky in "A Framework for Representing Knowledge" (1974) considered that mental images were active structures, or frames, which help us organize reality. He wrote: "Whenever one encounters a new situation (or makes a substantial change in one's viewpoint) one selects from memory a substantial structure called a frame: a remembered framework to be adapted to fit reality by changing details as necessary. A frame is a data-structure for representing a stereotypical situation, like being in a certain kind of room, or going to a child's birthday party. Attached to each frame are several kinds of information. Some of this information is about how to use the frame. Some is about what one can expect to happen next. Some is about what to do if these expectations are not confirmed."[3]

Minsky's frames or schema revolve around memory—an individual selects a remembered framework, but there is also a geographical analogy—a network of places that enables the rememberer to move from one frame to another. Maps and address books are tools that manage access to stored places. Clearly this has a relationship to the classical art of memory, but it can also be linked to theories of the picturesque landscape and questions of how the mind processes what is looked at in the landscape.

For example, Thomas Whately, in *Observations on Modern Gardening* (London 1770) recommends that the gardener must know how to select and discover the advantages of place, how to correct its defects and improve its beauties.[4] The gardener, furthermore, is a scenographer, offering carefully arranged scenes to the spectator, scenes that illicit specific sensations. Here is Whately's description of the garden at Dovedale:

The whole has the air of enchantment; the perpetual shifting of the scenes; the quick transitions; the total changes; then the forms all around, grotesque as chance can cast, wild as nature can produce, and various as imagination can invent; the force which seems to have been exerted to place some of the rocks where they are now fixed immovable; the magick (sic) by which others appear still to be suspended; the dark caverns; the illuminated recesses; the fleating (sic) shadows, and the gleams of light glancing on the sides, or trembling on the stream; and the loneliness and the stillness of the place, all crouding (sic) together on the mind, almost to realize the ideas which naturally present themselves in this region of romance and of fancy.[5]

Buildings were carefully placed in the landscape to excite the imagination, for Whately believed their effects to be instantaneous. Ruins, either natural or fictitious, were particularly useful for "All remains excite an enquiry into the former state of the edifice, and fix the mind in a contemplation on the use it was applied to; besides the characters expressed by their style and position, they suggest ideas which would not arise from the buildings if entire."[6] Whately was primarily concerned with the spectator's perception of the garden. He was delving in the realm of cognition: the experience of the various scenes in a walk, the emotions these scenes evoked, and the impressions that triggered the imagination.

A few decades later, William Derham's *Physico-Theology* (1813) would explain how objects were made more striking to the eye if the view was framed with the hands.[7] This was soon applied to viewing a landscape painting. So it was claimed "one sees a picture much stronger when the sidelights are broken all round by a proper holding up of the hands."[8] The picturesque tourist turned this "framing" into conventions: talking of "side-screens," "off skips," and "select distances." They went in search of their prey, the natural landscape, armed with a convex mirror called the Claude Glass. Coleridge noted how this device influenced perception. "In the country, all around us smile Good and Beauty—and the Images of this divine kalokayaton are miniaturized on the mind of the beholder, as a Landscape in a Convex Mirror."[9] The Claude Glass was a portable means of realizing an idealized landscape that conformed to picturesque principles. Viewing a miniaturized landscape through the flattening effects of its mirror-image made these landscape forms, as William Gilpin remarked, "something like the scenes of a playhouse, retiring behind each other."[10] In fact, the picturesque garden was composed in a series of framed vistas, "from the line that leads to the house, the foreground is the meadow, the mid-ground a winding stream with clumps and trees scattered about it, and the background is the rising of the hill and the line of trees to the ruined church."[11]

The picturesque frame is not dissimilar to Minsky's frames, both are information-processing structures of perception and not physical frames.[12] The picturesque frame involved a series of conventions: viewers expected to view the scenery of their England with a native flavor—it was a process of cultural self-education, stripped of all the supposed authority that Greek and Roman works of art imposed. Framed according to pastoral expectations, these scenes were meant to be an escape from the complexities of city life, a retreat into images of a golden age and of childhood innocence. In this ideally framed environment, life was sustained by Nature's bounty.[13]

The problem then is how to see the world, nature, and the land, when it is mediated by a framed perspective. The video artist Bill Viola remarked on the problem of unification between the viewer and the natural landscape when it is inevitably mediated by technology constructed so to limit or frame the world and all of its processes. How can these barriers between the viewer and perception be bridged? Bill Viola noted:

When I was out in the desert, in the South West, in '87, I brought all this equipment—different cameras, telescopes, infra-red cameras, super wide-angle lenses—and I started shooting during the first month. But then I ran into this block which it took me several years to recover from. I was unable to shoot. A lot of the time I was outdoors, sleeping in a tent, in this vast space, and this little thing, the camera, became a limiter. It's not a window on the world. You point it here, and you stand there, at this particular time and you have excluded everything else.

So during that period I couldn't work. I'd pick up the camera and it seemed like a joke that I could even consider that I could reflect the experience of this vast area and the world.[14]

Bill Viola's video work is all about communing with nature—intuiting the imma-nence of divinity in the natural world—opening oneself to the beauty that is the essence of that world. His work is all about the temporal process of perception using video as a medium of light that interacts with other sources of light be they the sun, headlights, fire, a table lamp. Trying to erase the distinction between the viewer and the moment of perception, Viola is also interested in exploring a particular perception of space that is peculiarly American.[15]

3 Associational models of perception

Place and the icons stored there engender associations. But associations may be open-ended; they may be evoked by place rather than found in a place. André Breton took a generative approach to writing. He claimed that automatic writing by paying attention to previously neglected associations was the "true photog-raphy of thought." In the spontaneous association of word and image, place and thought, it was a random generator like the camera, the phonograph, and the typewriter. "We do not have any talent," Breton claimed of his comrades, we are only "simple receptacles of so many echoes, modest recording instruments."[16] Surrealism was also an investigation of method, believing that procedures pro-duced inspiration or enabled discovery. The homonyms available in the word "expérience" (experience and experiment) and "recréation" (fun and re-cre-ation) were crucial. Breton's *Manifesto of Surrealism* (1924) stated the position "the failure of the old systems of reason and logic . . . and the need to find new investigatory procedures."[17]
Perhaps that is why Aragon's essay "A Feeling for Nature at the Buttes-Chaumont," in *Paris Peasant*[18] is often referred to as the occasion to rethink landscape with reference to a Freudian unconscious as well as an antidote to the modernist treatment that imposed functionalist geometries on landscape designs.[19] Living by chance, even going in search of it, the Surrealists felt a great power of enchantment that certain places, certain sights, and everyday objects held over them. This enchantment set up a kind of frisson between the spectator

and the environment, the subject and the object. Aragon was struck by the fact that when men painted they often reproduced on their canvases what their sight could register; they went on voyages in pursuit of that vision, and indeed they even liked gardens. But he was uneasy with what they called a feeling for nature. So he set out to examine this idea of nature, concluding that it was a narrow aesthetic embracing only that from which man was absent. This concept of nature had nothing to do with the mythical conception of the modern world that so attracted him. But then Aragon had to reconsider, for his myths of modernity extended throughout nature and that is why they held power over him for they occasioned the experience of frisson within him (Aragon, 136–38). So he concluded, "the true meaning of the word nature (is) the sense of the external world, and for me the sense of the unconscious . . . . Thus feeling for nature is simply another term for mythical sense" (139–40).

One night in a black mood of boredom, Aragon set out for a stroll with Marcel Noll and André Breton. Having nothing to do, they decided to go to Buttes-Chaumont. There at least, or so they assumed, they would depart on a marvelous hunt, a field of experimentation that might produce innumerable surprises. Theirs was not a retreat into the solitude nature so often promised. They hoped the park was closed for the night, because they sought a world of similarly adventurous and curious spirits who shared the desire to enter this shady forbidden zone and search for its hidden mysteries. They imagined this field of action, this laboratory under cover of night, was the setting for disconcerting scenes and special black dramas. Drunk with open-mindedness they entered the park (147–49).

From an bird's-eye perspective, the park looks "like a nightcap," or so Aragon described, a wedge with its main axis running west to east thrust into the old Quartier du Combat [fig.3]. There follows an entire description for three pages of the landscape plan that Alphand made in the 1860s, the three scenes the park was divided into, the various gates, the variety of elevations and knolls, etc. (151). But the most mysterious of all the forces of nature, Aragon thought, was the night. "The blood of the modern night is a singing light. Night bears tattoos, shifting patters of tattoos upon her breast. Her hair curlers are sparks, and where the smoke trails have just died men are straddling falling stars. The night has whistles and lakes of glimmers. She hangs like a fruit over the earth's coastline, like a haunch of beef in the cities' golden fist" (155).

In the densest part of the darkness of public gardens the desire for open air

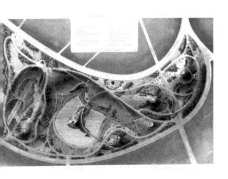

[Fig.3] Adolphe Alphand, plan for Parc de Buttes-Chaumont, Paris taken from *Adolphe Alphand. Les Promenades De Paris,* Princeton Architectural Press, 1984.

and peril, for love and rebellion, were intimately intertwined. "Let us stroll in this decor of desires, this decor filled with mental misdemeanors and with imaginary spasms . . . . The whole of human despair is there in search of pleasure. It is the hour of the frisson which bears an astonishing resemblance to a stroke of black ink. We are delighted to be inkwells" (158–59).

The three plunged into the night following a path towards the place of Violent Death or suicide bridge and then up toward the Belvedere. Aragon noted that many "(m)en pass their lives in the midst of magic precipices without even opening their eyes. They manipulate grim symbols innocently, their ignorant lips unwittingly mouth terrible incantations, phrases like revolvers . . . . After that, what hope for man to become aware of the enchantments that surround him?" (190). Then the path forks, one scene becomes picturesque with a little bridge and lots of scenery while the other view is awe-inspiring, with its cliff dropping straight down to the lake. The two paths meet again at a little Greco-Romantic temple. A grille suddenly blocks the path to the Belvedere. "Run the film backwards, grumbling as it rewinds: labyrinth, belvedere, the two twin footpaths, their farther and turn right" (192). They descend on marbled paving stones that bring back memories from childhood: jumping down staircases or along streets, only touching alternative slabs or stepping on the marble's streaks. And there in front there arises the marvelous gallant and trembling suspension bridge: they followed the sinking footpaths, around the lake with its dozy birds. "Occasionally, André Breton expresses himself in an English of rare elegance. The substance of his dissertation, which is substantially indistinguishable from the substantive air, is an ambiguity established between trees and words, the meadow resembles a limerick . . . and a little later it is Marcel Noll who peers between the gleams of light that crisscross through the fog to discover the charm of extraordinary voyages at the very back of the big grottoes forming nooks . . . along the south-east side of the island" (194).

Aragon's associative model of perception closely resembles dream states and reveals a fascination with intuitive cognition. Yet he wondered if he had an obligation to describe everything and thus lose the reader in the details or in the garden of bad faith? So he confessed, "I began to mingle the landscape with my words. I thought of tracing a map of the mind and, in pursuit of my reflections, proposed a path to the frisson" (198). He sought a spontaneous association between the word and landscape images, for language was an expression of psychic forces bringing the unconscious to the surface. But words could dull as well and fail to provoke the reader's imagination. Like the intervention of a film run backwards, he sought to make previously inaccessible information available and thus changed perception of oneself and the surrounding everyday landscape.

4 Cognition and the symbol processing paradigm

In the 1950s, MIT was a hotbed of investigations into cognitive processes: Norbert Weiner, the father of cybernetics, continued work on his theories of control systems revealing how bodies in motion achieve equilibrium through feedback loops carrying information from the environment back to the object. Noam Chomsky developed his Cartesian linguistics. Fusing symbolic logic with natural language, he studied how thought could be encoded in forms that could be manipulated purely by formal means. Language was construed as a sequence of symbols assembled according to certain prescribed rules or syntax. Meanwhile artificial intelligence experts envisioned the mind to be an information-processing machine, a manipulator of symbols and signs. The brain can acquire, store, and manipulate information. It can reason—by adding new information to its old stock and deriving new information from old—hence it is likened to a computer.

So it is not so surprising to find that Gyorgy Kepes, seeking to bridge the gap between artist and scientist, began to consider how information theories, cybernetic controls, and symbol manipulating processors could be applied to the manner in which the landscape was envisioned. Kepes participated in weekly discussions with Norbert Weiner at MIT in the late 1940s. Weiner's ideas of cybernetics and feedback loops or corrective equilibrium greatly influenced his work. From neurophysicist Warren S. McCulloch, he learned that the capacity to orient oneself in a given environment is based on the ability of the neurological system to discern invariance in continuous transformations. Thus Kepes reasoned, art could aid an individual to achieve a new equilibrium, to rediscover the invariant harmony and equilibrium beneath the constant flux and transformations of life."[20] In the opening statements of *The New Landscape in Art and Science*, Kepes commented, "This book is meant to be looked at more than read. It is a picture book arranged to bring attention to a newly emerged aspect of nature, hitherto invisible but now revealed by science and technology."[21]

The reader is expected "to see" and "to make connections for himself." The method used is text/image juxtapositions and implies the viewer knows how to see and how to fuse verbal communication with visual images. These juxtaposition create, by their interplay, a basic type of experience merging both the character of information and the poetry of images latent in the landscape. They alone tell a connected story. In the twentieth century, or so Kepes argued, we have become lost in an alien, menacing world. There is a "new landscape," a "second nature" defined as man-made environment and revealed by modern science [fig.4]. Appearance of things no longer reveal their true nature, images fake forms, forms cheat functions, functions are robbed of their natural sources. We need to make symbols of the things that naturally surround us, in order that they can evoke emotional responses and stimulate us by their palpable reality. "It is not with tools only that we domesticate our world. Sensed forms, images and symbols are as essential to us as palpable reality in exploring nature for human ends. Distilled from our experience and made our permanent possession, they provide a nexus between man and man and between man and nature. We make a map of our experience patterns, an inner model of the outer world, and we use this to organize our lives. Our natural "environment"—whatever impinges on us from outside—becomes our human "landscape"—a segment of nature fathomed by us and made our home" (Kepes, 18). The industrial landscape of the last 150 years has developed without finding what Walt Whitman called the "primal sanities of nature."

[Fig. 4] Lichtenberg figure, photograph of Prof. A.R.von Hippel, MIT, taken from *The New Landscape in Art and Science*, Gregory Kepes, Paul Theobald and Co., Chicago, 1956.

Our technical wonders have not provided us with the wide visions of harmony and order, but, increasing without plan, have jumbled the basic wealth of the mechanical era into a dazzling kaleidoscopic pattern which shocks and numbs our sensibilities . . . . The modern metropolis, a giant focus of our unsettled world, spreads out upon the land in widening rings of visual disorder. At its core, bludgeoning us with their vulgar images, massive structures blot out open space; industrial areas beyond are dumped with factory buildings and the dingy barracks where we house our poor; the residential fringes are dotted with characterless cottages repeated endlessly. Everywhere smoke and dirt screen out the sun; and our containers, advertisements, commercial entertainment, films, our home furnishings and clothes, our gestures and facial expression mount up to grotesque, formless aggregates lacking sincerity, scale and cleanliness (69).

This is the world that shapes our vision. These distorted environments have robbed us of the power to make our experience coherent. Visual creativity is thus impaired. We need new symbols, or so Kepes argued, to balance the technical landscape with man, to bring it into harmony with the seasons' rhythms, the breadth of the sky, and the resources of the land (70). When unprecedented things confront us, we become disoriented, confused, and shocked. Today, science has made the face of nature alien to us: too much information, too many inventions, and an exploded scale of things have made it imperative that we develop a way to map the world's new configurations with our senses and discover its potentialities for an orderly and secure human life. We need a new vision to bring the outer and inner worlds together, to regain a strengthening contact with nature. "Art and science are ordering activities of the human mind" (22).

Science looks for a pattern to the relations in nature, verifying its statements about natural processes. It collects quantifiable measures and expresses the found order in conceptual terms. Image-making is essential for both art and science. It defines goals, delimits the field of study, and offers models that anticipate the order relations that scientists will discover. "Visually, we judge our relation to the surrounding world through the shapes, sizes, texture and colors reflected into the retinas of our eyes. But we move and what is around us moves—advancing, retreating, expanding, contracting, growing, decaying. On the retina there is a fluid pattern of changing shapes, sizes, and colors: we are able to read these optical metamorphoses" (226).

This is the essence of symbol-making, the transformation of the ceaseless flow of sense data into clearly defined pictures, words, and concepts. "Symbol-making is based on transformations, on the changing of substances or the changing of forms... Today, the key to creative work is symbolic transformation: the translation of direct experience into symbols which sum up experience in communicable form . . . . This means that the traditional concept of an image as a mirror held in front of nature is obsolete. The new patterns are pictures of processes. They reveal hidden movements: images of movement within us and beyond us" (229, 231).

It would not take long before Kepes applied this symbol-making process to the image of the city, for images he believed were the generators of thinking and feeling; they were ordering devices and determined a sense of equilibrium in an environment constantly undergoing change. Already in 1944, Kepes had written: "To grasp spatial relationships and orient oneself in a metropolis today, among the intricate dimensions of streets, subways, elevated trains, and skyscrapers, requires a new way of seeing. The goal is a visual representation in which the most advanced knowledge of space is synchronized with the nature of the plastic experience. Space-time is order, and the image is an 'orderer.' Only the integration of these two aspects of order can make the language of vision what it should be: a vital weapon of progress."[22] Working collaboratively at MIT with Kevin Lynch, the two performed a study between 1954 and 1958 entitled "Perceptual Forms of the City." One of the outcomes would be Kevin Lynch's famous book *Image of the City* (1960).

If the man-made environment is to have an intelligent order, it must be reduced to a symbolic notation system. Its order depends on its imageability. But this model of cognition assumes that the mind is a symbol processing machine, and it leads to a passion for order. In its extreme it implies a separation of abstract symbols from their meaning, and it emphasizes the development of formal languages. All of this development, of course, closely follows the growth of computer/cognitive sciences in the 1950s and 1960s, where it was assumed that the computer was a good basis for understanding how the mind worked. In other words, the mind is considered to be like a computer, it operates according to a set of rules as if it were running a computer program. Thus Lynch analyzed the image of the city, dividing it into a precisely defined lexicon of symbols such as path, node, landmark, and district and developing a set of rules for assembling a well-formed city. Restricting interactions between the individual and the environment to the narrow range provided by its formalized domain, it becomes evident that we need to look beyond logic and the symbol processing paradigm to understand how the mind works and how the landscape/cityscape generates meaning.

5 Visual information and associative modes of perception

The last effect of computers on cognition involves the production of new forms of visual knowledge, new combinations of graphic images, and new manipulations of data constructions or dataspace. This new landscape of connections represents navigable online space where the document or dataspace becomes the form of encounter, and it involves not only representational forms but navigational structures as well. Form therefore entails both the visual representation of information and the organizational structures by which information can be assessed, visited, and explored.

Print places words in space—they are locked into position. A hierarchical series of spatial clues enables the reader to navigate the text. But a digital document is open-ended: edges no longer define its boundaries while the screen constitutes a "wander-ground" of journeys—sites of random or structured encounters where embedded layers in nested chains await excavation. Now it appears that information plus organizational structure plus navigational procedures creates the experience.[23]

Out of this electronically created terrain, information networks, electronic images, and virtual architecture—a new phenomenon has emerged—"the traceable grid" that exists in electronic space. This media volume provides us with a revised understanding of space as a conceptual space of image/word juxtapositions that go far beyond the symbol-processing procedures requested by Kepes and Lynch.[24]

An early example of this conceptual space can be found in the legacy of Robert Smithson. Familiarity with his earth works takes place through their documentation, their reproduction in photographs, films, and books [fig.5]. In his preoccupation with the Site/Nonsite, Smithson would visit a site, document it, and then select "samples" of rubble and rocks from it. These he would transport to a gallery space and display as a nonsite in an arrangement of maps, photographs, analogical samples and verbal captions that referenced the absent but specific site. The documentary information in the gallery site, actually constituted an actual site, while pointing to an abstract landscape somewhere beyond the confining boundaries of the gallery. He transgressed the gallery space with rocks and dirt, he dislocated the relationship between word and thing, he confused the boundary between fact and fiction. His works became an open-ended network of images and themes that traveled through other sites, other works of art, other writings and photographs—a network that opened on the boundless abysses of nature and the self.[25]

Another more recent example of conceptual space between the image and the text can be found in the huge book *S, M, L, XL* authored by Rem Koolhaas and Bruce Mau. This book, these projects, become a data space—a verbal-visual collage of alphabetical dictionary entries running down the margin of pages, juxtaposed with photographs that bleed out to the edge of their pages, juxtaposed against written commentary about projects. Take for example "Congestion Without Matter," OMA's competition project for Parc de la Villette, Paris of 1982: in this "terrain vague" between the greedy needs of the twentieth-century metropolis and the plankton of the suburbs—OMA designed a program that offered "Density without architecture, a culture of 'invisible' congestion."[26]

A series of color bird's-eye views of the model for Parc de la Villette lead the reader into the project. One in particular has a corner insert of Brandinelli's *Adam and Eve* [fig.6]. Is this to remind us of the Garden of Paradise from which we have been expelled, never to return? Elia Zenghelis, the cofounder of OMA, wrote "everything relating to nature, essentially, is doomed to disappearance. We are born, we die, we

[Fig.5] "Quasi-Infinities and the Waning of Space," by Robert Smithson, November 1966, Arts Magazine, taken from *Earthwards, Robert Smithson and Art after Babel,* Gary Shapiro, University of California Press, Berkeley, 1995, page 167.

disappear; only ideas, art, the artificial seem to offer some promise of permanence."[27] A few more pages and dictionary entries begin to appear along the margin juxtaposed with a double page color photographic spread of figures standing
on an open field arranged in a kind of meander [fig.7]. These figures are voters
in South Africa photographed by the Associated Press in 1994. On the margins
continues the third and fourth entries about Lille. The former explains the various
sports fields and walks to be found near the metropolis while the latter describes
the site plan of Eurolille—as a monster encompassing London, Brussels, and Paris.
Liminal defines a time and space betwixt and between meaning and action. And
so on go the entries of Liquefaction, Lite, and Lite City. These definitions and the
photograph appear—at least on the surface—to be accidental juxtaposition, but
they generate and disseminate meaning on their own. Standing in line to vote
are newly emancipated South Africans—just an image of people and landscape,
or a reminder of modernism's project, its emancipation from tradition, from the
tyranny of history and the academies, its social cause, its reforms of the city?
Connections and linkages are important but kept open and indeterminate.

There follow more birds-eye views of the model and more pages that continue the
format: dictionary entries on the left hand side of the page and the description
of La Villette on the right hand side. Finally there is the "Initial Hypothesis," Parc
de la Villette's program was much too large to create a park, in the recognizable
sense of the word. The latter would have provided a replica of nature with some
service facilities dotted about it. Instead this park would be an open ended,
constantly changing and adjusting park, just like the multiplicity and ambiguity
of the dictionary entries that undercut stable and definitive meaning. The park
contains an underlying principle of programmatic indeterminacy: how to combine
on a given field a series of activities that will interact and set off a chain reaction
of new, unpredictable events like those that might be engendered by the chain of
voters in South Africa? Or how to create a social condenser, an architectural trans-
former, based on horizontal strips of congestion that constitute the park?[28]

Horizontal strips and vertical entries set up an investigative process. Look up a
word and consider the information, then transfer the data from margins to site.
The horizontals and verticals establish the artificial confines of a gridded diagram
of space. The grid is the CIAM grille, the graphic notational system that enabled
comparisons to be made on 33 different cities and then projected forward onto
a homogenized and abstract functional city of modernity.[29] But OMA's system

[Fig.6] Image of Parc de la Villete model with corner insert of Bran-dinelli's *Adam and Eve,* taken from *S,M,L,XL,* O.M.A., Rem Koolhaas, Bruce Mau, 010 Publishers, 1995.

[Fig.7] Image of South African voters standing in line to vote, taken from *S,M,L,XL,* O.M.A., Rem Koolhaas, Bruce Mau, 010 Publishers, 1995.

is less rigid than the CIAM grille. It allows for free play, for on top of the grid are layered a network of points and a layer of infrastructure, intended to interact, disorient, blur with, and override elements in other layers. Just as the page layouts do, the reader faces two different projects—an alphabetical listing of words and an abstract layering of grids and points—and acknowledges the random play between them. This is not a designed landscape but a framework capable of absorbing an endless series of further meanings. It offers a spatial adventure derived from the alphabet. As Michel Foucault noted "the use of the alphabet as an arbitrary but efficacious encyclopedic order does not appear until the second half of the seventeenth century."[30] Its appearance, however, was revolutionary as it recast the very order of the universe by the way it linked words together and arranged them in space. There was an attempt to spatialize knowledge according to the perfect form of the circle and according to the multiple and dividing form of the tree. And Roland Barthes proclaimed, "Of the glossary, I keep only its most formal principle; the order of its units. This order, however, can be mischievous: it sometimes produces effects of meaning; and if these effects are not desired, the alphabet must be broken up to the advantage of a superior rule; that of the breach (heterology): to keep a meaning from 'taking.'"[31]

And so the appearance of lists, fragments, and associations as an ordering of experience performed on specific frames and handed down by habitual patterns of data assembled in alphabetical array yet drawn to experimentation and performance. Like the planes and layers of Parc de la Villette, the text shifts about from objective project description to personal anecdotes, from random facts to technical details. It generates a discourse in tension between objects and ground plane, between artifice and nature, between this space and that space. It is in the end an encounter, an adventure, a game, a shifting ground between architecture and landscape. This data space begins to play with the meaning system of architecture/landscape crossing over boundaries in both directions. It is a meaning system that constantly changes as it sets up a play between past and present forms, establishing ambivalent, open-ended conundrums and analogies that make it impossible to assign fixed meanings and allow form to emerge from the juxtapositions.

Notes

[1] Vanevar Bush, "As We May Think" *Atlantic Monthly* (July 1945). Quoted in Peter Storkerson and Janine Wong, "Hypertexts & The Art of Memory," *Visible Language* 31, 2 (1997): 134–5.

[2] William Bechtel and Adele Abrahamsen, *Connectionism and the Mind* (Cambridge, Mass: Basil Blackwell, 1991).

[3] Marvin Minsky, "A Framework for Representing Knowledge" in *The Psychology of Computer Vision*, ed. P. H. Winston (New York: McGraw Hill, 1975): 211–77. Quoted in Klaus Bartels, "The Box of Digital Images: The World as Computer Theater," *Diogenes* 41, no. 3 (1993): 50.

[4] Thomas Whately, *Observations on Modern Gardening* (London: T. Payne, 1770): 1–2. All quotations and discussion of Whately come from Katja Grillner, "Reality Bites: Real, Represented and Imaginary in the 18th-Century Landscape Garden," (unpublished paper, "Architecture-Imagining a Common Ground for Theory and Practice," University of Pennsylvania. Ph.D. Symposium, March 30, 1997).

[5] Whately, *Observations on Modern Gardening*: 114–15.

[6] Ibid., 131.

[7] Malcolm Andrews, *The Search for the Picturesque* (Stanford: Stanford University Press, 1989): 29.

[8] Ibid., 29.

[9] Ibid., footnote, 70. Gilpin noted that using a Claude Glass to view the countryside seen through the carriage window produced "A succession of high-coloured pictures . . . continually gliding before the eye. They are like the visions of the imagination; or the brilliant landscapes of a dream. Forms, and colours, in brightest array, fleet before us; and if the transient glance of a good composition happen to unite with them, we should give any price to fix, and appropriate the scene." By using different tinted glasses, moreover, the tourist could change the scenery altering time of day or the seasons. Mists, hot air, could create a tonal unity to angular landscapes and dissolve horizon lines. William Gilpin's tour-book *Observations on the River Wye* (1782) suggested that tourists go in pursuit of picturesque beauty. Many of the natural scenes along the River Wye were, in Gilpin's judgment remarkably correct, they were pictures (Andrews, 56). Rivers scenery was broken down into four parts: "the area, which is the river itself-, the tow side-screens, which are the opposite banks, and mark the perspective; and the

front-screen, which points out the winding of the rive." (Andrews, 89). Composed in simple parts, the Wye Valley nevertheless gave rise to an infinite variety of stage-set instantaneously arranged as the boat smoothly glided through them.

[10] Ibid.

[11] Ibid., 51.

[12] Bartels, "The Box of Digital Images": 61.

[13] Andrews, *The Search for the Picturesque.*

[14] Bill Viola. Quoted by Sean Cubitt, "On Interpretation: Bill Viola's The Passing," *Screen* 38, 2 (Summer, 1985): 117–18.

[15] Cubitt, "On Interpretation": 117–19.

[16] André Breton. Quoted in Robert B. Ray, *The Avant-Garde Finds Andy Hardy* (Cambridge: Harvard University Press, 1995): 75.

[17] Ray, *The Avant-Garde Finds Andy Hardy*: 45.

[18] Louis Aragon, "A Feeling for Nature at the Buttes-Chaumont," *Paris Peasant*, trans. Simon Watson Taylor (London: Pan Books, Ltd., 1971): 127–218.

[19] Denise Le Dantec and Jean-Pierre Le Dantec, *Reading the French Garden* (Cambridge: The M.I.T. Press, 1990): 231.

[20] Gyorgy Kepes, *The M.I.T. Years, 1945–1977.* (Cambridge: M.I.T. Press, 1978): 12.

[21] Gyorgy Kepes, *The New Landscape in Art and Science* (Chicago: Paul Theobold and Co., 1956): 17.

[22] Gyorgy Kepes, *Language of Vision* (Chicago: Paul Theobald and Company, 1964; originally published 1944): 67–68.

[23] Sharyn O'Mara and Katie Salen, "Dis[appearances]: Representational Strategies and Operational Needs in Codexspace and Screenspace," *Visible Language* 31,3 (1997): 260–85.

[24] Kathy Rae Huffman, "Video, Networks, and Architecture: Some Physical Realities of Electronic Space," *Electronic Culture: Technology and Visual Representation*, ed. Timothy Druckrey (New York: Aperture Foundation Inc., 1996): 200–201.

[25] Jessica Prinz, *Art Discoure/Discourse in Art* (New Brunswick, New Jersey: Rutgers University Press, 1991): 79–123.

[26] Rem Koolhaas and Bruce Mau, *S, M, L, XL* (New York: The Monacelli Press, 1996): 937.

[27] Quoted by Jacques Lucan, "The Architect of Modern life," in *Jacques Lucan, OMA – Rem Koolhaas Architecture 1970-1990* (New York: Princeton Architectural Press, 1991): 41.

[28] Koolhaas and Mau, *S, M, L, XL*: 921.

[29] Jean-Louis Cohen, "The Rational Rebel, or the Urban Agenda of OMA," in *Lucan, OMA – Rem Koolhaas*: 13.

[30] Michel Foucault, *The Order of Things* (New York: Pantheon Books, 1971): 38.

[31] Roland Barthes, *Roland Barthes* (Berkeley: University of California Press, 1977): 148.

The Messy Middle

Oppositional conditions creating a dynamic center

Coy Howard

You were born.
You will die.
In between, your life.

Architecture is a synthetic art requiring many skills. To do it well requires that we concern ourselves with it as a totality not as the exclusionary unity most often pursued. Unities can be easily achieved through a narrowing down and leaving out of experiential opportunities. Totalities, as all-embracing inclusions, require an opening up to the full range of experience, an enlargement of our sense of wonder and of paradox in the intervals and folds that surround us.

In seeking unities, instead of totalities, we often forget how disciplines change and how the core traditions of the discipline are preserved. All cultural pursuits possess a simultaneity of centrifugal and centripetal activities. Centrifugal activities are directed toward absorbing new information that exists at the distant periphery of the discipline. Centripetal activities are those that reinforce the core values of the discipline. Such activities are composed of the broadest knowledge perspectives and are focused on integration over the longest time frame. Our concerns should not be a tug-of-war but rather a vibration back and forth between the inventions at the edge and the wisdom at the center. Every whole event is inherently composed of a trinity of two opposites and a dynamic center, which is the resultant of the continuous interdependent transformative interaction of the two opposites. Physicists call this trinity the General Principle of Polarity. Philosophers call it Dialectical Logic. I call it Oppositional Inclusivity.

We must remember that the world is a vast totality with a dynamic process joining its contrary powers. This process of cross-pollination and transmutation is how the universe creates itself, and it is how we create. All truly creative products possess four qualities: unusualness, appropriateness, transformation, and condensation. It is the fourth attribute of condensation, the fusion of opposites into higher order totalities, that we must constantly confirm.This is a difficult challenge. One from which we often retreat.

In our retreat we often hide within the fallacies of simple location and misplaced concreteness. The fallacy of "simple location" occurs when we say to ourselves that architecture is primarily about space, or structure, or any other limited sub-set of its complex whole. "Misplaced concreteness" occurs when we start believing in the rhetoric about our work or its abstract representations rather than the evaluative results of lived experience within the work.

Oppositional Inclusivity in architecture is at its best a blend of the syntactical and semantic and the phenomenological and critical points of view. The syntactical point of view is the belief that the rules that we formulate, and the expression of those rules in the work, is what creates aesthetic experience. The semantic bias is the belief that the metaphors, similes, and associations bound together by narrative structure constitute the aesthetic core. The phenomenological perspective is the belief that materiality interfaced with our preconscious understanding of relational structures must be central in aesthetic experience. The critical value position, of course, warns of the dangers lying deep within the previous three, while positing that it is design's mission to tease out these hidden assumptions and make them revelatory in the work.

Our major task as architects is not revolution but the poetic preservation of diversity. To do this we must celebrate differences and be resistive to the domination of one value system over another. A strong personal aesthetic, resulting from a dynamic mix of these viewpoints, will be positioned to address the discipline's dual needs of change and continuity through its built-in resistance to the domination of one value system over another.

Three current issues before us as architects could strongly benefit from the maintenance of the kind of transformational balance I am speaking of. Human history, until very recently, has been concerned with the culturalization of nature. Current ecological awareness in the developed countries of the Western world suggests that the opposite position, the naturalization of culture, should, and hopefully will, become integrated into social policy and expressive modalities. This is the most recent manifestation of one of the great ongoing intellectual debates of the discipline: country versus city, craft versus machine, and the natural versus the industrial. Obviously, no single answer is possible in such debates. The truth, the winning positions (and they are multiple) are the ones full of the tension and drama of the fully expressed totality of human values.

A second concern is that of authentic experience versus mediated experience. Is high-tech going to replace high-touch? No one can long resist the seductive siren song of technology, nor should we. But to embrace and welcome something does not mean that one must reject something else. However, rejection is exactly what is happening. The far sense of vision, rather than the near senses of touch, hearing, and smell, is now preferred. Equally avoided are concerns for the the small, which provides a sense of scalefulness to architecture, and concerns for the decorative, which can animate and give expression to form.

The third issue, ethnocentricity versus multiculturalism, focuses us on questions of the range of our compassion, sensitivities, and expressive abilities.

Can our work speak to the diverse sensibilities of contemporary America and to that of the emerging world culture? Two modes of expression are possible within architecture: the "abstract" and the "representational." Within each of the two, three options exist.

In "abstract" expression we have geometric expression, organic expression, and hybrid expression, a conjoining of the geometric and the organic. In "representational" expression we have historical expression, eclectic expression, and the expression of stylistic metaphor. Unfortunately ninety percent of all contemporary architecture lies within only one of these options, geometric abstraction. Why should we limit ourselves to such narrowness and neglect the powerful use of symbolic and iconographic expression? By restricting our message to the purely abstract and indexical channels of communication we have removed architecture from the cultural concerns of the public, which has a strong preference for the representational and romantic.

Flip-flops of one-sided fads and fashions in ideas and sensibilities can produce a timely architecture. However, only oppositional conditions creating a constantly transforming center can produce an architecture of multivalence and longevity.

Topographic Memory
Bruce Lindsey

On my first trip to Phoenix I walked out of the Holiday Inn to an unexpected discovery. The sky is higher than Pittsburgh where I had spent the last 13 years. While I had been used to the high skies of Idaho growing up in a small town in the south of the state, the sky in Phoenix was even higher. It reminded me of something I had been aware of for sometime. The longer I am away from the landscapes of my youth the more I feel I am from them.

The structure of our memories is related to topography and landscape as well as language and architecture. Topography remembered is a kind of knowledge. This kind of knowing, like gesture precedes language, is generally felt before it is thought, and sets the context for our models of mind that structure our imaginations. We are consistently surprised when we see suddenly, as if for the first time, these structures appear in the things that we build. The degree to which this basic relationship is subsumed in our peripheral awareness is related to the degree of our surprise when we suddenly discover metaphors of mind in the way that a computer "thinks" or the beauty and complexity of how a city "evolves."

Re-envisioning Landscape/Architecture allows us to discover the strong correspondence between the topography of memory and the memory of landscape.

Augustus among the caverned hills of Carthage was astonished at the "mountains and hills of my high imaginations, the plains and caves and caverns of my memory, with its recesses of manifold and spacious chambers, wonderfully furnished with unmeasurable stores." Note how the metaphors of mind are the world it perceives (Jaynes, 1976).

Paul Virilio and Topographic Amnesia

In an essay entitled "A Topographical Amnesia," Paul Virilio makes a beautiful connection between the structure of our memory and the structure of the world. He compellingly suggests that this structure has been destroyed by the proliferation of manufactured images that do not require our imaginations. As our representations become more "real" and our capabilities to visualize things before unseen increase, we are losing what little power we had of imagining those things. The "topographical system" of our memory that corresponded to the spatial structure of the world has been struck by amnesia, and we are tragically forgetting how to remember. We may even more tragically be obliterating the concept of remembrance.

Virilio makes the connection between the structure of our thinking and the spatial structure of the world through the ancient technique of the Art of Memory or the Method of Loci.

This technique articulated by the Greek poet Simonides of Ceos in the first century A.D., and described by Cicero, consists of using a mental image of a city, building, and room as the locations for information to be remembered. Ordered in time and space the information could be remembered by traversing the space

of the imagined city in sequence and recovering the stored information. Used to memorize public orations, the technique was taught as part of the art of rhetoric. In the *Ad C. Herennium,* the only surviving text on the subject written by an anonymous Greek teacher of rhetoric (during the Middle Ages thought to be Cicero), memory is cited to be, "the treasure-house of inventions, the custodian of all parts of rhetoric." According to the *Ad C. Herennium,* memory was of two types: natural memory which you are born with, and artificial memory which could be improved by training (Quantrill 1987). Through the Method of Loci, the artificial memory could be improved and the whole of the architectural world could be used as a structure for memory.

The author of the *Ad C. Herennium* goes so far as to suggest the kinds of architecture that are best suited to the Method of Loci. Deserted, solitary, unfrequented buildings devoid of distraction from people, which might confuse the spatial order, are best (Quantrill 1987). Once established, the architectural framework could contain new information and also be purged of information allowing something new to occupy its place. The relationship of pieces of information to each other was architecturally related as in a dresser to the bedroom in which it was found. New combinations of information could be generated by different itineraries through the memory space. The replacement of the imagined architecture with actual architecture resulted in the Renaissance Memory Theatre where actors would recall their parts by focusing on a piece of the elaborate stage.

Architecture was a natural choice for the structure of the memory system, because it could support reciprocity between a structure of mind and the world "out there." It has distinct boundaries and is ordered both temporally and spatially. Spatialization is a fundamental act of cognition. We orient concepts in the space of our mind like concrete objects. Time, for example, which has no spatial dimension, cannot be understood without the spatial correspondence of past: behind, future:in front, and duration=interval. "You cannot, absolutely cannot think of time except by spatializing it ... This spatialization is characteristic of all conscious thought" (Jaynes 1976). The Method of Locus worked, in part, because of this correspondence between the spatial structure of our thought and that of architecture. It also touches on studies in cognitive mapping and perception, and as I will later suggest, has implications to landscape, the shape of the land, and its influence on our memories.

A similar correspondence between how we think and language is more commonly understood. We often think by talking to ourselves. The importance of thinking with images, especially for children, has experimental validation and suggests that we have the capacity to think in terms of all of our means of representations. It is also common that early memories become confused with photographs or home movies of the experience showing that memories are not only factual but also constructed. In asking students the question of how they think, a common answer is, "in movies in my head." Current revolutions in media, virtual reality, and global networks will certainly suggest new modes of thinking.

Virilio goes on in his essay to argue that this correspondence has been progressively destroyed by "visual prostheses ... (lenses, telescopes) which profoundly altered the contexts in which mental images were topographically stored and retrieved." These instruments allow our engagement to happen at a distance and transform experience into an image. Through an increasing abstraction, simplification and dislocation of language, and a preoccupation with detail, proliferated through the eye of the camera the enabling capacity of vision as described by Merleau-Ponty is "ruined by the banalization of a certain 'teletopology,'" which renders the imagination blind. The camera reverses the figure ground condition of experience and memory. While the shutter is open the eye is blocked. When time is captured experience is withheld. Again, an image separated from experience and context seduces through an emphasis on detail. The resulting amnesia causing a "rapid collapse of mnemonic consolidation."

Images, Words, and Landscape
Virilio offers no specific explanation for his use of the word "topographic" to refer to the structure of memory developed from the Method of Loci. The word comes from *topos* meaning place and *graphein*, to write. It seems likely that his use of the word would also come from the connection between the words *landscape* and *image*. Literally meaning a "portion of land which the eye can comprehend at a glance," landscape in its early usage meant not the view itself but a painting of the view. The English use of the word picturesque is related to the recent usage of the word and refers back to seventeenth-century French painters such as Claude Lorrain and Nicolas Poussin who popularized an idyllic vision of the natural world. The phrase "looking at the world through rose colored

glasses" stems from a Victorian practice of looking at a view through a small piece of colored glass called a Claude Glass, named after the painter. It has also come to mean a nostalgic and shallow attitude that emphasizes disengagement. The nineteenth-century invention of the "park" can be seen as a three-dimensional rendering of nature into a fixed condition or image.

The word landscape does not appear in indigenous languages. In her book *Lure of the Local*, Lucy Lippard quotes Joe Dale Tate Nevaquaya: "In the language of the Yuchi people, there are no words for lines of demarcation, boundaries, borders, or landscapes that are measured, surveyed, designated, and set aside as the sole possession of one." Yet the role of the landscape in organizing a frame

of mind is extremely important. Keith Basso in the book *Wisdom Sits in Places* describes the importance of this to the Western Apache, and, while the book is extraordinary in describing the complexity and beauty of this relationship, it is particularly evident in their use of language and place names. The language of the Western Apache in conversation is "cast in pervasively visual terms." Thinking is done primarily with images, and the role of the speaker is to convey these images to the listener. "Thinking, as Apache's conceive of it, consists in picturing to oneself and attending privately to the pictures. Speaking consists in depicting one's pictures for other people, who are thus invited to picture these depictions and respond to them with depictions of their own." This thinking and speaking in terms of mental pictures is facilitated with the use of place names. Place names support the image construction in the way the name describes the place and in the way many names have an associated "place" story that is recalled when the name is spoken. These stories, often with a moral implication, become part of the "wisdom" that is associated with the place. "Mountains and arroyos step in symbolically for grandmothers and uncles ... for geographical features have served the people for centuries as indispensable mnemonic pegs on which to hang the moral teachings of their history." The names of places often allow for a spatial orientation as in the translation of these names "Lizards Dart Away In Front, The Eastern Face Of A Mountain or Whiteness Spreads Out Descending To Water, a Sandstone Cliff Next To A Spring." They can also suggest how a place has changed over time when a name no longer "looks like the place."

Contemporary influences on our understanding of landscape as an image have come through such things as maps and aerial photography. The long views of Le Corbusier's later urban plans owe much to his first views of Barcelona from a plane. Seeing the city from above gave an emphasis to the whole that rendered the experience as a view. The Finnish architect Sverre Fehn speaks poetically about the conquering of the hill, allowing the horizon line to be moved, and the boundaries of vision extended. Current satellite images give us not only an unprecedented scale but also a seemingly infinite resolution to our vision and picture of the world. Virilio points out the political and military implications of this when he states that one of the strategies of war is the organization of land at a distance.

While the word landscape is connected to the word image, in J.B. Jackson's book *Discovering the Vernacular Landscape,* he goes further in uncovering the etymology of the word. What is of interest here are the component roots of the compound word, which refer to earth or soil and to shape as stemming from the word sheaf, which refers to a composition of similar elements also meaning a collection. Therefore, landscape as a "collection of lands" refers both to a distinct boundary, or plot, and "something like an organization or a system." While the word has always had an implication to ownership, property, or plot, Jackson states that the collection becomes significant because it is shared. He offers the following definition: " ... a composition of man-made or man-modified spaces to serve as infrastructure or background for our collective existence: and if background seems inappropriately modest we should remember that in our modern use of the word it means that which underscores not only our identity and presence, but our history."

This definition broadens the implications of landscape to include not just an image but an organization, not just of the land but of thinking through the land. Landscape as both an image and an organization is both a product of our perception and a structure of it. While the strength of the image may be resulting in what Virilio describes as a "progressive disintegration of a faith in perception" our faith in our environment to compensate may need to increase.

Topographic Memory

In my experience it is not only the landscape as an image or as an idea embedded in language that is important; it is in how landscape and the shape of the land literally makes an impression on our memories. In Pittsburgh where the Monongahela and the Allegheny Rivers meet to create the Ohio River the city finds its center in the figure of the Y that is formed. The steep banks of the Allegheny move up to Mount Washington where the coal fields that fueled the steel mills were located. The rolling topography prevents a long view of the city, and it is the clearly defined and easily remembered shape of the Y that pre-figures the place in the memory. The distinct and varied topography is also suggested as a reason that the 35 or so neighborhoods of the city have remained to a large degree intact and populated by specific ethnic groups. While navigating the streets where the phrase "you can't get there from here" was coined, the location of the rivers and the rare glimpses of the hills are always present in your mind as behind you, or on your right, or below. In discussion with friends who have grown up in the East, it seems that their amazement of the Western landscape is greater than a westerner going east. I suspect that this is related not only to the scale of the landscape but because of the ability to see the expanse.

When I envision the southern Idaho landscape of my youth it is certainly connected to a mental picture of the valley. Usually standing east looking west from above, toward Nampa with Boise and the Boise Mountains to my back and the Cascade Mountains in the background. It is also affected by the feeling of the gentle rise and the expanse of the horizon, that like the higher sky, is further away. It is always a surprise when we return to Idaho from Pittsburgh that the site of the horizon fulfills a forgotten longing for the long view that is absent in Pittsburgh. Perhaps this feeling is related to how the landscape affects that part of our memory that was described in the *Ad C. Herennium* as the natural memory – that part of the memory with which you are born but which is very susceptible to impression and long lasting in its influence. While it may also be that part of the brain that makes a person purchase an enormous sport utility vehicle with four-wheel drive, it more likely associates itself with the rolling hills instead of the manifold rooms of the artificial memory and provides an antidote to the Virilio's amnesia.

References

Keith H. Basso, *Wisdom Sits in Places* (Albuquerque, New Mexico: University of New Mexico Press, 1996).

J.B. Jackson, *Discovering the Vernacular Landscape* (New Haven and London, Yale University Press, 1984).

Julian Jaynes, *The Origin of Consciousness in the Breakdown of the Bicameral Mind* (Boston, MA: Houghton Mifflin Co., 1976).

Lucy R. Lippard, *The Lure of the Local* (New York: The New Press, 1997).

J. Douglas Porteous, *Landscapes of the Mind* (Toronto, Buffalo, London, University of Toronto Press, 1990).

Malcolm Quantrill, *The Environmental Memory* (New York, Schocken Books, 1987).

Simon Schama, *Landscape and Memory* (New York, Alfred A. Knoff, 1995).

Paul Virilio, *The Vision Machine* (Bloomington, Indiana: Indiana University Press, 1994).

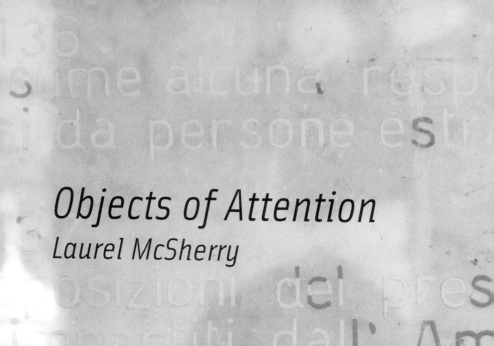

Objects of Attention
Laurel McSherry

Through the window opposite my desk I can see a garden. It is a narrow rectangle, home to jasmine and fennel, twelve apricot trees, and a rosemary hedge. I see trunks painted white. Soil that is brown. A hump of compost. A patch of shade. Above the garden, low clouds appear the color of mountains. If I didn't know better, I'd think the world all earth or sky. Squinting I can discern the profile of a hill. Darkness lifts from my keys. I no longer type from memory.

City lights help distinguish what is and is not ground. Distinguishing architecture from landscape is not as easy. What I do know is this: I sit in a chair, connected to the world through my eyes and a building, to a city both foreign and familiar, with histories pressed against and into each other. What I want to know is what makes places like this meaningful: how landscapes hold and give up memory. Yet this type of knowing isn't easy. Words like place and meaning are not absolute. My garden is a place, but so is this city. And what they mean, and to whom, is more than I can see.

What I can see, like the words I use to describe it, is a function of who I am; a function of time and place and perspective. To my mother, I'm her youngest daughter. To Nancy, a sister; to Kate, her friend. Last year to my university I was a title, a license, a stranger. This morning, by a window, I am a writer.

Daughter. Sister. Teacher. Friend. I write these words and think of what they mean to me; how meaning combines my own experiences with those of others. Although I am a daughter, I am not yet a mother. Having a sister shapes my thinking of what it takes to be one, something of what is expected of me, and part of what I expect in return. The same holds true for friends. For colleagues.

Night fades and my window scene grows complicated. Morning winds billow city birds. Other things enter and quickly change in appearance. Like green. Like smoke rising up to shift first its face and then its direction. Words play a part in generating what I know of this city. Creating, in fact, multiple cities. There is the city of the travel memoir. The city of poets and that of literature. There is the object city, the focus of scholarly work. Like those before me I too have wandered these physical and metaphysical topographies. My image of the city is both actual and invisible, flowing as much from material as from imagination. Daughter. Sister. Teacher. Friend. I say these words quietly and wonder how others might apply them to me. Like a garden, aspects of me can be observed, agreed upon, perhaps even widely shared. My height. The shape of my hands. The green in my eyes. Other aspects, however, are variable and highly personal.

The kind of daughter I am. The kind of sister. If I have been a good friend. If I am recognized as such.

From the window, the garden seems small, but I see much. I see time. I see labor. But what I notice—what I attend to—is still selective, varying with my background, my education, my mood. Neither words I've learned from science nor informed by my senses in isolation can sufficiently account for what I see. For each of us, seeing is like scrutinizing a painting. What we see depends on where we enter.

Daughter. Sister. Teacher. Friend. How uniformly uncertain are the images these words suggest; images fueled by internal analogies, by culturally shared expectations. The molding effect of words on perception is considerable. Do others see in me only what they want to? Are they disappointed to discover otherwise? Like landscapes, people have tangible and interpretive dimensions. Understanding them requires coalescing objective and subjective knowledge, of insights gained both directly and obliquely. Knowing is a dialogue between the suggestions of words and the substance of things.

Words may suggest a place to begin. But who I am is more than this—more than words or a box with absolute sides. I am not some fixed thing but rather a set of tendencies. I tend to go to movies on Fridays. I tend to speak fast. But tendencies are just that, subject to revision, to change, to improvement. Something else came up last Friday. I do slow down. Landscapes have tendencies too, patterns that invite expectations and predictions, even hope. But like the words used to describe me, they are imprecise. Like you and me, landscapes evolve.

There are many ways to see a garden, to see this city. Other ways to interpret and understand them. Yet, the molding effect of words on the meaning of landscape is considerable. Often spatial and symbolic categories shape what and how we see. Foreign. Familiar. These words may say something of these places. But as with teacher or friend each operates at a different degree of resolution and of wholeness. Like a garden, meaning is a human creation, more complex and subtle than it initially appears, like a story whose significance can only be understood after its telling.

It is autumn and I travel with a team of archaeologists to a rural region in central Italy. We have come to undertake a ground survey, to comb ancient fields for ceramic shards, and to confirm and date the occupation of land. Inexperienced in this work, I watch as the director spreads before us a topographic map onto which a grid of small boxes has been drawn. Line or field walking, I learn, proceeds in

stages, and much like contour mapping, selects its interval in response to the topography at hand. Our grid cells of 100 meters square means moderately sloping conditions and a scatter of nearly four kilometers.

It is morning. At the foot of a rocky hillside we assemble for the first of our hundred-meter legs. Two of us peel off laterally as anchors while the remaining three space out equally in between. Once in place we create a bright dotted line, each a point of intersection between a line of sight and a line of shoulders. Then together we begin, slowly, deliberately, counting each step aloud or silently in our heads.

We scissor along, halting frequently to pick up or scrutinize finds. But advancing the line is no easy task. Our route, governed by the placement of a grid, runs north/south, and so bears little resemblance to the geometry of plow lines and terraces visible before us. These structures, like the houses and fences that join them, run with rather than against the hillside, causing our paths to intersect them at odd and uncomfortable angles.

Although the survey lasted only a few days, its scenes lingered in memory long after returning home. Recalling one particular afternoon helped me to understand their meaning. It is day three, and we are tired and discouraged by a morning lost to rain. On the hillside, grassy fields have given way to muddy clearings, gentle slopes to impossibly steep ones. Repeatedly we are separated, beyond earshot, and wildly out of alignment. After nearly twenty minutes recovering positions, we finish the leg, call it quits, collect our gear, and ready for home.

Turning around, I look back on the path still visible behind me and reassemble in my mind what I passed by and through as a result of its placement. Like an animal surveying prey, at once I'm struck, absorbed by the details of the hill surrounding me, of the land before and beneath me. Following an inherited line had forced me to lay aside usual habits of perception and enter into a way of seeing I had never before apprehended. Not necessarily a greater intellectual understanding but a contact with my surroundings that included a certain identification with them. Although I'd studied landscapes for years, on the hillside that day I felt released from the ambition to make one. For the first time in a long time, I began to feel a small amount of hope.

In the car, we use the drive to recap the day, to share tales of what we saw and sensed and of hardships encountered and overcome. Although the paths we traveled were only meters apart, reports from the line—what we recall and how it was

arranged—vary considerably. From these accounts, each vivid, each enhancing and expanding, a collective image of the hillside emerges. These stories together create our knowledge of a place. Together these stories become landscape.

I believe that by examining a combination of features found in a landscape—together with variations and changes to them—we can begin to see that certain coherence that is landscape. For me, line walking was a first step, enabling me to contact a world exuberant with detail and alive with individualities. Line walking helped me to rediscover the wonder in the ordinary. At another level of resolution, by walking this random line I discovered the power residing in the combination of things, of the isolated with the collective. On the hillside that day, I found an art of relationships.

These days I challenge myself to see other landscapes this way; to learn what I might of familiar places—my neighborhood, a city—in ways derived largely from random encounters with them. Like walls on a hillside, I welcome interruptions as chances to attend to where I happen to be, to look on scenes with the intent of grasping wholeness, to wonder how the simple becomes extraordinary as a result of its context. But seeing this way isn't easy. Paying attention—remaining open-minded to what exists—is exhausting. But moving into the space of the objects I'm observing keeps me mindful of the potential qualities laying just beyond surfaces, and the possibilities of one day glimpsing a world outside customary generalizations, prejudices, and schemes.

Daughter. Sister. Teacher. Friend. Each word a concept crowded with mean-ing—voices of praise and those of criticism, histories pressed against and into each other. Like a landscape, these words are many and one, sometimes enhanc-ing, sometimes conflicting. At one level of resolution, they are parallel, at another, blended and informed. Above the city, morning clouds stretch to touch each other, and I'm keenly aware of the roundness of the world. Behind where I sit lies the ancient wall of a city, below it a river almost twice as old. My desk, this garden, this river, are axis points. If I were to spin the world—this Catherine wheel—replacing one scene with another, what would I see? Although something else might command my attention, this garden would remain both in the world and in memory, and so too its histories, its architectures, its stories. Spinning further, on other mornings, different words might fill these spaces. But for now, I look at this garden, and then closing my eyes think of others, other places, other rivers, and the words we would use to describe them.

Constructed Intention:
An Architecture of Place

Thoughts and observations pertaining to 8 Bedons Alley

Charles Menefee

On Landscape and Architecture

—The given landscape and architecture can be appreciated at multiple scales.

—The existing landscape and architecture at 8 Bedons Alley was modified by its occupants, previous specific usage(s), and evolution of properties around it.

—Modification of the existing building and landscape is limited by its structure and site boundaries, surrounding context, and social conventions of place.

—The landscape and architecture are defined by their location in a historic city with a preserved housing convention that regulates change.

—The landscape and architecture are more broadly defined by its surrounding natural features: the rivers and harbor, the Low Country, the climate.

—Modification of the structure opens architecture to landscape, extending the structure into the space of the garden.

—The landscape and architecture can be conceived as a state of mind—as an image held of the place and the city by those who call it home.

—The cohesion of building and landscape rejoins them with the pattern of the immediate landscape and identifies them with the community.

On Materials

—Material choices, while not formal choices, affect form.

—Materials have limits and qualities: pragmatic, sensual, and representative.

—Material choices convey perspective, demeanor, and character.

—Material units are combined to make the desired and necessary qualities. Adjacencies at the limits, corners, and edges are resolved to clarify intention.

On Craft

—Craft is developed from need and is defined through repetition and practice.

—The craft of construction is realized at multiple scales: at the scale of the hand craft humanizes construction, at the scale of furnishings enables occupation.

—The building is crafted to complement and honor the structure and landscape.

—The site is crafted to enhance its interactions with adjacent sites.

—The structure and site are crafted together to enrich the greater social and physical context of place.

On Joints and Junctures

—A joint is an opportunity for clarification of intent. A joint calls for an action appropriate to the articulation of a specific circumstance: contrast, connect, differentiate, separate, open, close, seal, bridge, and so on.

—A joint is created potential space that may be filled with another material but more often remains an opening.

—The form and proportions of a joint can be manipulated to accommodate occupation and aesthetic intention.

—Critical junctures occur not only within a structure but between structure and landscape.

—Structural/landscape junctures necessarily address issues of climate, physics, adjacency, and transition.

—Successful joints function to distinguish and unify and to separate and relate.

On Perception

—Landscape can be ignored; it can be merely observed; it can be occupied; it can be savored.

—The landscape is mutable: the perception of the landscape depends greatly on one's focus. Focus can be on the natural setting, the built landscape, the historical context. Focus can be colored by the time of the day or year, the slant of the sun or the presence of shadows, the persistence or absence of the wind, surrounding activities of construction or destruction, and the shifts in the political or economic climate.

—Architecture successfully realized is inseparable from the quality of the landscape by virtue of its physical presence; it can be background, foreground, or inconsequential, depending variably on its intention and the perception of those who occupy or observe it.

It is not necessary to integrate architecture with its landscape, but both structure and milieu can be enhanced by the effort to do so.

It's All One Thing

Michael Rotondi

This is an account of what my colleagues and I at RoTo learned from our four and one-half year experience in Indian country. It is not presented as a definitive description of Lakota culture, but it does represent in part a rich and complex culture that is a treasure of knowledge that I now believe to be essential to our survival as a species. There is a lot to learn from all indigenous people, and now is the time. As one elder told us when we came to visit "I know why you are here. You first came 200 years ago and were too impatient to listen and learn. Now you have returned for a second chance."

We began collaborating with the Sicangu Lakota of the Rosebud Reservation in South Dakota and the Lannan Foundation in New Mexico in March 1994 to plan a new campus and design several buildings, two of which were built: a Science and

Technology Center and a multipurpose building, which would be used primarily for ceremonial dancing and basketball. The combining of religion and sports in the latter building was initially a shocking surprise. How could these two types of activity occur in the same space? Understanding this, coming to terms with this through study, listening to stories, and direct experience of the awesome landscape, was primary to beginning an understanding of their culture. It is all one unified whole. It taught us how to see the relationship of the physical and spiritual worlds and the practical and profound. For most of us educated in the Euro-American world, these were separate aspects of our existence. They coexisted but were not seen or understood as interdependent. This was just the beginning of our education.

Before we started working on the project, we requested meetings with elders, the traditional teachers, to ask them for their wisdom, which was conveyed through stories. The duration of the stories could be twenty minutes or an entire evening. The elders somehow knew what needed to be told and how much could truly be understood at that point in time. They talked, and we listened and learned. The stories generally were about one grand teaching. We are one people and one planet. We are all related. Earth is a living organism: it is a multifaced single-functioning entity. Out of this emerged a knowledge and belief system that gives structure to their daily lives. Lakota lived in an extended territory that encompassed Eastern Wyoming (west), North Dakota (north), Missouri River (east), and Northern Oklahoma (south). They migrated across

 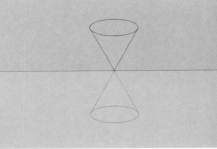

this landscape in a more or less clockwise manner following the sun and the buffalo (considered to be the sun on earth). Their survival was contingent on knowing the land intimately, which they did by "listening" to it and moving with its cycles and rhythms in a harmonically oscillating dance that characterized all of the created universe.

All the seasons were held in balance as were the diurnal, monthly, and annual cycles of the sun and the moon and the climate changes associated with their relationship with the earth. It was believed that humans could communicate with other forms of life and in doing so would become aware of larger cycles of time that can be described as time shared by all forms of life within a geographical area. Every entity had a part to play in the creation of the future, especially in sacred places to initiate the grand process of rebirth and renewal. Events occur in places, not in time.

Space/place determined the nature of relationships; time determined the meaning. The point of the stories, the focus of their prayers, and the purpose of the ceremonies such as yuwipi (sweat lodge), Spring Journey (through the Black Hills), and the Sun Dance was to acknowledge the unity and wholeness of all that exists and to make whole once again what had fallen apart.

They have an innate sense that human's relation to nature connects us with our inner development. The outer world was essential for the inner world; they were two aspects of one thing. The land could not be distinct from personal or collective identity. It was not merely coexistence; it was cocreation. The organism and

the environment were not separately determined. The environment was not a structure imposed on living beings from the outside but was in fact a creation of these beings. The environment was not an autonomous process but a reflection of the biology of the species.

In formulating their understanding of the world, Lakota do not discard any experience. Everything is included in the expanding sphere of knowledge and related to what is already known. Knowledge is derived from individual and communal experiences of daily life in keen observation of the environment and in the messages received from spirits in ceremonies, visions, and dreams. Knowledge is not independent of direct experience and abstract propositions are not the means to explore the nature and structure of the physical world.

Experiences lead to ideas not the reverse—both are inextricably linked. The full measure of each is enhanced by the other. Thus landscape is not theorized; it is lived upon. It is not merely a format for aesthetic notions of visual delight or a conceptual overlay of abstract thought. It is fundamentally about sustaining life in every way.

One Experience in the Landscape
Badlands, South Dakota

The Badlands formed five millions years ago when the Rocky Mountains in the western United States were forming. The Badlands, in the western section of

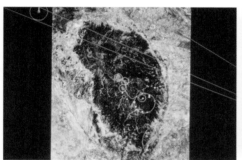 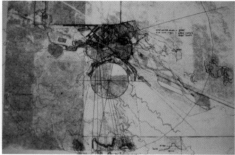

South Dakota, are flat, vertically shifted plateaus extending for miles. The exposed strata, 400 feet high in some areas, are an index of the earth's time scale. Humans are represented by twelve inches of grass and topsoil.

In 1996 as we were making our monthly three-hour drive from Rapid City to the Rosebud Reservation, we detoured through an area that is simply referred to as "The Prairie"; it is the only place in the Dakotas that appears to be a perfectly flat surface in every direction, as the prairie grasses extend to the horizon encompassing a complete 360 degrees. The earth is truly spherical from this vantage. The sun was setting on the northwestern horizon. It was late summer, the sky was clear and the sun yellow-orange. We had been standing still for thirty minutes with our depth of focus being the full extent of the space between us and the sun. There was extreme stillness. Our bodies could almost sense this infinite space. As the sun and the earth's horizon began to get close, the sun seemed to be setting, and as they met, this feeling immediately reversed itself. The sun was not setting, the earth was rising in rotation, and the sun was in a fixed position. This fact became a sensation. We were standing on the surface of the earth, a perfect sphere, with our bodies in space.

This experience lasted the duration of the rotation that eventually eclipsed the sun. We were in awe. The next evening, we described our experience on the prairie to some elders expecting an excited reaction to our great discovery. We did not get it. They gave us, instead, a warm look of satisfaction that we had begun to see what had always been present. This was an experience the Lakota turned into

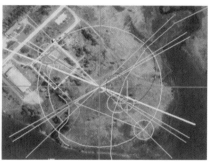 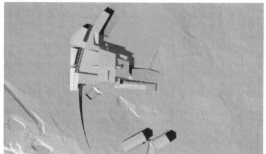

stories. They said, "This will happen again and again if you are open and free like young children, as you spend time on the land and 'listen' with no expectations; life's mysteries will be revealed over time."

Sinte Gleska University is the first and oldest tribal university in the Americas, started twenty-five years ago. The new campus is on a prairie adjacent to a lake. The planning, siting, and design of the campus was primarily generated by the spatial and diagrammatic structure of the traditional Lakota systems of movement and rest, the formal characteristics of the Lakota Universal Model (Kapemni), and Lakota numerology. This knowledge, recorded in the memory of elders, is expressed through stories, daily rituals, ceremonial dances, shelter constructions (tipi and yawipi), and temporary settlements. The challenge of our collaborative exploration was to find a contemporary form for traditional values and practices.

Historically, the Lakota were not stationary people. They migrated across the plains in accordance with the sun and followed the buffalo, the embodiment of sun on earth. Choosing sites for temporary settlement appropriate for enacting rituals and daily routines had precedence. Permanent settlements had no precedent except as imposed 120 years ago.

The tribal elders now believe that it is possible to establish a new precedent. Meeting with them, we learned how they located their camps, the basis for arranging their tipis, the size and configuration of the encampment, and the alignment of built structures with natural ones. The lines of movement and the

places of rest on earth are reflected in the sky, ever changing in a rhythmic and recurring cycle. Lakota myths and legends record the significance of this dynamic relationship of earth and sky, in which the horizon is the zone of human occupation. Their stories embody the concepts of mirroring, scaling, and nesting, all of which incorporate principles of order and systems of relationships between each and everything in the universe. All things are interconnected and interdependent. At all sizes and scales, the physical, aesthetic, and spiritual aspects are woven together.

For example, in the Lakota star knowledge, a system of astronomy and astrology, the configuration of stars known as animals or the "four-leggeds" and the "two-leggeds" (tayamni), are the stars at the center of the constellation, as well as their respective prairies in the Black Hills. No prefix or suffix identifies or distinguishes one from another because they are all Tayamni. Generally, the identity, and to some extent the definition of a place/person/thing, is provisional with regard to context, the relational system that it occupies at any given moment.

The essence of the Lakota star knowledge is embodied in the word "home." The Lakota star knowledge tells people they have a place on this earth. The Lakota star constellations that are mirrored on the land define and limit their homeland and designate "here." The star knowledge also tells people how to conduct themselves within this homeland. It gives a sacramental and moral basis for the use of their energy defining what work is and what to work for. (An excerpt from a letter to Michael Rotondi written by Ronald Goldman, May 1995.)

Traditional Lakota know all aspects of their landscape. The land has physical presence as well as spiritual meaning. Everything in it and on it exists in a dynamic balance based on reciprocity and respect. At the beginning of our work, we studied their texts, experienced the land, and listened to their stories. We began to see and understand all of it as one thing.

We postulated that if the form and physical characteristics of a site suggest connections to oral history, to a seasonal event, to a significant position of the sun, or to a significant constellation of a star, then by learning something about how people might move or where land might be manipulated we might reflect the traditional Lakota choreography. In this way, from the outset the campus was envisioned as an extension of the university's curriculum of Lakota studies.

We developed a hierarchy for primary siting decisions and diagrams of the campus based upon the number of "connections" or "correspondences" that occur in a reading of the natural landscape through the Lakota lens.

The Campus Plan attempted to integrate the man-made and natural site conditions as dictated by our reading or traditional Lakota spatial systems. We developed relational and multiscaled ordering systems. They were defined as NATURAL (experientially based), ABSTRACT (intellectually based), and MYTHOLOGICAL (spiritually based). Our site began at the scale of the Lakota homeland, defined by the known medicine wheels, such as Big Horn in Wyoming, understood to have defined the outer radius of the settlement and its geographical center of the Black Hills (Paha Sapa). We precisely mapped the relationship of

our campus circle in Antelope, South Dakota, to all the ceremonial sites in the Spring Journey, as well as to the paths of the corresponding constellations and sunsets. This process revealed a close relationship, exact in places, between the radial location of the Spring Journey sites and the timing of the ceremonies. The Lakota community received this information with great satisfaction, convinced that they had made a good choice for the campus site.

The increment in scale was the volume defined by the horizons visible from the site. Our analysis marked seven buttes to the south, a remarkable straight and directional fold in the landscape formed by the Keyapha River drainage, with visible horizontal and vertical edges formed by changes in prairie texture due to shifts in the underlying soil and so forth. As we pointed out these things to the

Lakota, we often heard stories about the landscape features. Through these oral histories, we continued to learn.

Three buildings were presented. Their design, construction logic, and building materials emerged from our belief that every aesthetic issue must be simultaneously practical. We developed these projects as instruments for teaching vocational education students the process, techniques, and skills of construction and as part of their economic development plan.

Most importantly, when we finally completed our work in late 1998, a process was well underway that would continue with their long-term project of "Rebuilding Their Nation," as Lionel Bordeaux said in his 1996 commencement speech:

In the beginning we were told that the human beings who walk upon the earth have been provided with all things necessary for life. We were instructed to carry a love for one another and to show a great respect for all beings of this earth. We were shown that our life exists with the tree life, that our well-being depends on the well-being of the vegetable life, that we are close relatives of the four-leggeds. In our way, Spiritual consciousness is the highest form of politics. (Statement by representatives of the Diné (Navajo), Lakota (Sioux), and Haudenosaunce (Iroquois Confederacy), 1978.)

Empooling
Peter Smithson

Where there is a sandy beach with rocks standing up from it, as the tide recedes small pools are left at certain places where the rocks cluster. It is, as this, that our urbanism acts; the formation of the buildings carry with it an empooling of the space-between. And as with the rock-pools, what is within that space-between seems extraordinarily vivid.[1]

[1] This is, in part, what accounts for the most asked-for photograph of The Economist Building being that of "The Man in the Bowler-Hat." Similarly, with those photographs of children at play at Robin Hood Gardens or the garden party at St. Hilda's.

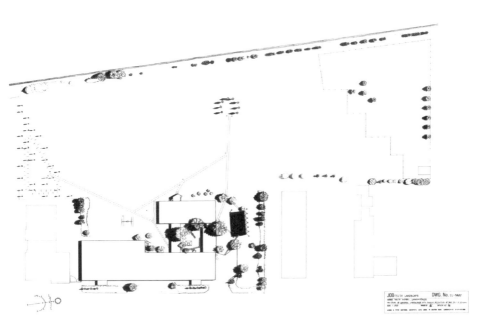

Landscape at Tecta, Lauenforde, Germany.
General plan with shadows projected at mid-July at 12 noon. The existing trees are shown at their present size 1995–1996, new trees are at the size as planted in autumn 1995.
Drawing: L.W., January 1996

What follows is a description of empoolings at the Tecta factory in Lauenforde.[2] Lauenforde is a small town on the River Weser south of Hamelin. In general terms it is on latitude 51° north between Hannover to the north and Kassel to the south. Tecta are manufacturers of modern furniture from the Heroic Period, the thirties, and from our own period—the 1950s to today. Our work there, it would seem, has been to give *more substance* to the original format of the factory, which was built in the 1960s: that is, storage, loading, and unloading—the machine activities—on the access road side, with the more human activities on the side toward the open landscape. We have—step by step—*opened* the factory in the direction of that landscape.

There seem to be three possible empoolings—at the entrance, in the garden court, and in the meadow behind.

[2] The Patron of all the work has been Axel Bruchhauser of Tecta, the furniture manufacturers.
Tecta Platforms (A.S.) 1990
Canteen Porch (A.S.) 1990
Toilet Tree (A.S.) 1986–1990
Yellow Lookout (A.S.) 1991
Sewing Room Porch (A.S.) 1992–1995
Stainless-Steel Fascia Bands (P.S.) 1995
Axel's Room Porch (P.S.) 1995
The Meadows (P.S.) 1996

At the Entrance

The access road side remains "shut" against intrusion and noise, except at the entrance.

The entrance space has been quietly changed by overlaying the existing black fascia band with polished stainless steel, which reflects back in a magically distorted way what lies before it . . . a screen of established mixed planting—sugar maple, spruce, pine, and birch, a few specimens of each. Within the enclosure created by this screen and its reflections, various devices have been deployed . . . to call attention to the factory's work[3] . . . to lead visitors to the entry.

[3] Interventions, adjustments, and cosmetic actions were stated as the necessary activities of the *Fourth Generation* in "Three Generations," see *ILA&UD Annual Report*, 1980–1981 (Urbino) and also "Staging the Possible," *Italian Thoughts*, Sweden, 1993, and *Italienische Gedanken*, Braunschweig, 1996.

In the Garden Court

For the people working in the factory the enclosed pool of quiet space of the garden court has been made accessible, both to look out into whilst washing one's hands—"one of the small pleasures of life"—and for getting into through a break in the wall of the canteen with a small, almost furniture-like, porch that projects out into the garden court.

The yellowness of the porch set amongst the branches of the two very large sugar maples, reflected back and forth from the stainless steel fascia bands, make the court with its miniature fountain into a true retreat.

The Canteen Porch, began the process of reorienting the factory toward the meadow.

In the Meadow

The meadow itself—already well-defined by a brook lined by trees on one long side—has been given more edge planting in the manner of the "side-screens" of eighteenth-century English landscape practice; so, as it were, to make it look into itself. Toward this meadow the factory is reoriented. There is, for example, an out-and-back path system with marker lanterns to keep the sense of the "internalness" of the meadow space. The "back" of the factory, now the meadow face, no longer unconsidered, becomes a "front," engaging with what lies before it.[4]

At a further re-entrant space off the meadow, Axel Bruchhausers' room is opened up on a diagonal to see to the meadow's furthest boundary. And, in the same way as the Canteen Porch, acts with the garden court; so here on the meadow-face the Porch acts with the meadow—overviewing and giving access from the factory to the landscape. The stainless-steel fascia band together with the concrete socle-band[5] bind the interventions into the factory ensemble and through the fascia reflections to the meadow.

This empooling has not been wholly consciously sought, it is in large part spontaneous, consequent to observation of, and invention from, the land-forms, the boundaries, and the direction of the sun's travel over the working day.

Behind it lies the realization that the focus of attention has shifted from the building as object to its action on the special shaping of the territory, and that shaping should be the dominant activity of our period[6] in the same way that housing was made the dominant activity of architects in the Heroic Period.

I refuse to abandon the idea that, as frequently in the past, "the territory" can evolve from a place of use into a work of art.

[4] This is one of the characteristics of "Conglomerate Ordering," see *ILA&UD Annual Report* 1986–1987 (Siena) and also "The Canon of Conglomerate Ordering," *Italian Thoughts*, Sweden, 1993 and *Italienische Gedanken*, Braunschweig, 1996.

[5] Banding also is a characteristic of "Conglomerate Ordering," see above.

[6] "The Binders," unpublished manuscript by author.

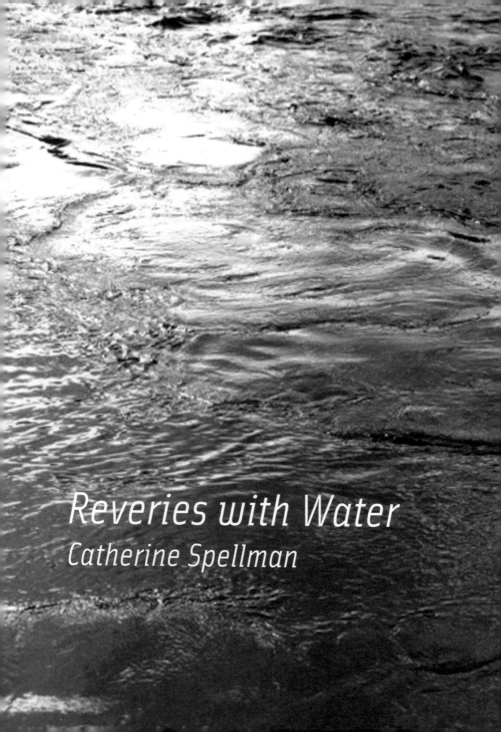

Reveries with Water
Catherine Spellman

In water lurk the mysteries of time. There is a kind of river of things, passing into being, and time is a violent torrent. For no sooner is each seen, then it has been carried away, and another is being carried by, and that, too, will be carried away.

Architecture is "both dream and function, it is an expression of utopia and instrument of convenience," it mediates between mental and physical realities to inspire us both spiritually and empirically. Thus, one of the challenges of architecture is to engage our imagination by making these realities apparent; to heighten phenomenal experience while simultaneously evoking meaning; and to develop this duality in response to the particularities of site and circumstance. Water—like fire, earth, and air—is an element in a pre-Socratic sense and therefore embodies both these realities. Just as the poet Muriel Rukeyser wrote that "the universe is made of stories, not of atoms," so too is water composed of stories, above and beyond its molecular fusion of hydrogen and oxygen. In Phoenix water could be used to play an essential role in the making of a poetic city that stimulates and relates to us as human beings. This study considers water in Phoenix as a means of exploring the relationship between oneiric and material phenomena in the making of architecture.

In desert cities such as Phoenix, water is the physical and spiritual essence of the place. Without water it would be impossible to inhabit desert environments, and yet here in Phoenix water is mostly invisible to the community it supports. Subconsciously we know that water is here, the grass is green, trees grow, pools are filled, but we do not consciously acknowledge, celebrate, or utilize water to enhance the quality of our community life or embellish our collective memory of this place. The project Water Ways explores the significance and meaning of water to the urban environment of Phoenix. We began with a broad study of the phenomena of water—considering its physical qualities, sources, systems, role in history, and inspiration to creative acts. Then we considered water in the context of Phoenix—where it comes from, how it is collected and distributed, how it has allowed the for growth, and what effect it has on the culture of this place.

This research raised certain questions that were explored through the design interventions: What do present and ancient systems of water reveal about the history and culture of a place? How does contained water differ in meaning from water left in a natural state and how does the container become a mediator between the natural and built environment? As the technology of water advances how has society's values and involvement in the urban environment changed, and how do traces of advancement influence a collective memory of a place? How have architectures in different regions of the world respond to, interact with, and give presence to water? What are the representational techniques that best capture the dual realities of water and how can these techniques be utilized in making architectures of water?

In memorable experiences of architecture, space, matter, remembrance, and time fuse into one single dimension, that penetrates the consciousness. As we identify ourselves with this space, this place, this moment, and these dimensions—they become ingredients of our very existence and enable us to place ourselves in the continuum of culture. The first collective memory of any culture is established with the act of settlement. Early cultures lived in a type of codependence that fostered a unification of the natural and the artificial. Survival depended on their ability to be amongst the forces of their surroundings. Within Central Arizona, the first known settlers were the Hohokam Indians (100 BC to AD 1450). They established a productive agriculturally based society with the construction of an elaborate irrigation water system. Following the slope of the land, the Hohokam constructed over 900 miles of major and arterial canals, connecting and uniting many villages with a common physical and social infrastructure.

Ultimately water is tied to the physical wellbeing and spiritual life of both early and present cultures that live in the desert. As well, water connects the past to the present because it flows in various imitations of time; the steady current of clock time, the ceaseless tide of universal time, the whirlpool psychological

time and the enigmatic mist mnemonic time. An understanding of its significance, to both body and mind, allows one to see the collapse of all temporal states onto the image of themselves reflected in the surface of water. This is why the reflective quality of water has such mesmerizing powers and has obtained so much presence in the arts and architecture.

The history of relationships between architecture and water exist in the layers of structures that support its distribution. The splendor that is Rome relies, in part, on a water network of tunnels, arcades and cisterns, imperial baths, monumental fountains, water terraces, public water spouts, private pressurized taps, and man-formed ponds from many epochs. The great Italian tourist Goethe describes an ancient aqueduct as "a succession of triumphal arches," expressing in a single phrase the architectural structure of the arcade, the value of the water they delivered, and the stereotypical Roman pride in conquest. The entire book VIII of Vitruvius' treatise is dedicated to the theme of water, its research, its nature, and the ways to transport and distribute it. Indeed, to supply water to a city is more than a service: it represents the collective effort needed to ensure the communal life of the settlement. It imposes a geometry, connects city to territory, exposes the palpability of water and it implies the psychological makeup of a culture. Here in Phoenix Water Ways is attempting to bring together the "dream and function" of urban life by re-considering the structures, presence, and memory of water.

Following is a list of the students that contributed to the Reveries with Water Project and examples of the work we produced: Monica Adley, Tim Boyle,

Water memory The important thing about memory is that you do not need to erase it to create a new memory. Memories exist in layers. They are not sequential, they do not follow the order of a line. Memories overlap each other, altering what and how we know a situa-tion. Memory effects who we are and how we are in the world. It is the layers of memory that makes us whole.

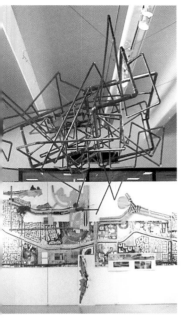

Doug Brown, Mike Clark, Luis Cruz, Katrin Denning, Christopher Haas, Brent Harris, Jim Harrison, Heidi Hesse, Victor Irizarry, Ankur Jain, Warisara Khajornkhanphet, Kathy McPhearson, Chris Van Oosten, Rob Rager, Brie Smith, Mary Spilotro, Johathon Spinner, Adam Strong.

We began our research by constructing a memory of water that would offer us the ability to see and understand its inner nature, how it functions, and what are its design possibilities. These water memories are achieved through perception and experience, precise recording, reflective thinking, and creative making with water. From this research we assembled a wall of images and descriptions that outline the meaning of water to us. The wall constructed with plexi-glass and transparent film conveys the reflective and transparent qualities of water while creating a surface which juxtaposes our collective memories of the substance. The list below describes the 12 categories we used to organize our research, which was then recorded graphically using drawings, models, tracings, maps, photographs, montages, collages, rayograms, etc.

Networks: a copper piping sculpture, that represents water manipulation by humans, and shows creation of space by infrastructure, densification, and overlapping of components. Part / Whole relationship. Members act individually and in masse, structure, connectors, functional elements, integration of differing objects, complexity. Chaotic system works as a trigger to the imagination, perhaps the first sketch of an architectural agenda a metaphor of water without water.

The tile piece records the absence of water and simultaneously the presence of the scars it leaves in the landscape. Here we see the abstract notion of surface water disappearing from the urban environment, evoking the power of the absence of water. The tiles acknowledge the embankment of the canal as place of participation, it is here that people gather and enjoy the space of the canal. The surface of the embankment is addressed throughout all the proposals.

The drawings are a recording of the students thoughts after researching water and experiencing the canal system.

One: a collage of the textural qualities of the canal embankment and the water. Thinking about how one holds the other.

Two: Parts and Pieces: isolating points of interest along the canal and bringing them together at one place. concentrating the power of the canal. Stiching together the horizon and surfaces that form the points of interest.

Three:the collage considers the source of the waters movement, the pull of gravity and the inclination of the topography. It empathsizes the relationship of the mountains to the canal system.

Four: a collage about the movement of water. Every new motion changes the direction and flow of the water. Here the motion of liquid ink changes the surface of the photograph.

Five: The Empty Bag Experience. the history rich canal has been frozen into a barren utility. A beacon is suggested that would bring attention back to the canal and to the site of a ready made container that offers the observer access to the cooling waters.

Interventions

At the mid-point of the semester, the studio decided to test some of our ideas through the construction of one to on scale interventions along the canal embankment. Each intervention addresses a water memory created by the initial research and the specific contextual possibilities of the site. With these interventions we were able to briefly create an amenity out of infrastructure, and observe how the public engaged it.

One: this project at the end of the canal explores the surface qualit of the water. A series of screens afford the dual view of depth and surface. The screen-rods act as both object occupying the site and subject receiving sections cut through the occupants' shadows as they interact with the installation.

Two: a forrest of site nails display tags that carry information about this particular place along the canal.

Three: Adjacent the canal is a collapsed water tank, recalling a time when the land was occupied by ranchers and their cattle. The photograph shows the quality of

1

2   3

space now held by the container and the lines of rope that re-unite this interior to the surrounding landscape

Four: The intervention is about making images in the folding axis—x,y,z. A telephone pole is selected as the site for the intervention. On the x-axis, mirrors activate the intervention as they reflect the pole. On the y-axis mirrors reflect a second pole which is far away. On the z axis mirors are laid down on the ground following the shape of the terrain of the embankment reflecting the water reflected onto the pole.

Five: a tapestry of stones found along the canal embankment shows the superimpositiion of two maps important to this artist—the map of the canal through Phoenix and the plan of his studio space. These two spaces when brought together create a third space along the embankment.

Six: Six foot bronze oars recall a time when one boated in the canal waters. Now forbidden the oars also remind us of the restrictions placed by the community on the canal use.

4

5

6

Water Way Sites

way n. 1.a line of communication between places. 2.the best route. 3.a method or style, a person's chosen course of action. 4.traveling distance. 5.the amount of difference between two states or conditions. 6.space free of obstacles so that people can pass 7.the route over which a person or thing is moving or would naturally move. 8.a specified direction 9.a manner 10.a habitual manner or course of action or events 11.a talent or skill 12.advance in some direction, progress. 13.a respect, a particular aspect of something. 14.a condition or state.

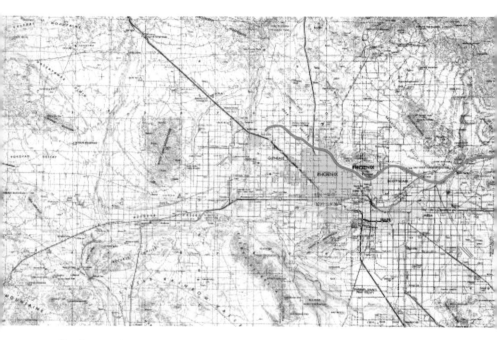

The Arizona Canal is the northern most canal on the irrigation system. It starts at the Gila Bend damn on the Pima Maricopa Indian Reservation, passes through Scottsdale and Phoenix and finishes at the Skunk River in Glendale on the west end of town. It is 38.5 miles in length flowing over 113 feet down hill across the metropolitan area.

In our initial survey, we selected 18 sites that had potential for a strong connection back to the community. The sites are sometimes at the intersection of two busy streets, crossing a public park or school, adjacent to commercial development, or connecting to an abandoned lot. Though extremely different in scale and

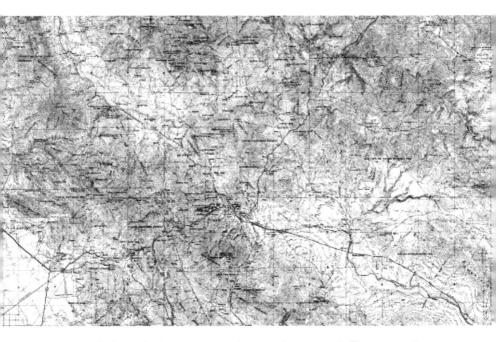

context each site evoked some memory of our previous research. These memories
in combination with the sites' possibility for physical connection to the community, tended to guide our design work. The initial design ideas are captured in 1 to
100 scale model/montages. These montages were used to outline and construct
series of design strategies that could be implemented at various points along the
canal. These strategies are illustrated with site photographs and collages.

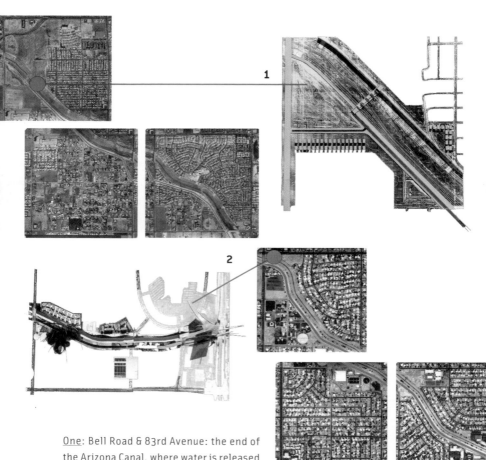

<u>One</u>: Bell Road & 83rd Avenue: the end of the Arizona Canal, where water is released into a wash that flows into the Skunk River and back into the Salt River, co-existence of different waters: rain over flow water from the ACDC, canal water, and river water. The proposal recognizes the interconnected scales of the canal system. This is the lowest elevation alone the canal system, a place where the urban edge meets the rural edge.

<u>Two</u>: 51st Avenue & West Cactus Road: here the ACDC is a canyon that divides the city into north an south. The ACDC is the memory of absent water and the water that might come in a 100 year flood. Pathways are proposed that cross the ACDC and become connectors between neighborhoods that are divided the empty space of the ACDC. These connectors are occupied with temporay programs such as a flee market, skate boarding, landscape, and outdoor theatre.

Three: Castles & Coasters, Water Filtration Center and Cortez Park, Dunlap Avenue & I-17, the proposal connects two urban parks, one active and the other calm, by interlacing the canal water into the sites. On I-17 water washes the overpass as it crosses the canal, an enormous shadow cast from a water screen puts the hard surfaces of the park into constant, placid movement. the space of the filtration center is covered with a steel grate that enables the visitor to 'walk on water,' and Cortez Park is periodically flooded with canal water.

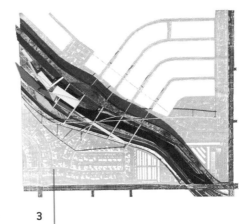

3

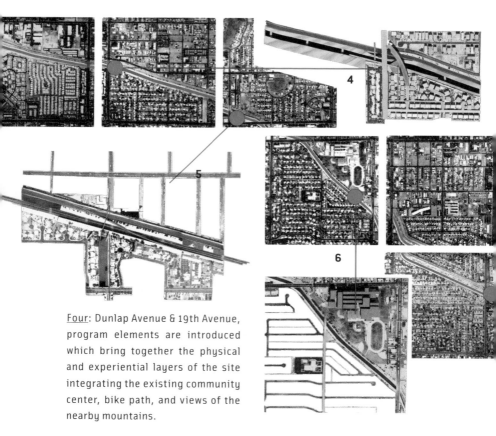

Four: Dunlap Avenue & 19th Avenue, program elements are introduced which bring together the physical and experiential layers of the site integrating the existing community center, bike path, and views of the nearby mountains.

Five: 15th Avenue & Dunlap Avenue, this site was once used by SRP employees as a camp ground/ living space whil they were working on the construction and then maintainance of the canal. The proposal suggests a urban pool that will allow neighborhood kids to play in the canal water as was done earlier in the century.

Six: Sunnyslope Highschool, Central Avenue & Dunlap Avenue, the site is best described as an island in a sea of suburbs. The proposal suggests a pedestrian bridge that will connect suburb and school.

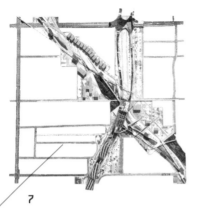

7

<u>Seven</u>: Highway 51 & Glendale Avenue, the freeway moves over the grid of the city like an aquaduct system iin the ancient Rome. The proposal merges the waterway with the freeway—creating overlapping elements—by projecting scences of water across the freeway.

<u>Eight</u>: 7th Street & Northern Avenue, this site is one of the few places where the original trees still survive. The proposal 're-plants' man-made trees that replace the ones that have not survived and makes a community garden that is fed with canal water.

8

<u>Nine</u>: Filter-Tower, 24th Street & Lincoln Avenue, this site contains one of the filtration plants along the canal, water functions in the city as a purifying and cleansing element. A 'Filter-Tower' mimics the uniqueness of the gates. The tower becomes a narrative of this process of cleansing/purification.

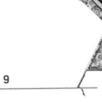

9

<u>Ten</u>: 40th Street & Stanford Drive, this proposal tries not to alter the terrain while it amplifies and celebrates experiences along the paths which are now hidden, muted, or ignored. The wash is accepted and celebrated as a water garden/ park. The ACDC becomes a huge, dark echo chamber, the noise of water flowing through it is amplified to the surface through passages and noise chambers. The noise covers the thin strip by the canal, creating a perceived cooling effect, through its presence.

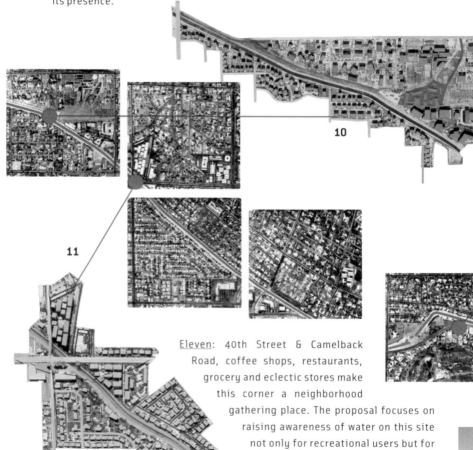

10

11

<u>Eleven</u>: 40th Street & Camelback Road, coffee shops, restaurants, grocery and eclectic stores make this corner a neighborhood gathering place. The proposal focuses on raising awareness of water on this site not only for recreational users but for motorists. Water is used in a dramatic way with shooting fountains, water overhead will be shed off creating places where people can share an umbrella and interact.

Twelve: Herberger Park, 56th Street & Indian School Road, the proposal mediates the level of the bank and the park, giving special attention to the trees. The
dynamic quality of the life of a tree will be contrasted by static constructions
with will remain after the trees die or are removed, so that, unlike the many
trees along the canal removed before these without a trace, these will remain
in some form.

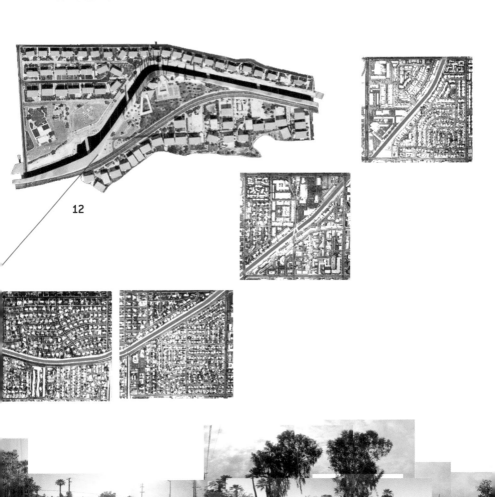

12

13

<u>Thirteen</u>: ARTComm, Cattle Track Road & McDonald Drive, the proposal suggests an Interdisciplinary Arts Community, that will recall the lifestyle and sensual richness of Scottsdale before development. This proposal would rely on the accentuation of the five senses.

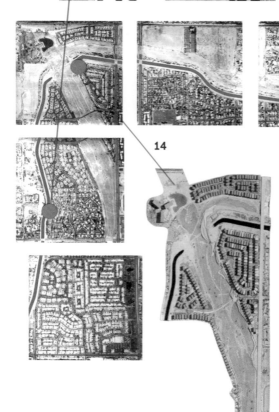

14

<u>Fourteen:</u> Indian Bend Wash, Hayden Road & Indian Bend Wash, the bank between the golf course and the neighborhood offers space for connections between the two. A neighborhood commons and multi-level plaza with recreational complexes is proposed.

<u>Fifteen:</u> Granite Reef Dam, the site is located on the east edge of the Phoenix Valley on the Salt River, south of the convergence of the Verde and the Salt Rivers and in the valley formed by the Red Mountain and Schelct's Butte. Presence of four waters at the site– the Salt River water, Verde river water, run-off water through the natural washes, and Colorado River.water in the CAP inform a proposal that mixes these watersin an elaborate water park.

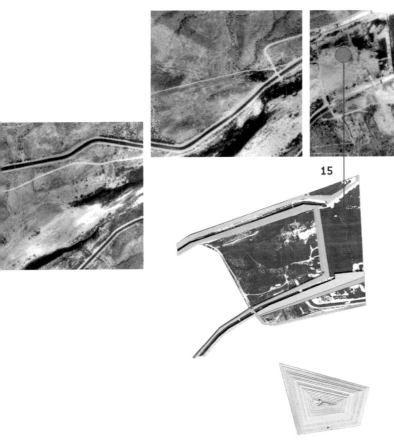

15

Tower Game. Each each student made an isometric construction. The Tower is a marker revealing the topographic change form the beginning to end of the canal (113 feet). Two towers [beginning and end] have the same elevation, thus one is 113 feet high and the other 113 feet deep. Each isometric construction addressed an aspect of the tower one its particular site. the drawings were superimposed onto each other resulting in coincidental conditions. These conditions trace the memory of past iterations and describe the erasure of the physicality of the original tower. To retain the memory of the tower, a type of analog is designed. Each site records a proposed construction that captures the ephemeral qualities of the towers. For example at the beginning a water maze is proposed that mixes the three separate water sources as they would mix if allowed to flow into the negative tower. At the end of the canal the constantly moving shadow of the tower is etched into the ground becoming a water park for neighborhood children.

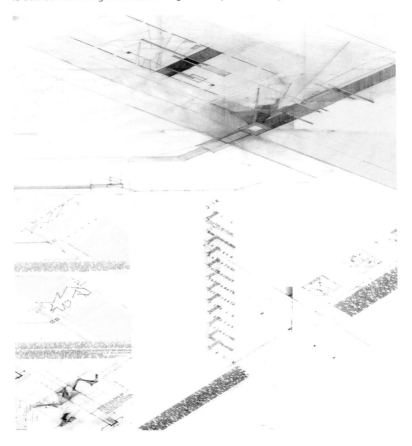

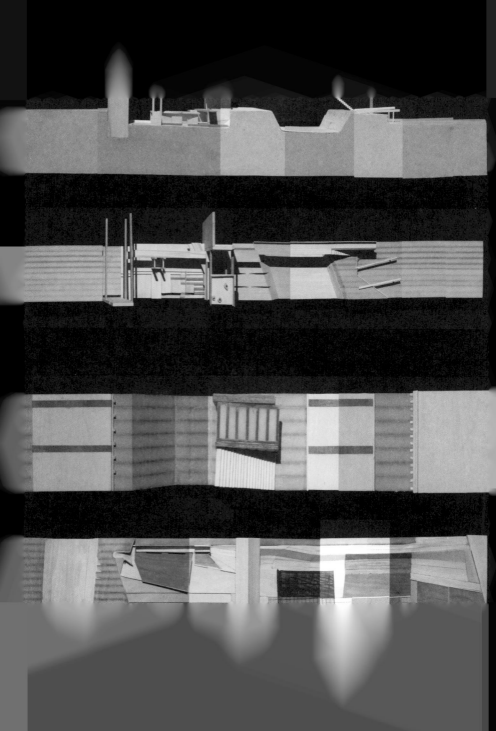

48th Street and Arizona Canal

The project at 48th street proposes that the leftover space adjacent to the shopping center become public gathering space in a way similar to gathering spaces along the canals during the 1950s. These spaces refer back to the conditions of the 1950s by exposing the workings of the canals at that time. For example, an underground water trough that crosses the site is opened again and used to feed a field of newly planted orange trees that replace the grove of trees lost with the construction of the mall. Or, the drainage channel on the east of the site is made accessible with a stair and viewing tower to watch the occasional rush of overflow water. And on the north side of the site a high-density housing project is proposed that re-introduces an ancient typology, dwelling along the canal.

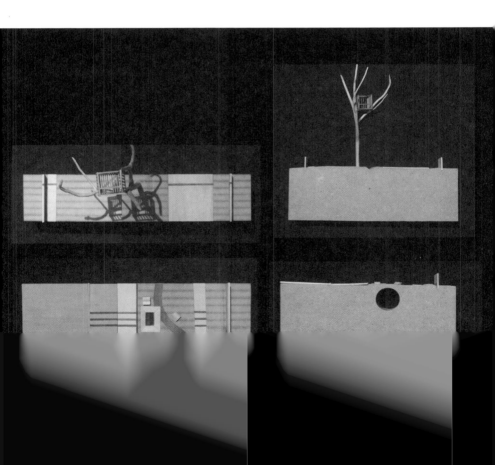

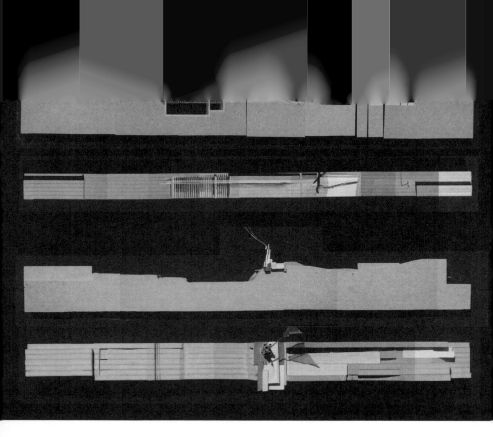

Northern Avenue and Arizona Canal

On the Northern Street site several of the eucalyptuses trees from the 1950s remain. They shade the canal and recall a day when life along the canal existed. This project makes use of this memory and proposes a vision of an environmentally considered park that creates a series of follies with the themes of water, earth, and wind.

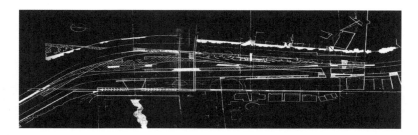

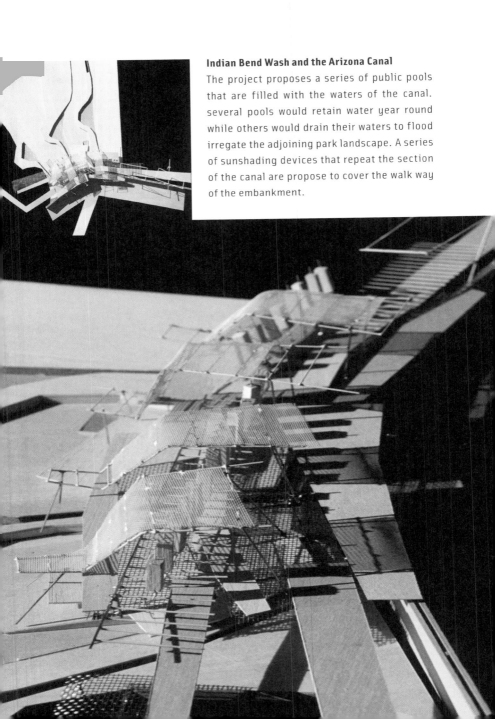

Indian Bend Wash and the Arizona Canal

The project proposes a series of public pools that are filled with the waters of the canal. several pools would retain water year round while others would drain their waters to flood irregate the adjoining park landscape. A series of sunshading devices that repeat the section of the canal are propose to cover the walk way of the embankment.

Water Exhibition

Finally, the studio wanted to heighten public awareness of our water system and its great potential to become a wonderful public amenity. The studio invited city officials, arts commissioners, and neighborhood association members from the three municipalities that the Arizona Canal crosses, to view the work in a public exhibition and participate in a group discussion about canal development. The exhibition was designed with the intention to display the work and simultaneously create a provoking experience with water. A system of temporary walls were constructed with wood and cloth. The walls contained water in motion which when lit from above reflected this movement on to the cloth walls. All drawings were displayed on transparent plexi-glass, therefore the motion of the water was superimposed onto the surface of the drawings. Section models through each project created several tight spaces that the visitor could pass through to view the work, thus experiencing tension and precarious quality of many of the design proposals.

City Proposals:
29 Drawings for
East West Hollywood

*Mary-Ann Ray
and Robert Mangurian*

Part One. Santa Monica Boulevard, A Gallery of Difference

This is a project that is part urban design and part cosmetics. It is a project that attempts to find deep meaning in shallow surfaces and shallow space. We were asked to look at a central street for the city of West Hollywood—Santa Monica Boulevard—in the context of their renovation program. Before committing more funds to the program, they were interested in having an overview from both an aesthetic and a functional viewpoint—a kind of master plan without being a master plan.

We began by looking closely at the designated eastern half of Santa Monica Boulevard within West Hollywood. Our reconnaissance involved looking closely and recording the street and surrounding area through many composite photographs. We decided to divide our analytical "eyes" into two ways of thinking and within the two a further divide.

One—*Thinking/seeing from the air and thinking/seeing from the ground.*
The aerial view came from studying the maps and plan drawings of the situation to look for patterns, both uniformities and exceptions. We tried to see this vertical view mapping exercise as a search for tendencies that could be seen as layers. The ground view came from direct experience on the street—from the car and on foot. Our main tools for the horizontal view were photographs and interviews.

Two—*Thinking that attempts to find commonalties and uniformities and that works to find the exceptions, differences, and anomalies.*
The bias of most planning and many architects is trying to make a place have an identity (at times we are also for this). Our parting of ways comes from making the identity emerge through the application of devices that gives the area a kind of uniformity—"stitching together," "blending in," and so on. While not being totally against this way of thinking, we attempted to see these "commonalties" as backgrounded, instead of providing "frames" for the great variety and diversity that exists along Santa Monica Boulevard. We also felt that the strong identity for this section of Santa Monica Boulevard could come from the hidden (and not so hidden) exceptions, oddities, and anomalies that exist. If Sunset Strip is known for its billboard gallery, then Santa Monica Boulevard—the east West Hollywood section—might be known for the gallery of difference/oddities.

We looked for use eccentricity, historical anomalies, things off-site that affected the site, oddities/landmarks (in the Smithsonian sense), the shape of the street, coloration and material palette, scale differences, dead-end streets, particular views, topographic eccentricity (and normalcy), text, night city, and finally patterns of normalcy and of the everyday.

Part Two. *Drawing On and To the Surface*

In our travels across and through the eastern half of the city of West Hollywood we have enthusiastically discovered and embraced many surprising things. We have found eccentric treasures, special situations, and a unique atmosphere. The projects that follow propose to strengthen and help draw to the surface these and other qualities of east West Hollywood.

The western portion of the city of West Hollywood is famous for its design culture, active nightlife, Halloween street-party extravaganza, Sunset Boulevard, and other highly publicized assets. The eastern half of the city is one of the most densely populated urban areas in the United States, rivaling parts of Manhattan but with a building stock of medium-sized, thin stucco-walled "dingbat" type apartments. The people who live in east West Hollywood are a diverse group, and many Russian immigrants live with extended families. This area seems to lack a sense of identity in the expression of its physical form, and the citizens are the first to agree with this. Running counter to this is the fact that the citizens strongly identify with subtle aspects of their "city." These subtle aspects below the surface, barely (if at all) visible, and often subconscious, are the very things our designs and plans attempted to mine for content.

The following is a series of speculative possibilities, interventions for Santa Monica Boulevard between Harper and La Brea, including Fairfax and La Brea Avenues in east West Hollywood. The ideas depicted here are presented in an often diagrammatic and exaggerated form in order to strongly relay some thoughts on the physical situation and possible future of the city. The proposals fall into ten primary categories:

I   Dead-end streets (Jefferson's jog)
II The district/street as a city gallery for art projects
III The miniature and the gigantic

IV Billboards and large signs reconsidered

V   Night life/night light

VI The potential of the perpendicular
    (side streets, building sides, or flanks as façades)

VII Additional oddities (enhancing the eccentric) and identifying (framing) the
    existing odd mix

VIII Working on the outdoor rooms (missing buildings)

IX Making something of the very hidden topography
    (perhaps this is an oddity)

X   Working on the transformation of the shop building
    (one-story dominant/two-story exception) — false fronts, makeovers,
    increasing transparencies, ganging up (clumping), and greening

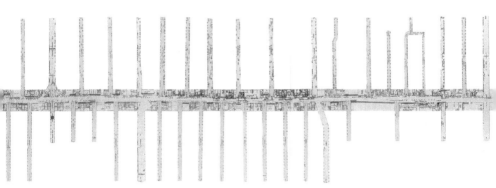

I. Dead-end streets, "Jefferson's Jog"—the Gigantic Bit-Map

President Thomas Jefferson left a physical index of democracy as he "drew" an
egalitarian one-mile square north/south/east/west grid superimposed over
the entire topography of the continental United States. One disturbance in the
system is the spherical geometry of the earth's surface. Santa Monica Boulevard
happens to be one of the places where the grid adjusts to the curvature of the
Earth—jogging as a bit-map would to conform to the geometry of the sphere.
Dead-end streets, a phenomenon that we have titled "Jefferson's Jog," identifies

as potential sites the buildings (or building clumps) that occupy the dead center of the dead-end streets and the potential view down and up these streets (from the dead-ended positions on Santa Monica Boulevard).

Proposals:

1. City porches on the north side of Santa Monica
   (looking down to Los Angeles proper)
2. City couches/chairs on the south side of Santa Monica
   (looking up to the Hollywood Hills)
3. Finding storefronts within view
   (that are ready for work and are at the dead-ends)

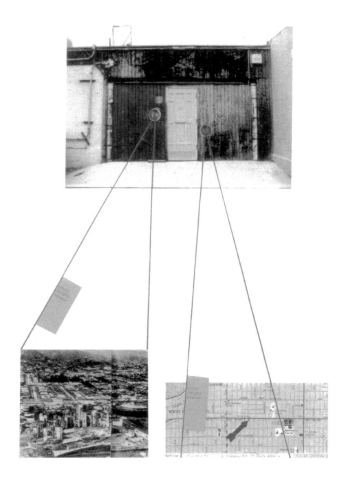

4. Fix the holes (where there are no buildings)
5. Other perceptual effects (sky windows and other visual refuge)
6. Marking the curb (mapping and registering the Jeffersonian grid, records of other things inscribed)

II. The district/street as a city gallery for art projects

Yes, there are a number of "Art Parks" throughout the world but never a decentralized museum/gallery that is really part of the city. The works would be of both installation types and works that require interior or protected exterior space.

Proposals:

7. Small projects/small budgets (projects that take up little space, little funds, but do something that could be big)
8. Alley projects: seams/connections (the open air city gallery/museum)
9. Peephole art (wide-angle lens, secrets to be found and viewed)

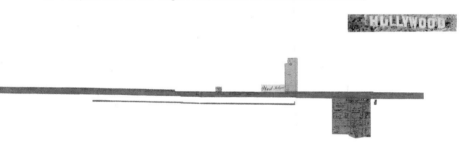

III. The miniature and the gigantic

We feel that the most effective areas to work within for this project involve the realm of the miniature and the gigantic (extreme scales). The "in-between" or medium-scaled features of the city—the buildings, streets, sidewalks, and vegetation—are costly and for the most part in place. The miniature includes the building wall/façade (we consider this not only to be a frontal element but also the "flank" façade, the horizontal façade, etc.) and moves within even smaller scale things. Yes, this would include the typical "street furniture" stuff but also things not normally considered (such as curb spots, doors, door knobs, particular signs, odd trees, etc.) The miniature posits the possibility of partial "makeovers" as opposed to the full modernizations of the façade. The gigantic sees the large-scale patterns having potential adjustments (again through the Commercial Revitalization Project). We have developed several "themes" for the gigantic that involve Santa Monica Boulevard along with Fairfax/La Brea as the large-scale armature. We have also found situations for an emerging large-scale playout through media like color or light, such as the blueing of the street stuff, the street trees, and large-scale lighting.

Proposals:

10. Other street furniture (taking the term as literally as possible—single chairs, bike racks, phone booths, shopping carts, and tables)

11. More street furniture (outdoor tables)

12. Blue zones

   (new blues, borrowed blues, other blues, and large-scale armatures)

13. Blue zones (mix with greened zones)

14. Kids' scale stuff/other scale (the miniature city becomes the normal city for the city dwellers with small bodies)

IV. Billboards and large signs reconsidered

We have explored possible alternatives to the typical billboard/large sign situation, with an eye toward the strong spatial possibilities within these elements. Yes, we are familiar with the ordinances limiting signage (and we do feel that these ordinances could be looked at again), but we feel that this territory needs to be revisited. The proposals include making building-like walls where there aren't any, making frontage extensions that help modernize and spatialize (but which aren't always venues for commercialization), back-lit lantern-like surfaces for street lighting, horizontal roof/porch "billboards," and green/planted surfaces.

Proposals:

15. Translucent walls on the south side

   (for single-story buildings: light fixtures for daytime)

16. Green boards (growing things raised up toward the sky)

17. Horizontal billboards ("Bladerunners," shade devices, and supplemental street lighting from glowing surfaces overhead)

V. Making something of the very hidden topography (perhaps this is an oddity)
The slope to the south of Santa Monica is subtle; the slope to the north is stronger and ends with the Hollywood Hills. Along Santa Monica Boulevard, there are some real conditions left (along the north side). We have thought of some things that make the topographic situation more apparent. One possibility is to propose a tilting back of façades along the north side of the street and a tilting in along the south side. Other projects are podiums, terraces, platforms, ramps, steps, waterfalls, and seating.

Note: This idea can be seen in the map entitled, "The Subtle Topography—The Shape of Flatland Moving into Foothills."

VI. Night life/night light
Night life/night light might provide the most economical use of funds. We have mapped some lighting potentials and have thought about an overall lighting plan. The plan is not precise and all encompassing but rather suggests types of lighting interventions. These are seen as partial or incomplete makeovers as opposed to the totalizing complete redo. Lighting works toward improving the sidewalk and street-crossing situation as well.

Proposals:
18. More blue (night blueing the street with blue light/blue reflective paint)
19. Light walls: lite walls (side streets with blank walls—perpendicular is lit)
20. Bright places (places to cross the street: lighting the few crosswalks)
21. Night trees: light trees (lighting the "black holes")

VII. The potential of the perpendicular (side streets, building sides)
Usually, we think that the façade or building front is where the action is. Along Santa Monica Boulevard, the dead-end streets present the classic façade condition. But, the pedestrian of the modern city is in a car, and the experience of the street (and districts) comes from this automotive experience—seeing through the windshield or sometimes a rearview mirror and entering the old walking city through the parking lot. Thus, the sides of buildings (or perpendicular projections) are usually more important than the fronts, revising the dominance of the true or street front in the walking city. We have found examples of this on Santa Monica Boulevard and elsewhere and will isolate situations where the building sides exist because of the open space along Santa Monica Boulevard. The side streets, because of their "dead-end" condition, present a side wall ready for action.

Proposal:
22. Side street thin buildings
    (news stands, thin grocers, shoeshines, keyshops, florists, etc.)

VIII. Additional oddities (enhancing the eccentric) and identifying (framing) the existing odd mix
Raising the condition of oddities is part of what is required here. We have found and described many oddities and treasures in our travels through east West Hollywood. The thrust toward difference (in the design of the façades) as opposed to a unifying trend appears as a clear tendency that we have strengthened. The unifying instinct must come from something else. And in some ways, a place that has an abundance of odd situations is in some strange way unified. The oddities project has led to proposals that find, frame, and enhance eccentricities.

Proposals:
23. Transforming the almost oddity
    (enhancing the eccentric—the house on the street)
24. Framing oddities
    (reverse peepholes: views from inside shop out toward found treasures)
25. Framing oddities
    (identifying the odd mix, framing from the inside-out)

IX. Working on the outdoor rooms (missing buildings)

The missing buildings along Santa Monica Boulevard seen in the normative urban design terms are problematic. In our terms, they certainly are there and have

presented some powerful possibilities. Doing the façade for the missing building combined with some greening instincts and night light have led to interesting project thoughts for these places. Also, the missing buildings are alternative spaces—as missing "teeth," they are alternates to the space of the street and the sidewalk—and can be strengthened through the Revitalization Program.

Note: No proposals have been specifically assigned to this category, but this idea can be seen in several other proposals.

X. Working on the transformation of the shop building (one-story dominant/ two-story exception)—possibilities

A. False fronts

Adding dimension to some of the building fronts might be a good idea. The scale of the city in constantly increasing. Those streets that remain from the older LA scale are lost in the shuffle. The increase in scale might not always be associated with commercialization. A translucent false front on the south side of the street becomes a solar light transmitter (and would work at night as a way of lighting up the street). Also, the false fronts might lead to the idea of "false sides."

B. Makeovers

We are excited about the quick, easy, and sleight-of-hand makeover—less a total remake of a façade but rather just nudging things. If the nudging is clever enough, the whole is transformed (without having to redo the whole).

Proposal:
26. Chain link fences (greening the chain link)

C. Increasing transparencies

The modern mall depends on transparency—seeing into the shop. This is possible and effective because of the closed environment (lower light level). The outdoor shopping street (the older model) has a hard time competing with the openness of mall space. We have looked into ways of opening up the existing store fronts. The south side of the street does not have the sun beating down on it and has an easier time with transparency. The north side requires some sun shading (perhaps in the form of a horizontal roof/lawn or other maneuver).

Proposals:

27. Increasing transparencies
    (increase the site of the storefront)
28. Increasing transparencies
    (illustrating building insides on building (out)sides)

D. Ganging up (clumping)

We are looking at possibilities of clumping—like things that form a place along Santa Monica or even a small district. Thus, the street might be seen as a strand of DNA with particular places (clumps) within a somewhat neutral background.

E. Greening

The possibilities of "greening" have been explored. Yes, trees, (and the existing pattern no doubt can be extended) but also things like walls of green, green façades, green coming from the tops of buildings, and other quite spectacular hanging gardens. If enough of this were accomplished, east West Hollywood would be a place to visit just to come see these vertical urban gardens.

Proposal:

29. Greening: green from tops
    ("hair" on buildings plus hanging gardens)

GREEN FROM TOPS: HAIR ON BUILDINGS proposes to make buildings appear as faces or characters along the street. The "façade" and the "face" would be one and the same. These hair-topped buildings would be achieved through plantings—long planting for Rapunzel-like characters and short grasses or reeds for the crew-cut look. The façade itself would then need to find clever ways to suggest other facial features—eyes, nose, cheeks, brows, mustache, mouth, chin, neck, shoulders, etc. Those façades/faces lucky enough to occur at an intersection would be able to add the ear and hair on the side wall!

Buildings that are also faces are big attractions in any city. People climb up behind the Spanish Steps in Rome just to see the Herziana Library entrance through the mouth of a grotesque face.

INCREASING TRANSPARENCIES proposes to find a way to make the storefront structure work within the current contemporary patterns of shopping. One of the situations that the public has gotten used to is the dominant and attractive transparency of the shopping center mall. The shop windows are almost all glass and the lighting within is brighter than the outside covered mall thus affording the ability to see deep within the shop. INCREASING TRANSPARENCIES states that some of the storefronts need to be altered to increase the visibility into the shop and, ideally, to deep within.

In proposing façade designs, some simple things might occur to promote the ODDITY. These proposals would fall into two categories—first, FRAMING ODDITIES, and second, ADDITIONAL ODDITIES. In FRAMING ODDITIES, views from inside shops would connect to a located existing oddity through "reverse" aimed peepholes that look out rather than in or though carefully positioned (window) frames that capture the "found treasures" through paradox.

BLUE ZONES is one of the projects that might effectively make visible a gigantic, or very large, pattern in West Hollywood. By proposing an adamant use of the color blue whenever possible, the city can enhance the existing commitment to the color as seen in the light posts and street furniture.

The current street blue is a very opaque blue. BLUE ZONES proposes adding other blues, perhaps blues borrowed from things like the sky. These might be blues that would be more silvery, phosphorescent, or shimmering. Through careful choices of colors, very luminous blues can be achieved through inexpensive layers of paint.

The façades of the shops and buildings along Santa Monica and Fairfax and La Brea would be encouraged to experiment with all kinds of "blueings." Blue windows might be installed in some of the shop windows so that as you looked in or out, a glowing blue world would be visible beyond.

This project shows the mixing of a BLUE ZONE with one of the zones of GREENING.

In ADDITIONAL ODDITIES, the odd remaining house and lawn left on the commercial street—Santa Monica Boulevard—is recognized and found to be something worth saving. It contributes to the story of a city of West Hollywood that encourages difference and the eccentric in both the people and the buildings/spaces that are a part of the city.

In order to enhance and transform this "almost oddity," several things could occur. The lawn might be made extra green and groomed. The house itself might be painted in "All-American" white on the siding, and a porch swing would be added at the front. Flower pots, patterned wallpaper, and figurines would appear in the windows, and these would be illuminated at night. A sweet picket fence based on a traditional historic American design would replace the chain link presently in place. From time to time, the fence would require white washing—recalling the adventures of Tom Sawyer.

Grassy Strata, Growing Wall would be achieved through the introduction of the box/trough, in a narrow projection from the building. The narrowness of the box and the selection of the grasses would ensure a tight fit to the building. The project demands a flush, wall-like appearance.

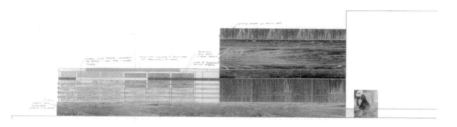

The maintenance of Grassy Strata, Growing Wall would be similar to that of a vertical garden or a tilted-up landscape. A timed drip irrigation system would be built into the façade, and the water moving down the wall would be expressed in an evocative way—a cooling spray, the sound of dripping water, a waterfall, a sun break and would conserve water usage by recycling water where possible. The selection of grasses would lean toward drought resistant plant material. The architecture of Grassy Strata, Growing Wall would be a "self-growing" architecture, a living architecture that would ebb and flow with the change of season, chroma shifts—blue-green to acid yellows, soft off-whites to deep reds, etc.

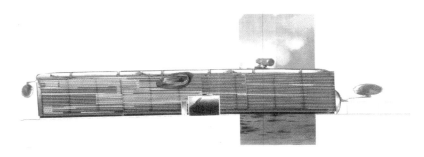

The available space at the northeast corner of the intersection of Detroit and Santa Monica could be transformed into a waterfall space. Attached to a metal trellis, Detroit's Radiator Waterfall would be outrigged mirrors, lights, and reflectors. These would allow light and images to bounce around and shimmer, and the colored reflectors would throw spots of colored light onto adjacent parts of the city. Also attached to the trellis would be sculptural shapes and ports— some bumper-like and automobile-like but at extra-large scales. These would then be chromed; in a sense the building would become a factory for working on itself and for making itself. At night, the grill or "radiator" would be back-lit, and the chromed accoutrements would be spot lit. A simple recycling pump would return water from a trough at the bottom up to a series of very small spouts at the top. The effect would be that of a translucent scrim, and since the space is open to the sky, these surfaces would be back-lit during the day. At night, artificial blue light would take over.

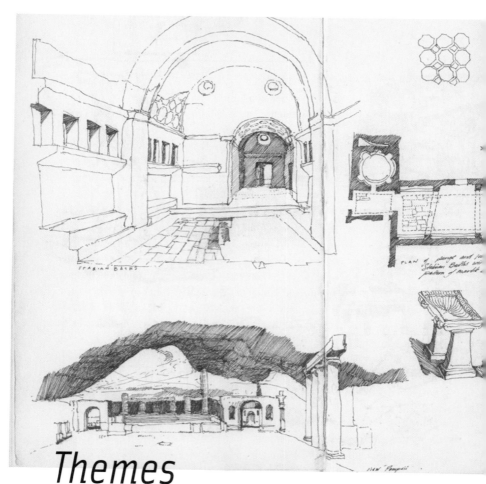

Themes
of the Architectural
Meta-Project
Martha LaGess

On Representation

An issue that will have exceptional importance to the design professions in the twenty-first century is the relationship between design and the conventions of representation. Recently, exponential growth in the use of computers and web-based communication systems in many design fields, including architecture and landscape architecture, has made it urgently necessary to reconsider this relationship. At the same time, its great scope and significance make it extremely difficult for design professionals to discuss, or even to think about.

On the one hand, this difficulty arises because design and representation seem indistinguishable from each other. Design first appears in the world as representations, and, vice versa, representation is always concretized as a particular design. On the other hand, design and representation can also be thought of as playing quite different parts in the design-construction process. Representation is often considered to be a "neutral" medium, translating between design as an activity—as thought—and design as a thing—as constructed object/environment. Put another way, although issues of representation are truly fundamental to design practice, most designers overlook them, either because they seem identical to or else quite separate from design concerns per se.

Nevertheless, in the age of design electronics the enigmatic relationship between design and representation has become a more visible and more interesting issue than before. And without giving in to any impulse to oversimplify the subtle and complex causes of this trend, it is desirable to point out two outstanding reasons for the change. The first reason is that the appearance of new, computer-empowered representational strategies and techniques—none of which can properly be called drawing—undermines the presumed identity of design and the old conventions of representation, especially the centuries-old conventions of orthographic projection and perspective. The second reason is that the new location for information (including information about the physical world)—the World Wide Web—is beginning to smudge modernity's boundary between fictional and real, between representations and the physical world. In the face of these changes, I believe that designers can (and must) reconsider the issues of representation explicitly, and perhaps one day, the twenty-first century will be thought of as the beginning of another kind of Renaissance.

The Postmodern

The Message and the Structure of the Message
(Since the author is an architect, the arguments put forward here refer to architecture; for the other design professions, similar stories could certainly be told.)

Most of us would agree that, in its day, the "Postmodern" profoundly affected the practice of architecture, just as the "electronic revolution" affects it now. Few, on the other hand, would think of these two "revolutions" as associated developments. We usually regard them as quite different historical phenomena, separated not only in time but also in subject matter. However, this impression of two entirely separate sets of concerns is quite misleading in regard to the issue of architectural representation. In that one area at least, a brief review of their (overlapping) histories reveals that the Postmodern and the Electronic Revolution can be treated as almost continuous.

Looking back at most of the drawings in architectural magazines of the early 1960s, we are struck by a kind of rationalism. At that time, drawings of ordinary American or European practices emphasized the value of clarity and technical precision in orthographic projections. Perspectives were assigned the role of projecting artistic or commercial value, and they were usually made only at, or near, the end of the project. In general, the practice of architectural design was strongly linked to the convention of orthographic projection and how it handled problems of form; measures and proportions that appeared in orthographic views were considered extremely important. For all but a few innovators, design seemed to be a matter of working out a logical, aesthetically pleasing, and commercially desirable solution to architectural issues as seen in building "slices": plan, section, elevation, and detail.

But during that decade, critical positions and alternative practices were multiplying within the discipline of architecture, as they were in other fields. We can recall this atmosphere with just a few examples (in no particular order and not necessarily the most important): there were the projects of Buckminster Fuller, Archigram, Dutch "social" architects such as Van Eyck and Hertzberger, and Frei Otto's structural/material experiments based on "natural" objects and forces. And there were so many books: Rossi's *Architecture of the City,* Venturi's *Complexity and Contradiction in Architecture,* and *Five Architects* (about Eisenmann, Graves,

Gwathmey, Hejduk, and Meier—not published until 1972) among them. All of these projects and publications were implicitly or explicitly critical of the authority and values of the contemporary architectural mainstream.

Any thorough architectural history of the period will need to account for how, and possibly why, the postmodern became the most popular form of experiment in a general atmosphere of experimentation in the 1960s and early 1970s. The postmodern was both a cataclysmic shift in general design interests and the gradual (and thematically related) general adoption of the working assumption that representation was an integral part of design itself. Representational experimentation came before the postmodern but had been a matter of only isolated experimental interest before the mid-1960s (like the famous drawings of Archigram) not an everyday working assumption in many practices as it became ten years later. In the early 1960s, collage and photomontage were still only isolated incidents in conventional orthographic and perspective representational practices—practices that seemed generally sufficient to explore architectural modernism's range of interests. But not long after Venturi's *Complexity and Contradiction,* it had become generally understood that inventing new drawing (and modeling) methods and inventing new architectural ideas was a reciprocal process. It began to seem impossible to have one without the other; it had become clear that new kinds of representations made new kinds of design issues visible.

In the 1970s and 1980s, this process of developing new design issues through representation, and vice versa, became a kind of cottage industry. Postmodern representational experiments revived a vast array of historical drawing techniques (especially from the Beaux Arts) and made many "technology transfers" from modern art: collage, frottage, overlays, and surrealist scale effects. Architectural representation, which formerly had semi-engineering status on one hand and an illustrative, advertisement-like status on the other hand, was completely transformed from the 1960s to the 1980s. New uses of composition, tone, color, pattern, figurative form, and text-as-image were introduced.

Everybody knows that the strongest postmodern interest was premodern movement architecture, including its history, philosophy, and formal vocabulary, but we tend to forget that semiotics/linguistics, social groups, and (for want of a better way of expression) architectural "mechanism" were of almost equal fascination. The explosion of drawing and modeling experiments carried these issues forward, and it was already during the postmodern that design problems ceased to be so strongly identified with orthographic projection.

To say this seems a little ironic of course, since there are so many memorable orthographic drawings among postmodern documents. Orthographic projection—simple orthographic projection as line drawing—had not become useless, but it had, to some extent, begun to seem less relevant. Problems of architectural language, historical connectivity, programmatic narrative, and material variety could not be seen directly in this type of drawing. The new problems required new forms of representation that would make them perceptible: tone, shadow, shading, and color could show design ideas that line drawings could not. Likewise, collaged plans, sections, and views could propose a complex intersection of design issues impossible to represent with standard orthographic views.

Before the postmodern, the architect had hovered between engineering and construction practices and art-related design practices. Engineering and construction called for analysis, measurement, calculation, and precision in drafting. Design demanded vision, judgement, and artistic drawing skills. Though rather uncomfortable, this situation had been stable since the nineteenth century; the problem of the status of the architecture discipline as a type of knowledge was certainly not fresh.

But after World War II and especially in the late 1950s and early 1960s, there had been considerable effort to tip the balance in favor of engineering by making design more rational. In post-Sputnik America, the general social trend toward the scientific seems to have found its architectural manifestation in the development of what were called "design methods." The postmodern reversed this tendency: during the postmodern 1970s and 1980s, proto-scientific "design methods" were first discredited and then largely forgotten. Architecture's connection with art was definitively reinforced through the revival of interest in everything premodern, especially the Beaux Arts.

Architectural representation was now to be treated as a special kind of graphic art. It became conceivable to include works of architects in art galleries and museum collections and even to open specialist galleries. Architectural representation was no longer to be regarded as a "transparent" technical tool, faithfully mirroring the "real" proposal or even as a commercial tool capable of selling a project. Now it was to be considered an artistic, rhetorical device that could "construct" a message on many levels. Architectural drawings had become works in themselves regardless of the building they were intended to represent. Marshall McCluhan's statement, "the medium is the message" also found its application in architecture.

Postmodern Dénouement

But from the mid-1980s, the sobering experiences of AIDS and financial hardship (following the 1987 stock market crash) took their toll on the mood of revolutionary optimism that had gripped architecture and design (and Western culture in general) since the 1960s. The rhetorical experiments of 1970s and 1980s representation and buildings were beginning to look a little thin and self-indulgent. And at the same time, postmodern had become too ordinary—"planner postmodernism." The representational experiments no longer seemed to produce new design ideas. Just as society had largely absorbed the lessons of the '60s and '70s social upheavals, mainstream architectural practice had absorbed the postmodern. Inevitably, its avant-garde appeal was lost.

From the architectural point of view at least, the postmodern was considered finished. Many people now strongly identified this label with a banal sort of historicism. This identification had a strange effect; it meant that works of formalist, linguistic experiment no longer seemed to be postmodern at all, even though they had arisen hand-in-hand with the works of historical allusion. The awareness of shared semiotic, programmatic, and social concerns, which had tied historical and nonhistorical work together, was repressed.

"Formalist" work, such as that of Peter Eisenmann, Bernard Tschumi, or Zaha Hadid, had seemed to be an integral part of the postmodern at the time. But after the mid-1980s, that kind of work began to seem as if it belonged to a completely different kind of critique of the modern, deconstruction, or perhaps, even part of a continuous development of modernism, all along. Many home truths of the postmodern (if it entertained the idea of "truths" at all) had begun to seem quaint, provincial, and even absurd. Criticisms of the "modern" project now seemed strange. The idea that architectural representation might have to do with the construction of a message was preserved; however, some interest in representation was salvaged from the postmodern ruins. A drawing could still be the architectural message—a series of collaged fragments of information, an objectified desire.

In the late 1980s, something like a modernist practice returned to many "design-oriented" offices. But interests such as figurative forms and space, nonhierarchical structures, and the architectural syntax were all preserved in new, apparently modernist projects. Many drawing techniques the postmodern had developed were still employed, even though the historical flavor that had been popular earlier was dropped. One might even argue that there were two stages of the postmodern—a first phase that emphasized the examination and revival of some premodern and extra-modern architectural interests and a second phase that incorporated first phase lessons into a revision of modern architecture's vocabulary.

The Electronic Revolution

First phase: Production
Today few would bother with the sort of debate that would be needed to distinguish different aspects of the postmodern. This is because the transition between what could be considered its first stage and what came afterward has been lost in the electronic era's shadow. Already in the administrative areas of wealthy and/or large practices in the mid-1980s, space had been made available for new machines: computers, printers, a fax machine, and probably one of the powerful new photocopiers. At the same time, computers had already appeared on some drafting desks. But they didn't multiply quickly, because most offices couldn't afford the strange and luxurious new "toys."
As the postmodern period in architecture ended, architectural representation's movement toward the arts lost momentum, went into reverse, and then stopped. Was this because the postmodern's intensive design-representational experimentation had been exhausted through its partisan's overexuberance? Or was it because the new electronic tools simply diverted architects' attentions elsewhere? Whatever the reasons, the first part of the electronic revolution in architecture could be called a "production" phase. At that time, the computer was used for engineering-related production, not art-related design. The postmodern raised design issues and issues of representation as if they were identical. The "production" phase of design electronics did the opposite: the computer entered design offices, and later schools, through the production "backdoor."

During the electronic revolution's "production phase," architecture firms invested in the new electronic machines for the sake of consultants, especially engineers. As more engineers used computers, architects were motivated to join them for the sake of "coordination." For both architects and engineers, transferring documents on disk was relatively easy compared to transferring hard copies, and the digital documents themselves made overlays more exact. Eventually, hand-drafting ceased to be an option for design practices with large commissions and sophisticated consultants. By the early 1990s, many more offices were computerized, and it became possible to define some entry-level architects' positions as "computer drafting."

As this situation developed, use of the computer seemed to polarize the profession into designers and producers, even more definitively than ever before. At its simplest, this was because producers used the machine and designers did not. But this was not the only reason; there were other more subtle reasons pertaining to the computer's origins and use. Scientists and mathematicians had created the computer and defined what it was able to do; so in the beginning, it seemed obvious that the computer could not, by definition, have anything to do with design, since design was obviously an art-oriented activity, the opposite of science. Even the fact that the computer was a machine seemed a sufficient argument that it could have nothing to do with art, since art seemed to require the free exercise of human judgement and skill. More particularly, it was clear that the precise, logical operations necessary for computer drafting were far from the lateral thinking and deliberate ambiguity of the skilled designer. Through the computer, the science versus art dilemma the architect had faced since the nineteenth century was exaggerated.

Second phase: Visualization

As the computer polarized design and production, it changed the balance of power between them, almost imperceptibly. Though architecture had long been divided into art-oriented design and technology-oriented production, these two aspects of the field had never been considered equals. Technology had always been treated as design's servant. And design was an art; no matter how much the image of technology, or even its practice, had influenced modern architecture, the modern architect remained some sort of artist, at heart. It was quite common to encourage a young person with drawing talent to become an architect.

Arguably, this was primarily because the art of drawing was the architect's primary means of design production. After all, according to the stories of art history, the history of modern architectural representation began in the Renaissance when architect and painter/sculptor were often the same person.

During the "production phase" of design electronics, design representation for the designer was still a matter of hand-drawing and, therefore, indisputably remained an art issue. Throughout this time, the word "technology" still seemed to mean something opposed to art: "technology" suggested engineering or construction, both part of the act of design realization not part of the design act itself. But when computer technology entered the realm of design representation for the designer directly, design art could no longer form a clear opposition to design realization technology. When this happened, the old distinction between art and technology in architecture began to fail. The power relation between design and production shifted as technology entered the realm of the design itself.

For the first few years of the 1990s, when the computer was commonly used for orthographic projections only, these documents were, in fact, often used for client presentations. But since the designers did not work on the computers directly, their means of design production remained unaffected. Furthermore, presentation drawing par excellence, perspective, remained a matter of handwork. Computer "set-ups" for perspectives were already possible, but the average architect couldn't render complicated drawings easily or quickly, so most perspectives were still completed by hand, even if they were begun by computer. There were specialist companies that could provide computer renderings for a substantial fee, but most architects still preferred the atmosphere of renderings in paint.

Software that made computer perspectives and rendering relatively easy and fast did not appear until the mid-1990s. Rendering was still a speciality and was still often provided by outside contractors, but now the designer could sit down with the computer perspective expert and see the project appear from many points of view quickly. This was a revelation. Since design electronics' first phase had affected production only, in most cases, most designers had remained relatively unaware of the new tools' powers. Suddenly, when fast computer rendering became available, the designer's job description changed. Representation was becoming a matter of technology rather than hand-produced art. The architect who had been a mature artist scrambled to become a technocrat.

Before this change, the designer as artist was an authority, like an atelier master, whether they produced their own drawings or not. The designer had been able to pick up pen or pencil to show beginners how to do their jobs. Now the "beginners" had to teach themselves, since the mature designer had no idea how to use the computer and, in most cases, was too busy, or too embarrassed, to learn. Soon the technician-beginners knew more about the new forms of representation than their bosses. Despite the visualization empowerment the computer offered to the designer, this new state of affairs undermined the traditional authority of design expertise. The mature architect was losing control of the means of design production. And, of course, the development of fast computer perspectives and rendering was only the first step in what many now think of as a kind of "hostile takeover" of the design art by computer representation technology. Animations, walk-throughs, virtual reality: from a certain point of view, all of these seem to have transferred power out of the hands of the architect designer and into the hands of the computer "technician." Quickly, computer programming, computer software, and computer documents were replacing the designer's ancient art of drawing, both in its manifestation as a noun, as the original marks on a support, and as a verb, as the magically coordinated and significant acts of hand, eye, and mind.

Third phase: Communication
While designers struggled to adjust their design processes (and office politics) to computerized production and visualization, another, far more significant, computer-driven change was taking place in the outside world: the World Wide Web's spectacular growth. Before the web, the Internet was a sort of centralized electronic library, but as everyone knows by now, the web allowed the individual document to link directly to others without passing a center, actual or virtual. With this capacity, the web also became a design consideration in its own right, in view of its impact on how individuals (and groups) use, and think about, public and private space.

In the design fields, the first signs of web communication explosion to come were "in-office" networks (and the apparently unrelated mobile phone phenomenon). Office networks were in use from the early 1990s, but it is safe to say that in the average design organization only the computing staff, and possibly the senior partners, had become aware of the general importance of computer networks before mid-decade. It was around that time that many began to redefine their in-office computer networks as intranets—networks that used web-based client/server technology for a limited, usually project-based audience. With intranets, the computer networks reached out of the office to external consultants.

Similar to intranets with the addition of further "outsider" access—for suppliers, contractors, clients, public authorities—extranets have been in use only since the very late 1990s. Externally hosted solutions for professional cooperation that employ specially written project management software also become available at approximately the same time. This is still a very young market in the year 2000. Late in the 1990s, the development of extranets only accelerated the networking process that intranets had already started. Intranets had already made it less important that the professional's body be located in an office, because the actual workplace could be the web. Those formerly trapped in the office could be farther away, and, at the same time, the formerly far away could seem closer together. The intranets had made the design office and its consultants sometimes seem like a single team; likewise, the extranets brought suppliers, contractors, and other project parties closer together.

The process of dissolving the office boundaries has eroded many of the former certainties of design practice. It has eroded the clear division of labor between the various design professions, the clear distinction between designers and non-designers, the clear division between people who do and don't work in a particular office for a particular company, and the clear separation between designer and construction site. For example, software that can calculate structural forces can be used by architects, as well as by engineers. Software that can easily produce three-dimensional images can be used by contractors, as well as by architects. Software that can be tied to databases can minimize the need for pricing experts. Software packages that can be programmed in the design office are bringing computer programmers into intimate dialogue with designers more frequently. And as these examples demonstrate, in the process of dissolving the office boundaries, new players have been added to every project team: the outside software companies and the internal computer experts.

Around the same time that the idea of extranets was being developed, software was written for an entirely new form of computer-enabled representation—solid modeling. It is arguable that one never really "draws" on computers in any case, but at least in the production and visualization phases of design computing, the documents issued looked like drawings. In solid modeling, the designer gives up even the appearance of drawing. In the world of solid modeling, information is chameleon-like; the "same" information can take on different forms. For example, project information can appear as the model, as its slices ("drawings"), as spreadsheets, as timelines. In this way, the site of the design act is no longer identified as "the drawing."

Solid modeling looks likely to replace the centuries-old drawing tradition as the primary means of representation within a few years. And at the same time, the embodiment of information as software and its files and the easy web-based transfer of this material is quickly revising the role of built fabric in society. Physical location and access to rich information sources (and thus to the development of knowledge and political power) are no longer identical. And perhaps more importantly, web communications are also mysteriously revising the relationship between the fictionality of images and narratives and the tactile physical world. Physical places, in some instances, are beginning to look like special episodes in some form of narrative. The increased presence of narrative in people's lives, however, far from decreasing the demand for physical places, increases it. The physical place and the web site form a reciprocal guarantee of each other's reality.

All these changes make the theoretical and practical impact of earlier design computing seem much less significant. It has become possible to look back with nostalgia at the time only a few years earlier. Even after the development of computer production and visualization techniques, it still seemed possible that a balance could be struck between the old ways of working—the old representation systems and processes—and the new computing world. This no longer seems to be a viable option; web-related changes have definitively separated designers, and the world they design for, from their precomputing assumptions and habits.

Semper Fidelis:
On Numbers in the Night
Peter D. Waldman

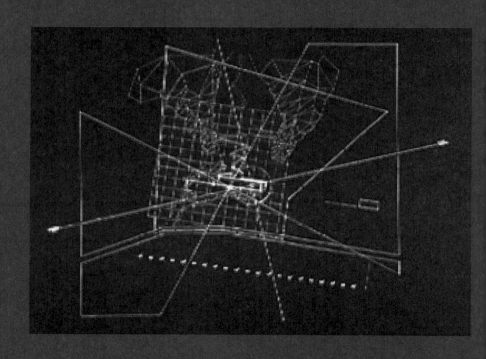

Semper has haunted me from the start. Ever since my student days I sought to ground the project by reducing the site to an enigmatic shadow line cast at high noon from a certainly more finite object conceived in my imagination. That dark enigmatic shadow line not only served the magnification of the emboldened artifice; it also provided a future ground for seeds awaiting germination in that fertile fissure. In those early days, I sought to compose architecture, not to construct it, and only traced out foundation plans in order to secure a building permit. I had the process backwards: my foundation plans were resultant not generative. It took me years to get over building poorly in my attempt to realize a finished vision rather than acknowledge that building may be about beginning and not finishing. Numbers in the Night are those hidden systems necessary to construct the imagination. These Numbers now haunt my process. I now take confidence in the utility of my own markings, in numbers as permutations rather than resolutions, and as reading site first in the most visceral of terms. My work now never seems to get beyond the specification of foundations for a garden, a building, or city. **Spatial Tales of Origin** begin with the site as found, with resources to be mapped initially by Nomads, then revealed as accountable by Surveyors, and transformed by the reflexive permutations of Lunatics. The Garden of Eden, however lost, intentionally preceeded the construction of the enduring City of Jerusalem. The circumstantial preconditions of the Site, tensioned by the predictability of the Sun and the Moon, determine the architecture of the lingering construction site. The temporal agenda that serves the genesis of the growth of the garden should also be requisite to the Specifications for Construction for building here on earth. To project the primacy of Specifications for Construction one must begin with the preconditions of the site and define architecture as the collaboration of the Gardener and the Engineer. The project of landscape and architecture is most powerfully manifested in the territories of the construction site, first revealing geological and historical evidence and then the elemental acts of each stage of the building process. **Parcel X in North Garden**, Virginia, is the subject of the text and trace of a lingering construction site, somewhere between Eden and Jerusalem, an oasis of modest tents and potent volcanoes, where colluvial slopes are mediated by inserted terraces and where enduring foundations and mercurial finishes are proudly displayed as numerous stress cracks, stains, and scars. It is hoped that Semper would be proud of this faithful cabalist in his persistence to attend to this first haunting lesson that resonates now as Numbers in the Night.

Draft Specification No. 1
In the Beginning

In the beginning God created Heaven and Earth, and all was without form.
"Genesis," *The Bible,* King James Version

On the Precise Responsibilities of Surveyors & Cabalists

1. *(In the Beginning)* is read routinely herein as a gerund, an ongoing activity to which one returns to trespass again and again throughout the construction process in the anticipation of ruin. **2.** *(Numbers in the Night)* is the specific speculation of an Architect as Surveyor and Cabalist who presupposes two simultaneous conditions necessary to strategize the Construction Site: One Condition *(Numbers)* presupposes accountability: the meters derived from the precision of the physics. The other condition *(in the Night)* is the myriad of permutations of orientation associated with evident fragments of several temporal logics resisting in the dark the absolute resolution of Cartesian thinking while making space for the coincidental rush of the nightmare, which others more discretely call the warehouse of the imagination. **Subtext (1+2) An architecture** may be simultaneously rendered accessible to the Surveyor by the diagrammatic clarity of its authoritative building systems determined by Gravity *(Caves/Tents)*, as well as rendered magical to the Cabalist by the permutations of distinct conjunctive Orientations *(the Megaron).*

Draft Specification No. 2
Ground Rules
The first architectural act is to break the ground; the second is to raise structure vertically to the sky. Semper

On Repositioning Within Landscapes of Aggression

3. *(On Repositioning)* begins with a tale of a surrogate instrumental act upon the site: the metamorphic body at the end of the day whose dynamic reorientations of ground rules commencing with one center and one flagellating line go on to retrace patterns of the spiral through the contrast of diurnal and nocturnal postures coming finally to rest in the ruinous condition of dust and ashes. On Repositioning presupposes that every architectural project since Genesis repeats the text of remarkable beginnings by rules first determined by the Sun, and then inverted time and again by the Mirrors of the Moon. On Repositioning presupposes reflectivity, a reflexive predictable cycle that regulates us by day and amazes us by night. Since the labyrinth of Knossos, the role of architecture has not only been to ground us here and now but to take us to terrific realms where no one has been before. **4.** *(Within Landscapes of Aggression)* is projected the construction site over time as the only possible location from which to witness the dual readings of Gravity and Orientation by distinct bodies now repositioning themselves with one another as collaborative and constructive citizens. The additive benchmarks of the Surveyor are always followed by the subtractive excavations of the Cabalist, and through these double crossed territories there is to be found on occasion the meander of the Nomad in search of other oases. **Subtext (3+4) The Surveyor and Cabalist** establish two distinct yet syncopated meters for the construction site. The Nomad, another kind of structuralist beyond the scope of this essay, reminds them of resources within the earth as evidence of geological and cultural structures beyond those of the geometry and mathematics of ideal form. **There are successive** logics projected here requiring first the mapping of a Spatial Tale of Origin and then identifying Landscapes of Aggression as a changing, reflexive repositioning of the construction site that is neither a passive armature nor a singularly linear process. The subject of this subtext is the frictional union of an enduring Syntax of Structure, as a chess game played out through the permutations of a topographic imagination.

Draft Specification No. 3
A Tale of a Gardener and an Engineer

For some time now, ever since my student days, I have been in the habit to return from studio late at night to jot down parti diagrams on a bedside sketchpad wedged between the cold stone floor and an imperfect spring mattress. In that unsupportive condition, I would deceive myself into thinking that structural clarity might be achieved by a few bold lines representing emphatic walls. Or was it rather the Cartesian forest of columns? The dilemma of either/or would haunt me for years. Abandoning sleep early in my adolescence, I tried to sleep recounting both parallel walls as well as the syncopation of grids. Three, no four; six, no seven; thirteen, no seventeen; often sixty-nine or was it ninety-six. To a reborn Cabalist, these numbers, which were supposed to stabilize my day's production, only haunted me by their permutations late into the night. More often than not I would try to clear this minefield shifting bodily orientations. **The dynamic body models** the construction site: vertical by day, horizontal by night, a spiral fetus in the beginning, decomposed as dust in the end. *(Numbers in the Night)* haunt those who attempt to appreciate the dynamic character of construction aggressively redefining site over time. The construction site is not about singularity but multiplicity, not resolution but dynamic negotiation. **For almost thirty-nine** years now I have been waking up exhausted but welcoming to my relief the bright light of day only to glance down to my horror on last night's intentional diagrams that could only be read as pentimenti, as marks and erasures, lineae occultae remaining unresolved, fragmentary, certainly incomplete and often frictional, blistered and scored into the grit of my pad. I was compelled by this sudden enlightenment to hide the evidence of a topographic imagination in an adjacent closet. But, perversely, I decided at some point to take confidence in the utility of my own night-time markings and now delight in strategizing site in the most visceral of physical terms. I read Specifications for Construction as instructions for alchemy, strategizing the soiling of foundations before burnishing eschatological finishes, defining architecture as the collaboration of both Gardeners and Engineers. **Structure as a visceral** conjunction of sequential frictions is appreciated most emphatically in terms of the lingering construction site, in revealing first the structure of the site in terms of both geological facts and historical fictions, then appreciating the elemental acts of each stage manifested by the building process, stressing the essential value of incomplete acts of ordinary individuals repeating routin familiar tasks. **The construction site** as armature meters the spatial realm where citizen and stranger move with distinct rhythms, where light levels are leveraged by Lunatics, and weathering obscures some measures and accentuates others. If the warehouse of the imagination is illuminated by darkness, the armatures of structure, and the inventory of Caves and Tents, then the preconditions of dark labyrinths and shadowy forests provide for an architecture that transposes authoritative orders associated with the bright light of day. Tanazaki's *In Praise of Shadows* and Picasso's *Guernica* both identify the light bulb as the phenomenal plague of the preenlightenment imagination where now nothing is hidden, and "terra incognita" is erased from all world maps.

Draft Specification No. 4
Eden then Jerusalem

Structure before enclosure is a precondition to dwelling within Architecture and provides the last evidence of the postoccupation ruin. **Building as a verb,** as an instrumental deformative act, is manifested through successive territorial transformations, Semperian Landscapes of Aggression, conventionally conceived as the short-term construction site and resistively perceived as the long-term scarred territory of repositioned topographic engagements. **Starting with the foundations** of Parcel X, a syntax of structure is the festering frictional determinant of a spatial tale of origin negotiating the spatial territory defined by both concentric gravity and eccentric orientation. The initial retaining wall splits to frame a gap as it emerges from the ground to permit the summer solstice morning light to enter the Basement of Parcel X. Then shining steel studs before they are enclosed with the copper skin cast magical shadows for a brief moment in collaboration with the adjacent stand of ancient tulip poplars. This magic is merely represented now by the regular markings of the burnished standing seam sleeves that meter the copper shield from sunrise to sunset. **Gravity is invariant,** pulling vectors constantly to the center of the earth. Orientation is temporal, yet recurrent, inscribing each day with an arc of three horizons marking variant sunrise, high noon, and sunset. Gravity and Orientation are then the only benchmarks agreed upon by Surveyors and Cabalists who provide the constituent characteristics of an architect. Ever since Genesis, architecture has been conceived as both physical and temporal, metering the space first between heaven and earth, ephemeral vapors and the topographic imagination, ultimately establishing the recurrent paradigms of Eden and Jerusalem, the cyclic garden and the resistive city. It is not the point of this essay to assume that the City and the Garden began as one. Rather, by bracketing the debate with Genesis and then Exodus, I am suggesting that the world as construction site was the structured place before cities, buildings, or gardens, but that building *(as a verb)* in its incompleteness was there first in its progressive state. The moment of finish, i.e., Paradise as a walled-in garden, led to prerequisite abandonment as with Sodom and Gomorrah. Structure as Order mediates with the world of nature first. Only then does architecture fix a world within.

Draft Specification No. 5
Places Left Unfinished at the Time of Creation
On that first terrific night, Crusoe had to choose between a cave or a tent. He chose both. Daniel Defoe, *Robinson Crusoe*

5. *(Specifications for Construction)* is the conventional model of directing distinct sequences of trades negotiating foundations, frames, and finishes in order to describe architecture as a process of consequent construction. I have found it useful over the years to teach the reading of architectural artifacts initially through constituent parts—walls and frames, attics and basements, doors and windows—constructed, occupied, and maintained by individuals and groups as Recurrent Dualities that place architecture in the role of the conjunction itself. It is to be argued here that if there is a text to be read, then architecture is the specification of a constructive and frictional process of building up as well as weathering down, of the resistive as well as the vulnerable. **6.** *(Enumeration of Lessons Learned)* is identified as the responsibility to make manifest precedents and ongoing research through this *proglomena* for a modestly metered dwelling located at the forest edge. Parcel X is an ancient and familiar tale, an architectural primer recounting the enduring codes and components of our discipline, demonstrating a syntax of structure all too forgotten in the current amnesia.

Subtext (5+6) This essay on the useful routine of originating Specifications for Construction is to take delight in both Science and Magic: lessons of structuring site reconsidered by Ariadne and taught to Theseus long, long ago and far, far away. Her probable descendent, Robinson Crusoe knew well how to read both the Sun and the Moon in a recurrent structural covenant with Gravity and Orientation. Their ongoing reading skills demonstrate the still fecund space of syncopated structures to be considered again as required reading, a primer perhaps, for the architectural imagination of their collective descendants.

Draft Specification No. 6
On Noah's Ark

Specifications for Construction are prefaced by a section enumerating the pre-conditions of the site before construction. The preconditions of Parcel X record a site already full, not empty, of geological fissures and colluvial soil where ancient forests of vertical tulip poplar trees are metered by cattle fences and punctuated by camping sites of Nomadic origin. Then the first eight sections of Specifications for Construction determine the strategic repositioning of dynamic constructional sequences or trades for the material and temporal metering of space. **Yet, the final eight** sections of Specifications for Construction retreat from this frictional process with provisions for external and internal finishes as if to stabilize or fix the now objectified armature. Building as a verb, as ongoing constructional process, is in crisis if one accepts the notion of substantial completion, with the assemblage of a checklist, which comes from the assumption that structures are invariant and thus should not creak or leak. There are alternatives to an impoverished and pretentious architecture that conventionally values more the resolution or stabilization of structure over the vitality of stress scars and watermarks. I suggest an architecture that celebrates the instrumentality of construction sites as progressive. The spatial tales of origin recounted in Speci- fications for Construction should begin and end with yet another eschatological beginning, always found in water and watermarks, soil and stain, in darkness and an encrusted patina, in fire and in ash, in secret springs and manhole, and finally lightning rods. **Conventional wisdom** perpetuates the passivity and immutability of architectural structure achieving static resolution rather than celebrating as landscape architecture the ongoing evidence of dynamic and competing loads in the anticipation of growth and change. **Conventional wisdom** perpetuates con- structional paradigms as singular: walls or frames, caves or tents, complete an authoritative onto themselves, rather than as contingent, incomplete, in stress if not in failure, vulnerable and certainly oppositional if not multiple as in the model of the megaron. **Conventional wisdom** perpetuates the typological notion that architectural structure is externally imposed upon the site by Surveyors implanting benchmarks, leased cranes lifting prefabricated frames and walls of immutable meters kept secret in the dark interiors of Masonic lodges rather than revealing specifically topological notion that structure may be internally quarried first from resources within the site, by Cabalists who generate innu- merable permutations determined by the measure of a digit as well as the arc of a crane. **The builders of** ancient structures used the immediate site as resource to inventory most of their material: the forest for timber, the mountain for stone. The construction methods however were ancient secrets passed down from gen- eration to generation and from other lands and cultures far, far away. **In this alternative vision** of primitive or archetype construction site the Surveyor takes one's coordinates from the aforementioned three horizons particular to the site; the mason is an alchemist first, at home in the quarry as well as the Lodge; the framer, a journeyman, is equally at home in the forest as well as the bright light of day. The preconditions of alchemical Masonic structures are found in surface clay and transformed in the kiln, while the instrumentalities of the framer are the ax and the sawmill. Geological projections and colluvial faults, Noah's Ark at Mount Ararat are structural paradigms of immediate geologic as well as distant mythic dimensions.

Draft Specification No. 7
The Volcano is Also a Tent

On Enumerating Lessons Learned

1. At Princeton in the 1960s, one generation was taught that modern Architects were obliged to build with light, but precise, structural armatures that hovered above the ground. **2. A decade later,** another generation was taught in the same school that the Architect had obligations to reconfirm the order of this world and, as such, should no longer reveal the extension of space with frames but reconfirm the finiteness of rooms with substantial walls. **3. Slow to learn** or resistive as a young teacher in the 1970s, I offered an alternative model to the polarized students: wall and frame in frictional and evasive engagement in the model of the megaron, inverted in the basilica, and reappropriated by Le Corbusier distinctly in his early and later works. **4. An earlier project,** Maison du Weekend, employs primitive and contemporary structural paradigms of great mass and ephemeral lightness echoed in the north wall diptych of Parcel X as concrete walls and glass block panels within steel frames. These two projects establish a record of strategic repositioning of visceral structures requiring both the conjunction of inviolate frame as well as the shadowy weight of buried foundations, grottoes, and metered cells. **5. The later projects** of Le Corbusier, Ronchamp and the Heidi Weber Pavilion coincidentally consider the repositioning of massive and light structures and use the distinct resources of their immediate construction sites. Ronchamp in part is a tent that looks like a cave, part rubble of a former sanctuary, part gunnite over a veiled steel fabric, with a heavy concrete cloud of a roof floating on point supports. The memorial pyramid in front pays tribute as inversion to the enigmatic Sphinx of Gizeh or the Italic Temple of Giove at Terracina. The Heidi Weber Pavilion establishes a memorable horizon through the projection and inversion of the Alps as distant pyramids tensioning the insistent horizon of the park as it meets the Zurich Sea. In addition the light, modular framing of its insistent metering belies the vast grotto bar contained within. These two precedents reconsider their immediate topographic situations in two distinct conjunctions of Caves and Tents as they face one another in frictional engagement from their mountain locations at the edge of a delimitated spatial sea. **6. These two projects** serve now as brief references for reconciling terrains through Parcel X. The insistent horizons of the floor and the roof are in contrast to the oblique

Preconditions: Oasis

Day 1: Campsite

Day 2: Palisades and Prism pole

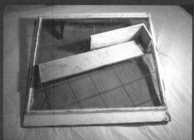

Day 2: Palisades and Plinth

Day 3: Steel Meters

Day 4: Shield

Day 5: Packing Crates

Day 6: New Terrace

section of the site. The copper shield is an unrelenting ruler as well as having the character of a fine tooth-comb. The Volcano is also a Tent encamped once again upon the site. The hearth is a grotto, an outrigger ark beneath the kaleidoscopic box that merely frames the Sun and the Moon. This essay on the visceral choreography of the Construction Site is an apology for Parcel X, a temporal encampment where the steel frame creaks and the rain shields do not leak (too much). **7. This project is part of** a generational study of climatic dwellings commenced with the Parasol House for the same clients in Houston more than a decade ago. These two campers arrive, one with a ruler, the other with a compass. **On the first day,** a tent is pitched not far from the pre-existing well. A campfire establishes the ash traces of man's first nightmare. **The second morning** begins the process of clearing the site as a staging area for construction. The eastern boundary is the first to be surveyed; a prism pole is left to frame the sun, and the first partial palisade is built and braced against the cold north wind. At noon a plinth is extended to the full southern edge of the site. That evening at the western boundary, X-bracing records the setting of the sun in the brittle surface of this first parterre. Between the palisade and the plinth, the now weary nomads rest under the light of a full moon. **The third morning** begins the process of erecting a steel framework based on a 26-foot meter to give another measure to this now cleared and leveled site. A fireplace is created to the south and a totem somewhere beyond the precinct to the north. **On the fourth day,** a shield is erected to challenge the southern exposure. Steel studs, lead-coated copper siding, metered Hope's doors become an incessant backdrop. Thereupon, an armature of eye hooks and guide wires with a mind of their own collaborate with wisteria vines to mask this pretentious straightedge. **On the fifth day**, a trailer arrives with kitchen stuff and household goods. Hidden behind the back of this masque of urban decorum, the trailer is raised up on blocks to serve temporarily as a cookhouse/outhouse. Nearby, another tent is set up to guard the goods. Under the hot noon sun a parasol is stretched to form a framed ground plane hovering above the previous plinth. From this new terrace one can recover the horizon previously denied by this undulating topography. Late in the day, glass curtain walls seal off the east and the west with unsentimental anonymity, while a glass-block panel of equal size makes prismatic the northern exposure. **On the sixth day,** a manhole reveals the secrets of the cistern beneath a labyrinth of packing crates; a study is perched above; a volcanic lens points to south; and the ground begins to heave. On that sixth night the elderly collaborators find rest in a hammock suspended within this armature of the first campsite and dream now of how similar the first move was to the last. **On the seventh day,** it is rumored a wall rises to the north where the totemic stake once distinguished within from without. Its iridescent face now contains an extended aperture, some say barbeque, while others whisper funeral pyre. Only the blind arthritic dog knows for sure the destination of this portal. In the nomadic North American condition, one can never tell if your next move is to be your last. Precautions should be taken to secure both daydreams and nightmares; ancient flues must guard deep cisterns; household goods must be kept at a distance while the preconditions of the site punctuate this campsite from within. This Genesis of Revelation is the ancient rite of all Nomads who know that the City and the Garden have origins on the Oasis.

Projects and Interpretations: Architectural Strategies of Enric Miralles
Catherine Spellman

The work of Catalan architect Enric Miralles are inspire interpretation and creative reading. Miralles' work receives international acclaim for its sensitivity to place, interpretation of culture, expression of structure, and creative reading of program. His work tells us that each new situation offers specific truths that reveal the history, geography, and culture of a place and that each new project should reinterpret these truths to bring meaning to the project. This paper offers a series of interpretive readings that suggest strategies present in Miralles´ work. These interpretations focus on the uncanny ability of the projects to respond to the context of a particular place. The interpretations discuss the relationship of a structure to the physical qualities of a site (geography, topography, figure/field relationships), the perceptual experiences of the site, the formal properties of site expressed in a language of folded forms, the methods of collecting and translating material in the design process, and the influence of structure and technology.

Constructing the Site

Giacometti figures are both united to and separated from the base they stand on. The figures emerge from their sites, made of the same material and formed with the same hand. The figures and their site are both in a state of intimate dialogue and abstract distance. Jean-Paul Sartre in his essay on Giacometti's sculpture comments that "his figures are solitary, but when placed together, in whatever combination, they are united by their solitude, to suddenly form a small magical society." The tension

that Sartre describes is created when a figure is placed in a state of abstract reference to its site. This becomes a recurrent theme in Miralles' work, which tends to advoid a direct and coherent relationship to the site.

In Miralles' work, there is a clear intention of redefining the site for the new building. He does this by drawing a strong relationship between the abstract idea that orders the project and the specific realities of the site. The physical form of the project emerges from this relationship. However, the ideas that give form to the project are not fixed to the specific form of the site. Ideas are abstract and nonspecific. John Hejduk equates this method of designing the site to the methods of a painter. Hejduk states, "The painter starts with the real world and works toward abstraction, and when he is finished with a work it is abstracted from the so-called real world. But architecture takes two lines. The architect starts with the abstract world, and due to the nature of his work, works toward the real world. The significant architect is one who, when finished with a work, is as close to that original abstraction as he could possibly be . . . and that is also what distinguished architects from builders." (Montaner 1990)

Igualada Cemetery

Miralles' finished projects maintain a close connection to the original idea and also establish a relationship to the realities of the given site. At the Igualada Cemetery, for example, the idea that the shape of the landscape would be directed by the procession path of a funeral guided the layout of the project. The contour lines that form the edge of the project are both continuous with, and disconnected from, the natural slope of the site. The project reveals how Miralles can frame the existing topographical order by overlaying the abstract order of the program.

In another example, the Boarding School in Morella repeats the form of the medieval complex that is set

Morella Boarding School

Pérgola Avinguda Icària, Barcelona

in the mountain in the distance. The school follows the orientation and gesture of the retaining walls and terracing walls of the complex, fitting into the landscape in a similar way. As the school steps down the mountainside, its rooftops become the new ground surface of the mountain providing exterior places for children to gather. At the Eurythmics Sports Center in Alicante, its large flat roof provides a planar surface that is juxtaposed against the mountain in the distance, echoing the view of the mountains from the sea. At the Avinguda Icària, in the 1992 Olympic Village, the roof structures are intended to inhabit the center of the avenue, like the trees that inhabit the center of the Ramblas in Barcelona's medieval quarter.

Archaeology in Reverse

In order for a landscape to be transformed into a place of inhabitation, an act of reversed archaeology occurs. This process is one of etching ideas, abstract and specific, into the ground. Rather than removing the earth to uncover the traces of past human life and culture, traces are embedded into the earth to mark the movements of future life and culture. To work in construction is to transform the topography of a place. Miralles points out that topography is the combination of the Greek word topos—*place*—and *graphy*—writing. Etymologically, it means the writing in a place. The construction of a building reflects its archaeology; it is literally the meticulous description of a particular place in terms of its inhabitation (Miralles 1994).

The Huesca Basketball Stadium works as an example of this reversed archaeology. The project is sited in a leftover space between the city center and a park that defines the western edge of the city. The siting of the project was intended to tie the city center and park together through a series of public spaces that mitigate the scale of each. The decision to excavate the site and set the stadium into the ground at the base of the hill allowed the roof of the project to continue the line of the trees up to the edge of the city. From the other direction, the hard urban surfaces are continued through the public play spaces that reflect the activities of the basketball stadium.

This east/west symmetry is repeated along a north/south axis, giving shape to the limits of the project.

Huesca Basketball Stadium

Folding the Cloth

In the sculpture *Saint Teresa in Ecstasy* by Fillippo Bernini, the folds of the cloth, sculpted in stone, reveal everything about the meaning of the sculpture. These folds convey the shape of the figures, their movement and relationship to each other, the direction of the incoming light, the flow of air, and the passage of a moment. Indeed, in the folds Bernini reveals the emotion and tension of the story being told. The cloth unites the figure with the theatrical stage set of clouds and falling rays of light.

Huesca, model of roof

A sense of turbulent motion and suspenseful activity draws the viewer into the scene, bringing them into the drama of the moment. With these folding,

twisted figures, Bernini has found ways to bring home to the faithful an intensified experience of the supernatural (Wittkower 1980).

Like Bernini's sculptures, the folded forms in Miralles' architecture reveal the stories or events of the buildings. The tilted roofs, inclined walls, sequences of connected inside/outside spaces, and overlapping circulation systems reveal the ways that the life of the building is acted out by its occupants. In many of Miralles' projects it is difficult to discern what is building and what is ground.

At the Huesca Basketball Stadium for example, the space of the outdoor playing fields are continuous with the edge condition of the storage rooms, which overlap with the entrance pathway into the stadium. Here the entry porches are placed between the stadium and the ground, and the exterior plazas mitigate

Olympic Archery Pavilion, roof structure

the scale difference between building and ground by overlapping the space of both. At Igualada Cemetery, the space of the pathway slides into the space of the sacristy, forming the wall that holds back the change in grade of the landscape. At the Archery Pavilion for the 1992 Olympics, the edge of the playing field curves and becomes one with the entrance pathway, that in turn bends and becomes continuous with the wall system and entry to the changing rooms. In the overlapping spaces, activities that are not strictly programmed by the games find a place to happen.

All this amounts to an architecture that can reflect the independence and life of Baroque space.

Taking a Walk

Prevalent in Miralles' projects is the theme of walking. To understand the nature, organization, and meaning of his architecture, one must walk through it. Reading the drawings will not suffice; it is not an architecture that is generated from the mathematical order of the plan; it is one that is related to movement and events (Curtis 1991). Miralles' projects aim to make a correct fit  between an event and a place for an event to happen; they invite participation and require you to move through them to understand their order.

Walking in a Miralles project, one is reminded of Thoreau's essay "On Walking." Thoreau uses walking as a metaphor to describe the essence of writing and the complexity of nature. Thoreau states, "No wealth can buy the requisite leisure, freedom, and independence, which are the capital in this profession. For many years I have walked almost every day, and sometimes for several days together. An absolutely new prospective walk is a great happiness, and I can still get this any afternoon. Two or three hours walking will carry me to as strange a country as I expect ever to see" (Thoreau 1860). Thoreau celebrates the free-flowing, unstructured nature of the walk as a kind of mental research, which he connects with the virtue of wilderness and a space that is conducive to writing.

Miralles' projects place great emphasis on public routes from the exterior through the interiors. At the Gymnastic Stadium in Alicante, a series of stairs and ramps become an architectural element applied to the front of the building that leads the visitor through, around, and up to the various levels of activity. In much the same way as the escalators at the Pompidou Center in Paris or the ramps at Le Corbusier's Carpenter Arts Center in Cambridge, Miralles' circulation systems are about providing the visitor with a clear sense of orientation and direction. William Curtis points out that this sense of movement is similar to that discussed by Geoffrey Scott in *The Architecture of Humanism*. Curtis writes, "Through these spaces we can conceive ourselves to move; these masses are capable, like our lives, of pressure and resistance; these lines, should we follow or describe them, might be our path and our gesture" (1991).

Alicante, public walks

Alicante, interior entry

At the La Llauna School in Badalona, the experience of the space is that of walking along a busy street where the sidewalk accommodates a plethora of activities and possibility of endless happenstance occurrences. One has the sense in this school that students are being prepared for the social life of the streets of Barcelona, and they are invited to bring their city experiences along with them into class. At La Llauna the theme of the building as street is spelled out rather laboriously at the ground level with the aid of actual streetlights and other urban paraphernalia. Higher up, the corridors are so wide as not to be corridors at all, but places of multiple functions for students milling around between classes (Curtis 1991).

La Llauna School, Badalona

At the Civic Center in Hostalets, we find another project that is placed on the boundary between the city and its periphery. The project continues the

Hostalets Civic Center

movement of the city street, through the project, and up a series of ramps to terraces that allow you to look out over the distant rural landscape. This ramped circulation through the building organizes the functions on both the interior and exterior. Hostalets is a small town to the north of Barcelona, and the municipality needed a gathering space for diverse social and cultural events: a reading room, a bar, a place for casual performances, and a miniature stadium for courts on one side of the site. In effect, the architects synthesized the notions of stadium, social theater, and collective bevedere of terraces in a single building that is organized around the theme of walking.

Seeing the View

Annie Dillard, in her article "Seeing," ponders the qualities of a framed vision of the world. Dillard states, "I used to be able to see flying insects in the air. I'd look ahead and see, not the row of hemlocks across the road, but the air in front of it. My eyes would focus along that column of air, picking out flying insects. But I lost interest, I guess, for I dropped the habit. Now I can see birds. Probably some people can look at the grass at their feet and discover all the crawling creatures. I would like to know grasses and hedges and care. Then my least journey into the world would be a field trip, a series of happy recognitions" (1994).

Miralles can see. His architecture attempts to help focus the view of the occupant, to alert them to the wonders of the context around them. The projects are about framing the view of the occupant as they move through the space. In this sense they are not tectonic; in spite of the presence of ramps, various stairways, and strategic windows, the projects offer views of the external and internal workings of the building.

Externally, the projects show a concern for the approach to and away from the building. The site is structured to frame the building and to make the building a part of the natural path of movement. Through framed views, the project becomes a part of the landscape. At Huesca, for example, the hill that forms the entrance into the stadium reduces the scale of the building, fitting it graciously into the distant landscape. Internally, the circulation system is formed to reveal the makings of the building, to display the events, and to allow you to read multiple activities of the project. In many ways, Miralles' interiors have the qualities of a Vermeer painting where layers of light and space are revealed through windows and doors that open onto each other.

Huesca, approach to outdoor courts

This Vermeer-like quality can be seen in all Miralles' projects but in particular in the Civic Center at Hostalets de Balenyà. William Curtis has said of this building that, "it comes close to the generative image of architecture as a social landscape since it is made up from interlocking platforms and layers of thin walls traversed by ramps and stairs. The image of the institution is of events suspended above the earth protected from the weather by slicing and interpenetrating roofs, which play against the rise and fall of the land" (1991).

At the Editorial Headquarters in Madrid, planes of birch veneer plywood are used to frame views and focus the visitor's glance on the various happenings in the space. The abstract planes create a series of shifted, overlapping spaces that move the visitor's eye through the space. At the Archery Pavilion in Barcelona, a series of windows is created for the viewer that reveal the structural workings

Civic Center, Hostalets de Balenyà   Editorial Headquarters, Madrid   Archery Pavilion, Barcelona

*. . . the materials with which one
works, with purpose in and of themselves, disjointed and independent
. . . a series of proposals has guided
this work.
And each of them has independent
evolution and consequences. . . It is
a basic drawing. A line drawing that
defines the future of this project.
Even though it would be more adequate to say that the drawing is an
imaginary map of that place . . . this
transformation gives new names to
things like path, rivers, and crossroads. . . We know that the landscape does not pre-exist by itself. I
become a landscape by living in that
place. There is no landscape without
human meaning. In this sense this
place already existed. . . However,
in order to work on it, the landscape
must be transformed into a map.
In other words an imaginary map.
. . . A document that allows entry
and exit to the concrete reality of
that place. Until any figure cut out
against the sky, where it once was
hidden, could be described clearly
on the map.*

Enric Miralles, *Documentos de
Arquitectura*

of the building. An internalized and abstracted understanding of the space, juxtaposed with the windows, allows you to see out. These internal views give the visitor another level of understanding of the workings of the project.

On Collecting Material

Every passion borders on the chaotic, but the collector's passion borders on the chaos of memories.
Walter Benjamin, "Unpacking My Library"

An architect collects personal and societal memories and experiences that are sifted and transformed as he/she reconsiders the relative parameters of an architectural project and specific site. The architect then develops a new construct out of this accumulated past experience and the material and abstract realities of the architectural project. The collection of memories is the architects' greatest resource. But memory is ephemeral, and architects must work with actual material resources. Miralles' most prevalent method of design is concerned with the translation of ideas and memories into physical material that can be manipulated during the design process.

His methods of translation evolve around the act of drawing. In Miralles' work, drawing is not only a tool of communication but also a means of thinking and finding one's way in the design process. Drawing, as Miralles explains, is a place where the maker and the ideas can be together externally on the surface of the paper. It is also a way of creating a dialogue between members of the studio. Reading a Miralles drawing is not simple. The lines are mostly made in one thin lineweight. Many layers of information about the project's spatial configuration and construction are drawn on the same surface of paper. This reinforces the intention to convey abstract ideas, offering multiple readings of the project. William Curtis points out that "Miralles' drawings are like hieroglyphs full of hidden ideas and meanings, but they are also musical scores for the orchestration of human activities and the terrain" (1991). Implicit in the lines is material, structure, light, space, view, and detail. His drawings contain a series of gestures that are repeated in variation throughout the projects. These gestures, as explained by Miralles, are born out of a series of specific interests rather than out of an interest in specific style. Sometimes the sources of these interests are found in the work of others— borrowed ideas as opposed to borrowed form.

One Holds Another

Michelangelo liked to draw figures in contact with one another. He was a master at capturing the form and shape of the body, conveying the structure of bone and muscle that would allow one figure to support another. Here, the force of gravity can be seen passing through the figure of Christ as he becomes an instrument of compression on the brink of buckling under the weight of the figure upon his shoulders. The effort of structure is made visible to the viewer who is brought into its reality in the most straightforward way.

Miralles' projects possess similar concerns for direct structural expression and exploration of the possibilities of technology—

not in terms of sophisticated mechanisms or structural gymnastics, but in terms of simple laws of gravity and statics that are visibly revealed throughout the projects. At the Archery Pavilion built for the 1992 Olympics, for example, the tilts of the roof express the variety of angles that can be supported by the columns below. At the Alicante

Archery Pavilion, Barcelona

Gymnastics Center, the forces that play on a column are expressed by dividing the column into parts of tension, compression, and balance. At Igualada Cemetery, the structure of the tombs' support become the foundations that hold back the excavation of the site. At the Civic Center in Hostalets de Balenyà, the giant girders that define the vertical dimension of each level are clearly supported by the concrete walls that create the horizontal limit of the space.

With this attitude toward structural expression, Miralles works within a system of relating the parts to the whole—which is to say that Miralles likes each building element to maintain its identity while becoming a part of the system of connections that hold the entire structure together. Like a child's erector set, the pieces could be assembled in endless combinations, however, the necessities of the program and concepts give order to the forming of space. In the process of construction, Miralles is interested in "the freedom from the doubts of design" that construction provides (Zaera-Polo 1995). Construction is guided by many known factors: the time it takes concrete to dry, the weight a single column can hold, the length a cantilever can extend, the distance a beam can span. These entities determine many things in the building. They give guidance to design.

Miralles tends to operate by variations, considering what any element of architecture can do and how it could be made to do multiple things. He never works by reduction, but attempts to reveal all the possibilities and multiplexes of the

Alicante Sports Stadium   Igualada Cemetery   Hostalets de Balenyà Civic Center

construction. An example that he offers is that of the wall. He states, "When I think about the construction of a wall, I think about all the possibilities that a wall could contain. I think about a wall and think about a niche that could reveal the depth of the wall, the structure that makes the wall possible, the ability of the wall to screen, or reveal the activity behind it. Of its use as a means to hold up the roof" (interview withZaera-Polo 1995). This attitude of working through variation requires an understanding of the possibilities and constraints of the building community. The projects are driven by the standard building practices of a particular region, rather than the universal standards of a particular material.

Conclusion

Miralles' body of work is one that has creatively and consistently responded to the parameters of an existing situation. It has described the surroundings out of which it emerged, and to a greater or lesser degree, it has conditioned those sur-roundings. His architecture includes memories of and gestures to the buildings, the street, the neighborhood, and the region in which it is set. It incorporates the people and how they live—now, in the past, and in the future. It considers the history of place. Through its openness, it questions where context actually begins and where it ends. In describing the building process, Miralles says, "It turns us into privileged observers. Thus the mode and the construction returns us to thought about the origin of our path. This air, now enclosed, ought to express the absence of what existed there. On the other hand, what appears here is something that we would never have thought possible there. The empty space cannot disap-pear after working on it. It is an expression of this absence. Only architecture can bring it about, not by allusion, nor by displacement, nor by emptying, nor by omission or oversight. Silence is the response to the new distance that has been defined in terms of what exists" (Miralles 1995).

References

Walter Benjamin, "Unpacking My Library," in *Illuminations* (New York: Schocken, 1969).

Peter Buchanan, "Dialogue and Distillation: The Architecture of Enric Miralles and Carme Pinós," in *The Architecture of Enric Miralles and Carme Pinós* (New York: Sites/Lumen Books, 1990).

William Curtis, "Mental Maps and Social Landscapes, The Architecture of Miralles and Pinós," in *El Croquis 49/50* (Madrid: El Croquis, 1991).

Annie Dillard, "Seeing," in *The Art of the Personal Essay*, edited by Phillip Lopate (New York: Anchor Books, 1994).

Documentos de Arquitectura. Unpublished pamphlet.

John Hejduk, personal notes of the author.

Enric Miralles, lecture notes and personal notes of the author.

Josep Maria Montaner, "Basic Formal Concepts in Miralles' and Pinós' Work," in *The Architecture of Enric Miralles and Carme Pinós* (New York: Sites/Lumen Books, 1990).

Jean-Paul Sartre, "The Paintings of Giacometti," in *Situations* (Greenwich, Conn.: Fawcett Publications, 1965).

Geoffry Scott, *The Architecture of Humanism* (New York: Charles Scribner Sons, 1924).

Henry David Thoreau, "Walking," in *The Art of the Personal Essay*, edited by Phillip Lopate (New York: Anchor Book, 1994).

Alexander Tzonis and Liane Leaivre, "Critical Regionalism," in *The Critical Landscape*, edited by Jasper de Haan (Rotterdam: 010 Publishers, 1996).

Rudolf Wittkower, "The Age of the High Baroque," in *Art and Architecture in Italy 1600–1750* (New York: Penguin Books, 1980).

Alejandro Zaera-Polo, "A Conversation with Enric Miralles," in *El Croquis #72: Enric Miralles 1995* (Madrid: El Croquis, 1995).

Last Horizon
Albert Pope

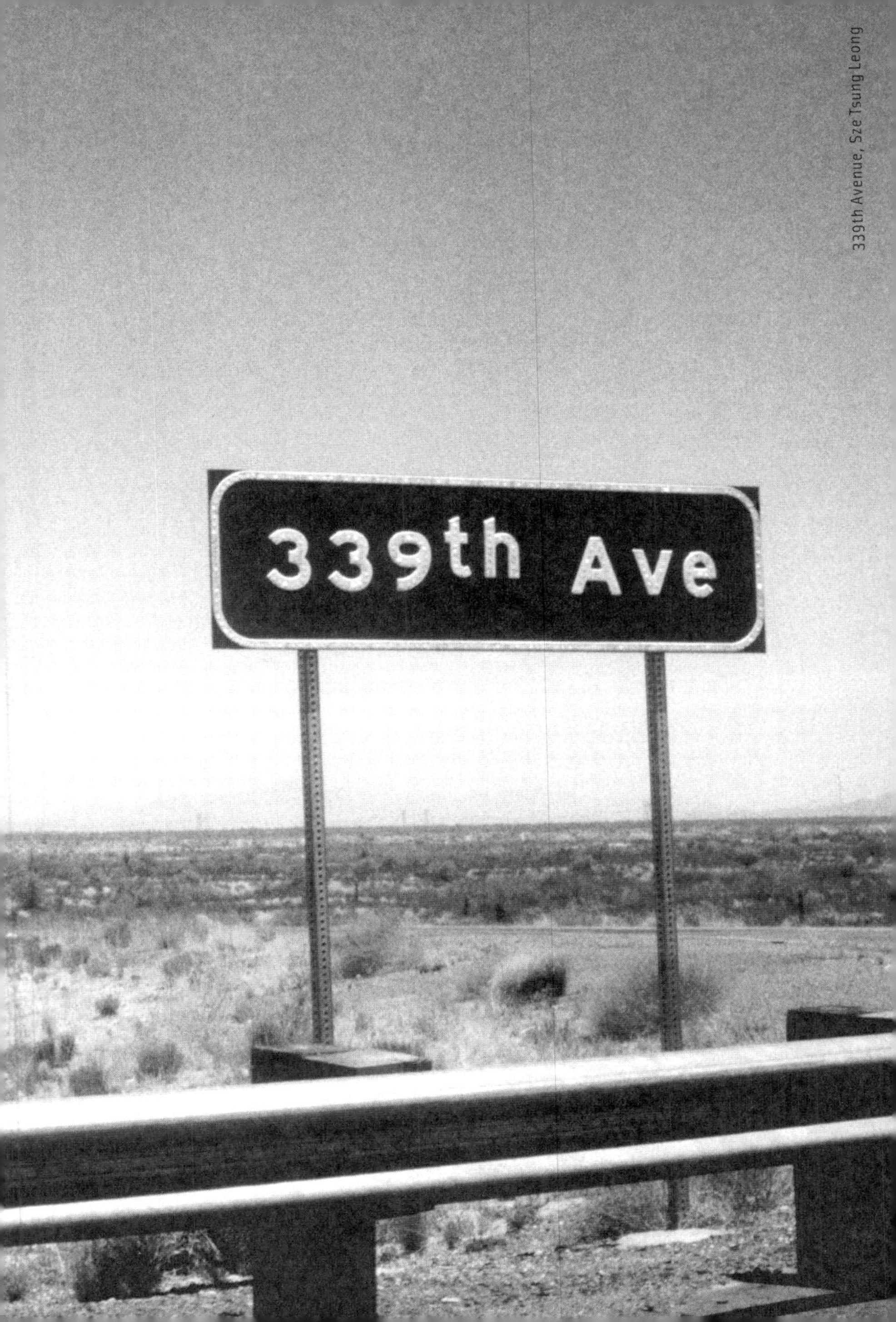

339th Avenue, Sze Tsung Leong

Introduction: Horizon

If you want to find out how various cultures understand the natural world, go to their cities, locate the leading edge of new construction, and observe the strategic transformations taking place. Regardless of how banal or impoverished the processes of urbanization may have become, the significance of the actual movement from the natural to the urban cannot be overstated. The urban horizon—any urban horizon—is where the world comes into being and is thereafter systematically redefined. The urban horizon is the site at which the natural and the urban engage and through this engagement are revealed. The urban and the natural are dialectically interrelated; one cannot exist without the other. It is only through the city that we can "think" the natural world, and this is true whether you are in Lagos, West Covina, or Fukuoka. There is no transparent experience of the natural nor is there anything essential that fixes its meaning for all time. The idea that our understanding of the natural is historically relative or "constructed" is by now commonplace, yet it nevertheless remains true that without these constructions, specifically urban constructions, there is no cognizance.

As the urban and the natural are so integrated in their meaning, it follows that an extraordinary transformation in the way we see and understand the urban would be mirrored by a transformation in the way we see and understand the natural. An extraordinary transformation of the urban did take place sometime around 1950 when the continuos gridiron city of the nineteenth century gave way to the discontinuous cul-de-sac city of the twentieth century. This essay will attempt to show how the radical fragmentation at work in both the urban and the natural environments describe a singular continuum or "world" in formation at the leading edge(s) of urban expansion.

The health of the eye seems to demand a horizon. We are never tired so long as we can see far enough. Emerson, *Nature.*

Modes of Expansion

In order to understand the urban/natural demarcation, it is necessary to know something about the mechanics of urban expansion. The continuous gridded city of the nineteenth century and the discontinuous cul-de-sac city of the twentieth both expand in very different ways. Each distinct mode of expansion is decisive with respect to how the urban and the natural come to exist and how they form, or fail to form, a consolidated urban frontier.

Idea of Grid Continuity

In opposition to its historical reputation as an industrial slum, the nineteenth-century city was first and foremost an open city, and this openness was the result of its infinitely extensible gridiron of streets. Representative examples of the nineteenth-century gridiron—the Cerdà Plan of Barcelona, the by-law streets of London, the massive Kreuzberg district in Berlin, the Commissioner's Plan of Manhattan—all established a historical trend of ever greater continuities in urban form. By the middle of the nineteenth century, gridiron expansion would not be thwarted by fortified walls, preexisting construction, agricultural allotments, or topographic features. Transcending all historical land-use patterns, the ubiquitous gridiron of "city streets" defined an open, universal matrix of space that was wholly unique to the nineteenth century. These uniquenesses can be analyzed and described in many ways. What we will attempt is to describe the nineteenth-century city by analyzing its unprecedented mode of expansion. Specifically, we would like to explore the implications of its consolidated urban frontier.

What is radical about the nineteenth-century grid expansion is that it preempted the purposeful design of discrete urban districts or quarters. Gridded streets are not designed per se, they are simply deployed, "unrolled," or extended out street by street, block by block, at whatever rate the markets will bear. This standardized, automated form of urban expansion was not a new type of planning but was, rather, a new type of antiplanning that eliminated nothing less than the agency of deliberate design intervention. It was a reflection on the status of the city that, in the nineteenth century, its accepted mode of production was paced, not by the combined effect of economic, political, or cultural interests, but by the unmediated rhythm of urban/industrial expansion. For example, in Chicago, gridiron streets were not laid out by an urban "designer" focusing on a unique place surrounded by historically specific communities on a peculiar great lake locked into time. It was, instead, the result of a routine application of a spatial strategy unceremoniously executed by a handful of ruthless speculators. What the Hathaway Plan of Chicago (1834) initiated was less the design of any specific urban district—business district, residential district, industrial district, port, they would all fill in later—as it was a totalizing spatial field. Bearing little relation to the reflexive matrix of solids and voids that historically constituted urban fabric, this new field would both grow autonomously and measure out to infinity.

Considered only as city streets, each one of them would have to end. As a vector in a universal spatial field, however, they would have no outward terminus in their organization of all territories to the west. Chicago would ceaselessly move toward the horizon to become coincident to it. It was this totalizing aspect—the grid as a global matrix—that gave it the qualities of the universal. These qualities made it possible to move, not only Chicago, but also the most insignificant of local crossroads, onto the plane of the world.

Consolidated Horizon

This so-called plane of the world was most clearly revealed, not as a plane, however, but as a line, the line of the urban frontier. As the nineteenth-century city is not the result of singular building campaigns, it does not grow incrementally by discretely designed sectors, districts, quartiers, subdivisions, or neighborhoods. Instead it grows continuously, like a floodtide, an assembly line, or a fast-moving stain or spill. In the nineteenth century, the frontier literally coincided, not with a city wall or an urban greenbelt or an agricultural allotment, but with the line of the horizon. (As a universally extensive field it would have to have a global reach.) And it is in this sense of the frontier and horizon coinciding that the nineteenth-century city can correctly be said to have constructed the only truly open city in the history of the world. This frontier was, of course, much more than the leading edge of urban construction. It was, in a way that is peculiar to the nineteenth century, a concrete meditation on the relation between the urban and the natural. In the United States, it constituted a view of the world that was confident of its technologies, possessed of its future, living on the edge of a continent whose conquest was inevitable. The city edge was that unified front from which the battle against nature and for bodily survival would be ceaselessly waged. As a massive construction site, its very audacity spoke of certain victory.

Site

More than a specific construction site, then, more than the place where universal space is literally produced, the nineteenth-century urban frontier forms the nexus of an urban and natural world that it has called into being. This line is certainly conceptual, but it is also, and more significantly, actual. Being actual it has specific character that can be reported upon as did the British planner Patrick Abercrombie on a visit to Berlin just prior to the outbreak of the First World War. Out on the periphery of the city he noted with some alarm: " . . . as she grows, she does not straggle out with small roads and peddling suburban houses, but slowly pushes her wide town streets and colossal tenement blocks over the open country, turning it at one stroke into full-blown city" (Hall 1988, 33). In one short sentence, Abercrombie produces a fantastic image of the autonomous forces ("she grows") of industrialized urban production as revealed at its leading edge. Its mechanical character ("at one stroke"), its unprecedented scale ("wide town streets and colossal tenement blocks") and the miraculous speed of its construction all join to suggest the shock of some new force existing in the world. What seems to have impressed Abercrombie the most, however, was the sudden, methodical, even violent consumption of "open country" by something so clearly its opposite.

The Destruction of the Hinterland

Like many turn-of-the-century industrial societies that found their productivity to depend upon a permanent state of war (or a permanent addiction to a war economy), turn-of-the-century cities often seemed to require a continuous state of urban development. Industrialized urban construction, like industrialized warfare (like industrialized forestry, industrialized agriculture, industrialized meatpacking, industrialized mining) evoked, not only the image of a "battle" against natural forces, but also the sense that nature was so much raw material to fuel so much (more) industrial output. Massive slag heaps, rank slaughterhouses, logged over forests, depleted farmland, poisoned wells, and abandoned quarries all shamelessly marked the hinterlands of the nineteenth-century gridiron city, attesting to its most immediate relation to the natural world. These sites were not the effects of centuries-old practices of cultivation, they were instead sites that could only be described as devastation.

This unprecedented violation of the natural presented some problems. If nature was to be only raw material used to feed the inexhaustible appetite of aggressive urban/industrial expansion, it would become necessary to construct an alibi, to mitigate the long association of the natural with the centuries-old cultures that grew out of specific land use. "The natural" would have to be reconstructed as something beyond human intervention—something heavily idealized and altogether remote—in order to compensate for the violence routinely done by new industrial practices. In other words, the violation of the natural in the immediate sense required the idealization of the natural in its remote sense. Thus at midcentury, a romantic cult of wilderness predictably emerged as compensation for the relentless plundering of the urban hinterland. In a quick progression from Wordsworth to Thoreau to Muir, environmental advocacy was born. (In 1866, the word "ecology" was coined by the German biologist Ernst Haeckel.) Nature was, for the first time, not something that you lived in—not to mention something that you were—but something out there in a splendid isolation. It became what we today understand as wilderness, a term that was reinvented in the second half of the nineteenth century. This remoteness of authentic nature relieved the inconvenient concern over the brutal extraction of resources closer to home. With a rarefied reverence for "Nature" now held safely in reserve (Yellowstone was established as the first national park in the world in 1874), wilderness advocates provided an apology for the aggressive exploitation of the world.

Little needs to be added to the discussion of this historical paradox. As William Cronon has noted, "only people whose relation to the land was already alienated could hold up wilderness as a model for human life in nature" (date, 80). Enough has been said concerning the railroad cut that ran tangent to Walden Pond at the time of Thoreau's infamous occupation or, fifty years later, to the ironies of a "Prairie School" emerging at precisely the moment that the prairie ecosystem collapsed under the onslaught of industrial farming. In the nineteenth century, forests, alpine landscapes, vast oceanic expanses, polar wastelands, and even prairies became cultural apologies for the ruination caused by resource extraction. In the lexicon of the romantic poets, these landscapes came to symbolize an ideal of wilderness, which was, by very definition, remote from the abuses of industrial processes. Thoreau's well-known admonition that "in wildness is the preservation of the world" means very little in hindsight. In wildness is the preservation of our sanity, our historical traditions, and the amelioration of our guilt. As for the rest of the world, all that was now no longer natural, it could now be exploited with impunity.

Collapse of Space

The idea of wilderness was forged not only by the romantic poets but also by the gentlemen-scholars and proto-geographers who constructed the specific relation of the urban to the natural on a model that would come to be known as known as Central Place Theory. In 1826 Johann Heinrich von Thunen first pub-lished a book called *The Isolated State* where he sketched out the principle of urban expansion based on its interrelation with concentric zones of cultivated land. The determining factor was distance in relation to the economies of trans-portation. Rents would fall off as distance from the (urban) market increased creating a gradient of decreasing cultivation moving out from the center. Thus he described a first zone next to the city containing intensive agriculture. He described a second zone containing extensive agriculture (unrotated crops), a third zone containing open range for livestock, a fourth zone used for trapping and hunting, and a fifth and final zone as "wilderness." Far from revolutionary, von Thunen's isolated state was an updated, scientific restatement of the binding interrelation between the city and its hinterland.

Insomuch as wilderness advocates regard only the fifth or wilderness zone as authentic nature, their effect was to reclassify the four intermediate zones of greater and lesser cultivation as "not-nature" and lump them together with the city as the spoils of industrialization. Flying in the face of the new ideas about wilderness, Central Place Theory made obvious those intermediate landscapes of increasing environmental cultivation/devastation that could no longer be clearly understood as either urban or wild. The industrialists and the naturalists alike had little use for such mediation. For the industrialist, what was formerly nature must be culturally deregulated and opened up to maximum utility; for the naturalist, nature must be upheld as the seat of the sacred, pure and unsullied by industrialized society, in order to reclaim its maximum authenticity. By the middle of the nineteenth century, Nature could either be so understood as so much industrial fodder or the face of God. Needless to say, that much of the world escapes such classification.

Thus, at the end of the nineteenth century, we return to the urban frontier and note the collapse, in real space, of its neat binary classifications. With all the brutal technique of industrialized farming, logging, and mining, there was no way to hold up the urban frontier as anything approximating the natural. Through these techniques, the city had extended its influence far beyond its built-up edges. (By the turn of the century, the city was more natural in appearance than a logged-over forest or a newly created dustbowl.) All of the historically negotiated spaces—the spaces of significant interrelation between the man-made and the natural—could not be made to conform to a single boundary line that is the urban frontier. But what had disappeared in actual fact, lived on in the minds of those who took it upon themselves to classify the earth. The line between the man-made and the natural had been gradually obliterated by industrial practices but lived on in the simplistic logic of the poets, naturalists, and industrialists.

The coherent gridded edge of the nineteenth-century city began to falter as the century wore on. Such a consolidated urban front had literally reproduced the exclusive relation between the urban and the natural formed in tandem by the industrialists and the naturalists. What would eventually emerge was not a consolidated frontier but a hinterland of both rich and degraded interrelations between the natural and the urban. Simply stated, the grid frontier eventually came to mark, not an exclusive or reductive polarity, but the collapse of the natural and the urban into an inscrutable, entropic muddle that, for want of easy classification, came to be systematically ignored. As industrial practices persisted, the idea of the natural could no longer adhere to the formerly urban or agrarian world. Clearly, the nineteenth-century conception of the urban horizon would have to dramatically change.

Duality

Emerson's deceptively simple proclamation that "we are never tired so long as we can see far enough" leaves us in some doubt as to where exactly he chooses to make his stand. He is clearly on some kind of frontier facing toward an open horizon with the fallen world of the industrial city at some uncertain distance behind his back. The question of his location is crucial. Not eight years after the publication of *Nature*, the locus of the wild would recede to the new gates of John Muir's Yosemite (first protected in 1864, declared a national park in 1890). Was

Emerson, then, standing on the perimeter of Concord's grid or had he by now focused in on the great North American wilderness areas soon to be protected by federal law? (The question is rhetorical. In 1871 Emerson, at age 68, would visit Yosemite and meet John Muir. Muir insisted Emerson come with him on a camping trip and sleep out in the open. Emerson refused immediately boarding a train back to Concord (Richardson date, 565).

So concrete was the idea of continuous gridiron expansion, an actual built line between the natural and the urban, that it sustained an intractable duality that still, remarkably, haunts us to this day. Transcendental philosophy and protected wilderness areas notwithstanding, the specific meaning of the urban or the natural in the nineteenth century is less important than the fact that both were set up in a strictly exclusive relation. As a debilitating polarity, the exclusive construction of the urban and the natural preempts any and all gradients of potential and shadings of meaning commonly associated with a cultivated/devastated middle ground. Despite profound transformations in the way we see, think, and construct the city, despite all that has happened in the intervening century, we remain very much held hostage to this binary construction.

Abandoned Frontier

As the urban and the natural are so integrated in their meaning, it follows that an extraordinary transformation in the way we see and understand the urban would be mirrored by a transformation in the way we see and understand the natural. An extraordinary transformation of the urban took place sometime around 1950, when the continuous gridiron city of the nineteenth century gave way to the discontinuous cul-de-sac city of the twentieth century. We will now attempt to show how the radical transformation in the urban environment relates to a radical transformation in our understanding of the natural. As was the case with the nineteenth-century city, this relation can be understood by looking at the mechanics of discontinuous urban expansion or of radical grid fragmentation. Specifically we must again look at how the urban and the natural come to exist at the decisive line(s) of the urban frontier.

Sometime around 1950, the universal space of the gridiron street ceased production, possibly forever, and the relation of the city to its natural setting was transformed. Evidence of this extraordinary transformation is apparent enough.

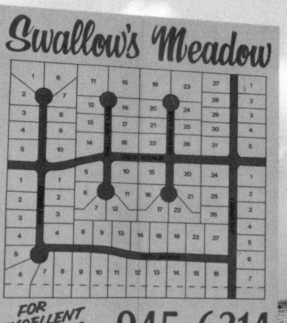

Swallow's Meadow

FOR EXCELLENT HOME SITES CALL: **945-6314**

Driving west out of Phoenix on Interstate 10 toward Los Angeles, several miles past any signs of human inhabitation, you unexpectedly come across an exit for 339th Avenue. The exit is marked by a standard green interstate sign that indicates little more than a narrow line of unkempt asphalt that quickly recedes to the horizon. As conceived, 339th Avenue was an arrogant claim on the open desert, staked out in belief that the open urban frontier and the all-pervasive horizon were coincident. As the Phoenix grid was first laid out and repeatedly deployed, the unobstructed expansion of urban space toward the horizon would have seemed as obvious as the horizon itself. Today, the unabashed arrogance of land speculators imagining thousands upon thousands of urban blocks—a major metropolis—springing up on the northern edge of the Sonoran Desert seems both ludicrous and funny.

Given hindsight, however, this old "Avenue" appears to be more than a monument to bureaucratic persistence. It is instead a poignant holdover from a way of imagining the city that is now fifty years extinct. The continuities of space moving through the original gridiron of Phoenix and connecting it to the prominent expanse of the desert horizon have been lost to the urban imagination. The grid has long since imploded, its extension preempted by hundreds of closed, discontinuous subdivisions now cutting off the continuities of original gridiron expansion. Phoenix is today ranked among the fastest-growing urban regions in the United States, pushing out into the desert at the fantastic rate of one acre per hour. Yet this expansion is being made not toward, but altogether in spite of, the desert horizon. Now on the "outside," 339th Avenue has been cut off by a sea change in urban thought. It is a phantom urban block occupying the desert as a monument to another set of possibilities—to a time when those continuities were so obvious, so inevitable, as to generate out of a small desert town no less than 339 streets. Today, the 339th Avenue exit off Interstate 10 is the very image of an abandoned urban frontier.

If the city does establish our relation to the natural world, then the foreclosure of both the open gridiron and the urban horizon suggests a present, urgent need to rearticulate that relation. More than urgent, it must be said that the present alienation from the world is at best politically suspect and, at worst, cynical and suicidal. Such extreme alienation would come to pass when the idea of nature is no longer physically or factually supported by concrete realities such as those we construct by our own industry. Without such support, our alienation from the world becomes complete or replaced, as it were, by amateur rock climbing, sport utility vehicles, eco-tourism, and animal shows on the Nature Channel. Given such a high degree of alienation, our understanding of the world reverts to something wholly atavistic as do the arguments for "resource management" and "sustainability," which are equivalent today to advanced stages of corporate greenwashing. We certainly know that twentieth-century technologies driven by nineteenth-century ideas is a formula for heat death, yet it is precisely this death that we must contend with today. In this regard, it is necessary to imagine the implosion of 339th Avenue and to confront an entirely new urban context that has transformed our way of seeing and thinking the world. If we are no longer drawn, like Emerson, toward the urban horizon, to what, then, are we drawn?

Driving away from Merida down highway 261 one becomes aware of the indifferent horizon. Quite apathetically it rests on the ground devouring everything that looks like something. One is always crossing the horizon, yet it always remains distant. In this line where the sky meets the earth, objects cease to exist. Since the car was at all times on some leftover horizon, one might say that the car was imprisoned in a line, a line which is in no way linear. The distance seemed to put restrictions on all forward movement, thus bringing the car to a series of countless standstills. How could one advance on the horizon if it was already present under the wheels? A horizon is something else other than a horizon; it is closedness in openness, it is an enchanted region where down is up. Space can be approached, but time is far away. Time is devoid of objects when one displaces destinations. The car kept going on the same horizon. (Smithson 1974, 119)

With the midcentury closure of the open urban frontier, the vital connection between the city and the horizon collapses. Rather than attract, as it did for Emerson, the horizon suddenly seemed to repel. Robert Smithson makes a curious counterpoint to Emerson, one century hence. From the expansiveness of a healthy eye to some kind of horizontal entrapment, the horizon becomes, by 1969, a sign and symbol of our alienation from the natural world. Yet Smithson is not indisposed for lack of an open prospect. He is, instead, perversely attracted to his alienation seeking redemption in the natural in spite of, if not because of, our many desecrations.

Modes of Expansion

At some point around the middle of the twentieth century, the universal field of the gridded frontier extension ceased its movement toward the horizon. At that moment, the indispensable continuity upon which every land grant, every lot and block, every state and county boundary, and every farm road and trading post was fixed, disappeared. In that abrupt cessation of outward movement, what constituted its natural complement also vanished as an actual site. From this point on, there would be no single leading edge of urban construction, no clear and simple boundary between what is urban and what is natural. In destroying the binary structure of the nineteenth-century urban frontier, grid fragmentation rewrote, in physical space, our understanding of the world. Yet, for all the obvious signs that universal gridded space had been summarily abandoned, the conceptual frontier, the way we "think" the natural and the urban, changed not a bit.

Idea of Grid Fragmentation

Grid fragmentation is as essential to the twentieth-century city as grid continuity was to the nineteenth-century city. The midcentury transformation from the open, continuous grid to the closed, fragmented grid is the decisive event of twentieth-century urban development. Today, it is the pivot around which our understanding of the urban and the natural derives. In order to comprehend this relation it is necessary to know something about the mechanics of grid fragmentation and its specific mode of expansion. The significance of this new relation will once again be revealed in the status and disposition of the urban frontier.

At the beginning of the century a major innovation in urban infrastructure was proposed by various individuals and planning groups all loosely associated with the Garden City movement. This innovation sought to replace the open gridiron structure of the nineteenth-century city with the closed configuration of the grid fragment or spine. In direct opposition to autonomous grid expansion, the spine was a closed or finite figure surrounded by a significant spatial buffer. The grid fragment took the form of hierarchical axes that were surrounded by generous park-like open spaces or green belts. The isolated configuration was presented as a separate, so-called garden "city." The incrementally planned garden grid fragment was conceived as an alternative to the indifferent, mechanical extension of the metropolitan gridiron. As adapted in Radiant City slabs-in-the-park or the single-family housing tract, the Garden City grid frag-ment forms the basis of the predominant modes of postwar urban production. While each grid fragment was complete in itself, their axes could be combined and linked together with other fragments via an interurban transportation sys-tem. Unlike the leveling of difference by the universal grid, the aggregation of discontinuous spines and residual spaces exhibited enormous flexibility. They could accommodate significant variations imposed by preexisting built conditions or irregular landscape features. They could conform to natural ridgelines or valleys, bound the edge of a forest, describe the curve of a lake, or twist toward the sun. With their population limits and low densities, Garden City spines could provide children with ample green space and protect them from dangerous through-traffic, provide buffers to industry, construct natural firebreaks, and minimize the destructive effects of aerial warfare. They could also provide an insidious, invisible barrier to race and class. Through a gen-eral dispersal, the grid fragment could ameliorate the metropolis's dangerous abuse of the land and restore its alienated citizens to the redemptive values of the natural world. Being discontinuous, the system could conveniently reduce infrastructure costs as it required less paved surface and shorter utility runs than a continuous gridiron pattern.

There was, however, more at stake with grid fragmentation than such expedien-cies could explain. As a significant number of fragments came to be dispersed, an evanescent, polynuclear field would emerge to replace the totalizing space of the nineteenth-century gridiron. As adapted by Le Corbusier, Wright, and Hilberseimer, and subsequently by developers all over the world, the Garden City model must be understood as more than just a change of density, the accom-modation of a new style, or a growing taste for urban greenery. The dissipation of the urban infrastructure was not just a simple lowering of urban density or the reversal of a figure/ground diagram. It was a frontal assault on the open metropolitan grid and its vast spatial horizon. The radically discontinuous grids common to today's postwar periphery are the direct heirs of the aggre-gate spines that constituted the Garden City's utopian vision. With the arrival of the discontinuous, polynuclear field, there would no longer be a single, leading edge of urban construction.

The idea of a vast hinterland of space—an endless reservoir of space manifest at the urban horizon and latent in every open street and boulevard—had lost its relevance. Long before federal bureaucrats got around to administering the national forests, managing the G.I. Bill, stockpiling nuclear waste, or funding the massive interstate highway system, the open urban horizon had become a thing of the past. What was left was not grand; what was left was a series of fractured edges bordering residual spaces, which were of seemingly little use to anyone.

Fractured Horizon

As opposed to the street-by-street deployment of continuous gridiron blocks, garden "cities" were to grow as highly planned, isolated increments each designed, in total, for specific sites by specific planners. While the Garden City movement sought to overturn the "antiplanning" of the nineteenth-century city by the planning of discrete settlements, it proposed something quite different from the districts or quarters of traditional cities. Unlike traditional urban districts, garden cities were complete in themselves and could never add up to any greater whole that could become a city, let alone a metropolis. They instead constituted autonomous, inward-focused units strictly limited in size. As discrete units of growth, then, they did not expand along a single, consolidated urban frontier as the nineteenth-century city did. Instead, their mode of expansion would fracture that frontier. By necessity, each unit of expansion would move out into the open space beyond the leading edge of gridded construction and establish entirely autonomous, ex-urban nuclei.

The nineteenth-century urban frontier described by Abercrombie would be radically transformed by these new processes of fragmentation and extension. The single leading edge of urban construction would split into a thousand pieces each with a relatively small nuclei establishing their own center, periphery, and edge. This drastic reduction of the increment of urban expansion, from the frontier of a single metropolitan entity to a myriad of small edges—the edges of so-called villages and towns—constituted an entirely different way of conceiving and constructing the world.

There is, however, more to grid fragmentation than the identification of the relatively smaller units of urban expansion and their apparent leap out beyond the gridded perimeter. In addition to these properties, it is important to note the internal behavior of the ex-urban units themselves. As they move outward beyond the frontier of nineteenth-century gridded construction, each of these units turn inward on themselves to form autonomous enclaves. This simultaneous inward turning and outward moving action is the key to fragmented urban expansion. There is an observable ratio between the inward-turning and outward-moving motion of contemporary urban form. In order to move out, the fragmented units must turn in or, conversely, in order to turn in, the fragmented units must invariably move out. This simultaneous inward-turning and outward-moving action is responsible for the disintegration of the consolidated frontier. In contrast to the coincidence of the boundless grid and the horizon, the horizon of the discontinuous city can be described as "imploded" by way of its internal centrifuge. Thus it is that a relatively small nuclei can collapse inward while moving outward—disconnected and utterly exposed—into open space.

Built out of the dynamics of each individual unit of expansion, a field of loosely linked ex-urban nuclei begins to take shape. As in the individual nuclei, there are observable ratios between size, location, and surrounding open space inherent to the ordering of this field. The larger ex-urban units become, the farther they must overreach the existing line of urban construction. The farther these units overreach the existing line of urban construction, the more insulated they must become. The more insulated the units must become, the greater their need for a larger excess of space or spatial buffer. Thus from the outward-moving and inward-turning nuclei, a coherent polynuclear field emerges succeeding the continuous, universal space of urban and agrarian grids. In the interstices of the diverging grid fragments an alternative to universal space opens up. The production of an alternative to the totalizing space of the universal grid should not be viewed as coincidental or residual to the processes of contemporary urban production.

The horizon within which the contemporary city is contained is something other than a single, infinite horizon. As described by Robert Smithson, it is a kind of "closedness in openness" or a condition in which openness is preempted and the extent of the horizon becomes encompassed, as in the circumference of an island. The nineteenth-century's urban frontier has not been lost, it has been displaced; it has been internalized. It is no longer the greater setting for the city (where the horizons coincide), it is a circumference contained within itself. As it is imploded inward it also multiplies forming a polynuclear field with commensurate properties. Amusement parks, wilderness areas, corporate subdivisions, commercial malls, and bird sanctuaries all constitute this field. Instead of seeking out the open expansiveness of the nineteenth-century frontier, we now require, if not demand, other existential situations. Instead of openness and outwardness, we now seek out islands, refuges, shelters, asylum, retreats, sanctuaries, cloisters, havens. This dramatic reversal in the fundamental characteristics of the worlds we routinely construct are all-telling. It suggests a reorganization of our most basic, instinctual habits of being-in-the-world. Nothing less is at stake in the reconstruction of the urban and the natural, which has taken place over the preceding half-century.

Following that, one would presume that, along with the fracturing and implosion of the actual urban edge, a fracturing of the antagonistic nineteenth-century dualism between the urban and the natural would also occur. We would now like to demonstrate how this dualism was not overcome but was surreptitiously sustained by the new mechanics of grid fragmentation. Today, we seek the frontier that is not a frontier, and we discover an island that is not an island.

Not Urban, Not Agrarian, and Not Wild

This overreaching of boundary by discrete ex-urban units indicates that a profound transformation in the way we construct the urban and the natural has, in concrete fact, taken place. That does not mean, however, that we are aware of, let alone coherent about, the significance of such a transformation. Regardless of the retaditaire conceptions that we may implicitly hold with regard to nature (the latest fashion in safari vehicles, Gore-Tex® jackets, and ski resorts for example), the actual world that we have constructed places us within an entirely new existential relation between the urban and the natural, whether we are able to grasp that relation or not. One cannot overstate the profound differences between a world predicated on a continuous urban field of universal or global dimension and a world predicated on a discontinuous urban field of inward looking grid fragments isolated in space. Considered existentially, the occupants of these two worlds would be very different people with very different prospects and very different lifestyles and utterly divergent values with regard to the surrounding world. The fact that few can account for the difference between the open gridiron of yesterday and the closed corporate subdivision of today, in no way mitigates these differences.

The collapse of the nineteenth-century urban horizon and the reconfiguration of the world into a series of discontinuous urban and wilderness islands can only be understood retroactively. The fact that the national park system and the Garden City movement emerged and flourished at the same time would not have been emphasized in the 1890s. Yet who today would miss the relation between the 1901 publication of John Muir's *Our National Parks* and the 1902 publication of Ebenezer Howard's *Garden City of To-morrow?* A broader sense of ecological fragmentation emerges today where the fragmentation of the city into cul-de-sac patterns is the result of the same forces that fragments wild habitat into a handful of national parks and wilderness areas. It was not until these two tendencies began to merge into analogous "monocultures" (such as the affinity between shopping malls and tree farms) that their fundamental relation became apparent.

Yet this transformation from open to closed, continuity to fragmentation, and horizon to circumference does not tell the whole story. Along with these new fragments something else comes into the world: the excess of space outside of the now isolated islands of the urban, the agrarian, and the wild. This wholesale transformation from a seamless continuity of the urban and agrarian grid to the discontinuous archipelago of isolated grid fragments opens up a new type of "residual" space that is literally uncharted and, given the present lack of adequate conceptual footholds, unchartable. Given this century's dramatic refinement of destructive technologies and associated practices, and the subsequent need for ever-larger staging areas, extraction sites, and dumping grounds, it is at least conceivable that the demand for conceptually blind, unchartable land was as urgent as the demand for urban and wilderness enclaves. If ancient cultural prohibitions precluded the fouling of the urban, the agrarian, and the wild, where else would the sites required by new "dirty" technologies and practices go?

Discontinuity and Spatial Production

Is it possible to imagine that the aim of these island enclaves was never the enclave itself, but the residuum of underconceptualized space that it inadvertently produces? In order to answer this very paranoid question it is necessary to examine the spatial remainder of grid fragmentation and emphasize what may at first seem to be its most obvious aspects.

The processes of grid fragmentation produce a field of linked spines floating in a sea of residual space. This type of urban construction constitutes the predominant mode of space-making at work in the city today. As fragments are deployed, space emerges, but it emerges, not as a primary effect of urban construction, but as its residue or excess. Thus, a highly polarized, external condition appears: a condition that could not have existed in the universal urban field of the nineteenth-century city. This unprecedented urban "outside" of space is significant in two respects. First, it constitutes the predominant type of space produced in the city today (rivaling the historical importance of piazzas, squares, or corridor streets), and second, despite its predominance, it exists as a remainder, or excess; it goes virtually unseen and remains negatively defined and underconceptualized.

As originally conceived by Garden City advocates and modern city planners, the production of such space was not inadvertent at all. Quite the contrary, the production of open space by grid fragmentation was a distinguishing feature for Howard as it was for Le Corbusier and Hilberseimer. At this point, however, it may be useful to ask if grid fragmentation really produced idyllic urban open space as Garden City advocates and modern masters believed, or did it produce something else, something unexpected, some excess far beyond the control of those who unwittingly set it into motion? The rhetoric was always of openness, nature, an abundance of light and air, parks, greenbelts, allotment gardens, and good health. While many sang the praises of grid fragmentation, few were really capable of understanding, let alone supervising, its consequences or controlling its meaning. As the fragmented grid was realized in postwar residential tracts and slab cities, the spines and supergrids did produce an excess of open space. Yet, the residuum of grid fragmentation is unlike any type of urban space that has existed in the past; it was certainly unlike the ludicrous rural or "town" models that the Garden City drew from. This is because the space produced by grid fragmentation defied all of the known modes of spatial classification present at the time of its emergence. In this regard it was, as it remains today, completely misclassified along the lines of a binary logic now half a century obsolete.

This inability to classify is directly related to the collapse of the urban horizon where the boundaries between the urban and the natural were highly concentrated and meticulously maintained. Historically, there was no doubt as to where the leading edge of urban construction was located. On one side there was a predominance of the urban, on the other there was a predominance of the natural, such that when this hard edge collapsed through the processes of grid fragmentation, our ability to imagine what came next collapsed as well. This is because what came next—the residual spaces of grid fragmentation—formed no consolidated boundary upon which to base clear conceptions. Without such boundaries the residual spaces of grid fragmentation could only be defined negatively as "not urban" or "not natural." If the world is imagined as being simply divided between urban and natural then such space that was neither simply could not exist. It would, as it has, drop off the mental map, existing outside of criteria too crudely configured to account for it. This is why contemporary space goes unseen, and underconceptualized and why it falls into dereliction and abandonment or, worse, violent exploitation. Unlike the Garden City advocates intention to design and produce space—green belts, parks, agricultural allotments—the character of space produced today constitutes a nefarious gray zone open to whatever activities it would serve to obscure. This is because it defies the easy classification of the gridiron frontier, yet it has developed no classification schema of its own. With this production of obscurant space, the city—the traditional site of social well-being—began to devour itself.

Conceptually Blinded

The upshot is that our ability to conceive and construct alternative ideas of the urban and the natural has not kept up with our ability to actually produce these alternatives in real space. The fact that we are all but blind to this production is of no consequence. Many have tried, and are currently trying, to strike conceptual footholds. Yet, apparently, the simplistic classifications of the past maintain their grip upon our collective imagination.

With regard to collective imagination, our present conceptual shortfall constitutes a dangerous gap, for it is clear that the environmental crises we confront today will not be met by ever more efficient "management" of "resources" as sustainability advocates routinely argue. Only cultural change can overcome the exploitative nineteenth-century practices that see these crises as a problem of environmental stewardship, fully external to ourselves. Today, such practices betray an outmoded mindset where detachment from the natural only reproduces our tendency to see it as something other, as something antagonistic, which must ultimately yield to our purposes. Our inherited binary logic has given us this much, yet, it is by now so blindingly present as to make it impossible to see that such an idea of stewardship is delivering precisely its opposite.

The greater urgency we have today is due to the fact that, as our collective imaginations have faltered, our collective effectiveness has been greatly increased by managerial efficiencies and exquisite technologies now routinely put to the sacking of the earth. One often gets the feeling that what passes for nature is only that one percent of the world that is locked up in national and state parks. Likewise, what passes for the urban is what is locked up behind the wall of a subdivision, the perimeter of a shopping mall, or the gate of an office park. In our stunted urban imaginations, the subdivision gate opens directly onto the national park or wilderness area. (Why else do we drive our sport utility vehicles every single day but to quickly cross to the other side?) It is our inability to loosen the bonds of binary classification—the strict maintenance of the urban and the natural—that forces us into these opposing and ever-diminishing worlds. Today, what passes for the natural and the urban constitute a miniscule world of technically managed landscapes whose only true amenity is an absence of ambiguity. This, of course, leaves a lot left over to suffer the degradations of neglect. All that is left underconceptualized is accordingly left undervalued, and this, in total, is the bulk of the world.

If our ability to escape our received ideas of the urban and the natural has not kept up with our ability to reconstruct them in real space, then it is time to learn from what we actually make but may not yet understand. It is necessary to revise our conception of the urban horizon now fractured by the proliferation ex-urban nuclei and their spatial residuum. If we would look today at the urban frontier we would see not Emerson's wilderness sublime but an obscured landscape of entropic degradation and waste possessing a wild beauty we are as yet unable to explain. It is through the opening up of this world that we can recover our conceptual blind spots and start to think about a possible "preservation of the world."

References

Ralph Waldo Emerson, *Nature; Adresses and Lectures*, 1849.

Johann Heinrich von Thunen, *The Isolated State*, 1826.

Ebenezer Howard, *Garden City of To-morrow?* London, 1902.

John Muir, *Our National Parks*. Cambridge, 1901.

Robert Smithson, *Incidents of Mirror Travel in the Yucatan*, 1974.

Robert Smithson, *The Writings of Robert Smithson*, edited by Jack Flam (New York: New York University Press, 1979).

Terrors and Pleasures
of the (New) Automaton
David Heymann

*Imagine a room filled
with thousands of live butterflies
and you're right
in the middle of them.*

1 Future Attractions

This is what happens in a Butterfly Museum. Butterfly chrysalides and larvae from various parts of the world—though primarily from butterfly ranches in Central and South America, home to more visually startling species—are brought into a large, greenhouse-like glass structure. Here the mechanically controlled environment mocks the rain forest. At night it rains, and during the day there are periodic bouts of mist. The chrysalides, pinned to bark or sticks, are set out to hatch on frames behind open-ended protective glass shields. You can watch the slow unfolding of the butterflies, their wings drying and hardening. It's like a very small, very crowded maternity ward.

Once emerged, the butterflies are free to fly about the space, feeding from ubiquitous fruit plates and nectar trays, alighting on real and artificial plants and trees and on visitors—coupling and fluttering in general. There are no predators. The architecture requires a minimum of flight obstructions and sharp edges. After a few weeks—depending on the species—these butterflies die, having lived out their splendid lives. In the meantime, replacements will have been brought in to be born. Carcasses are removed every morning, and attendants quietly dispose of those butterflies that die during hours.

A visitor buys a ticket for an appointed time and enters with a group. Prior to being allowed into the live room, groups are shown a video or given a lecture on the biology of these remarkable creatures, their fragility, and, by extension, the fragility of their environment. The sources for the chrysalides are roughly identified and exonerated. The entire enterprise is cast in the light of doing the right thing environmentally. The word *nature* is frequently used, though complex distinctions between wild and otherwise are not made. The visitors are admonished to stay on the trails and to watch their footing on the continually moist surfaces. Checklists—laminated, with color photographs of the species one might see—are passed out. For all intents and purposes you are entering the wilderness.

An air lock, a dark tunnel, water, a ramp up into light: still, entry to the large live room is frequently accompanied by initial disappointment. Only gradually does the eye become facile at spotting the butterflies. Then suddenly they are everywhere, overwhelmingly (in Houston's there are several thousand): in the air, on the ground, under leaves, on feeding stations, and often landing on the brightly colored shirts that repeat visitors know to wear (and the museum promotes). The trails loop around and back on themselves, passing various microenvironments. Everywhere there are people being cautious, pointing and whispering—no guard rails interfere. There is a surfeit of complicated camera lenses. Afterwards there will be a gift shop. Surprisingly, or perhaps not, it is possible to purchase real butterflies, mounted, in glass frames.

If the largish to large city that you probably live in or near does not yet have its own Butterfly Museum, well, you can be certain that somewhere someone is planning one. And if you have never been in a Butterfly Museum, then you are distinctly slacking, my friend, in experiencing the peculiar terrors and pleasures that only the consumption of Nature in the late twentieth century is capable of offering. A new Automaton is here, a mechanized, moralized pleasure dome, ready to educate the children and entertain the adults (which may be the same thing) and able to confound the skeptics, who lament, "it could not, should not be done."

2 Jewelry

In 1994, the Houston Museum of Natural History reopened its extensively renovated building.[1] Originally built in 1964, the museum for many years maintained a low hum in the landscape. You don't need a picture to know the type: think travertine-clad warehouse, think state office building. Despite the grade school groups on obligatory field trips, the large building felt dim and undervisited. The exhibits—an odd mishmash of sporadic donations, heavy on petroleum exploration, without an evident overall curation—never seemed to change. The whole languished in that pleasant and/or frustrating torpor endemic to hot and humid cities. Outside, one entered Hermann Park, of the City Beautiful variety; it too going inexorably to seed. Houston at that time was a city with—in the language of the museum—a substantial inertial mass, with an overwhelming tendency toward entropy.

[Fig. 1] Exterior view, Cockrell Butterfly Center, Museum of Natural History, Houston, Texas. Hoover and Associates, architects, 1994. (Photograph by Ronald J. Zaguli, RJZ images)

Then came the early 1980s. Houston underwent a stretch of extremely rapid growth, fueled by high oil prices, that brought nearly a million new inhabitants to the city. During roughly the same period—on a larger cultural scale—a new breed of self-promoting museum was gradually supplanting the quiet-repository museum in the scramble to secure ever more scant funding. Coincidentally, baby boomers, then coming into their own as parents, were seeking out safe places for children to be entertained, and for themselves to meet, in the evolving urban landscape, and the newly aggressive museums precisely filled this niche.

Given this evolution, the Museum of Natural History was further benefited because the role of nature in society—the definition of nature itself—was also changing. If the archetypal television image of nature in the 1960s is a National Geographic special documenting some essentially amoral system of cause and effect—a mantis eats her mate, postcoitally—free from, but threatened by, the invasion of humankind, certainly for the 1980s and 1990s, it has to be nature as pitchman for, among others, beer (Tap the Rockies!) and, especially, sports utility vehicles (sting rays swim past: the camera swoops up continuously, through pounding surf—a beach, gulls—up and over a vertiginous coastal range to find a Jeep Grand Cherokee parked on a dormant volcano—spectral sunshine, orchestral overture).

Much has, of course, been made of the irony in this, but there is, arguably, no irony here at all. Certainly the last thirty years has seen a profound shift away from nature as understood in the National Geographic example above. Does anyone still believe that there are natural environments free of the consequences of human presence, even if at a distance (acid rain, the ozone layer, global warming, etc.)? Perhaps in a sort of |martyrdom, it seems the notion of nature as amoral has been supplanted by the notion of the natural as very moral. Visit any elementary school: see if George Washington is held up for more substantial veneration and respect than the little blue penguin. Nature, when we had it, just was. Now that we don't have it, nature is very good.

The elevation of the natural has, of course, been exacerbated by the extraordinary growth of urban areas. The relationship of the concept of nature and the fact of cities, while clearly an issue of startling complexity, has nonetheless one characteristic particular to the issues at hand. Historically, Nature and City are linked by a perverse inversion: the urban realm is sensed to be man-made, the greater is the demand for the natural. But what natural is understood to be also

changes as a consequence of increasing urbanization. As Robert Nash has pointed out, a rest stop
in Minnesota may be wild to a resident of New York
City, but it is civilization for a trucker coming down
from the Yukon.[2] The definition of nature exists on a
sliding scale of authenticity according to our normative environment. As that environment increasingly
becomes an urbanity understood to be artificial,
what is acceptably natural slides increasingly from
actually wild to apparently wild.

Today there is an extraordinary demand for the natural as a consequence of the extraordinary increase
in urbanization. At the same time, there is a reduced
supply of the natural as once defined: free of human
intervention. The awareness of this change has
merely increased the demand. But—luckily?—our
definition of nature has been changing too, and it
should be possible—because our frame of reference
is ever sliding toward the urban—to accept as natural things that were once patently understood to be
human fabrications.[3]

The Museum of Natural Science rose to this larger
challenge rather well. Around its original travertine
box—mute, opaque, a storage house mausoleum—it
added a series of spectacle objects—a planetarium,
an Imax theater, the Butterfly Center—interconnected by a shopping mall-like public arcade with
gift shops and cafe (the total expansion was 65,000
square feet). The original building too was brought
up to date, and exhibitions were revamped and substantially curated, filling gaps in the original line up.
The educational endeavors were expanded, as were
the social ones: openings became events, galleries
were named after patrons, extraordinary collections
were donated, and so on.

[Fig. 2] Interior view, Cockrell
Butterfly Center, Houston, Texas.
(Photograph by the author)
[Fig. 3] In the butterfly forest.
(Photograph by the author)

Still, the real jewel of the renovation was and remains the butterflies, housed in their jewel-like setting—a truncated glass and steel cone, set prominently at the end of the pedestrian arcade, where it is also most visible to drivers on the nearby main arterials. The Butterfly Center is entirely isolated: it is an aquarium of sky. To enter it—after the obligatory video sermon—you drop below grade. Coming through an air lock, you are at the base of a pit into which is pouring, from sources unknown, a waterfall. A ramp spirals up from this pit through a descending mist. The walls—gunnite—are modeled as a Yucatan sink hole. The sense that all is a sham vanishes as a very large—it is easily the size of a well-fed bat—iridescent blue butterfly appears, flapping lazily.

Gradually the foliage begins: the ramp comes to grade at the base of an immense tree (it is actually stained concrete). The butterflies appear in earnest, and the path branches, doubling back in the opposite direction about the pit, through and throughout a dense, wet, semicircular forest of flowering plants and shrubs, butterflies everywhere. Eventually these various paths come together at the base of a ramp-stair, which ascends further into the glass cone to a point just under-neath the waterfall's lip (still above that the cone continues for another half of its height). Here are the vitrines—Inca motifs abound—where the butterflies are born. Another air lock admits you into the cliff—check your clothing for strays!—and you enter the museum's vast preserved butterfly and moth collection. It is a staggering, maze-like display, like a fantastic over-ripe jewelry store.

It is all jewelry. Where once the museum had formed a blank edge to the park, now it has set out this faceted glass emerald, like a new geometric emissary. While the park has declined (Nature-as-we-once-knew-it), attendance at the museum has skyrocketed. To see the butterflies it is recommended that you have advance reservations on busier days. It is, after all, not like going to a museum: the insects are alive! It isn't until you are inside that you begin to wonder if maybe that somehow might not problematically be the point, but the thought flitters away before you can put a pin through its abdomen.

3 Bodysnatchers

The evolution in our understanding of what constitutes the natural is curiously coincident with the
shift from the Modern reliance on essence to the
after-Modern fascination with and dependence on
image. These evolutions may or may not be linked
in some chicken and egg fashion to changes in the
theoretical concerns of various cultural endeavors—Film, Photography, Art, and Architecture—but
it would be hard to argue, since, in the case of making more Nature, as the increased demand would
have us do, it is by definition impossible to make in
any other way except by image and especially by the
control thereof.

In this regard, the design of the Cockrell Butterfly
Center utilizes a series of strategies to generate a
phantasm of nature.[4] These strategies are perhaps
familiar—they are variations of methods already
widely at work in the designed landscape—and may
be of interest to you, since in all likelihood you,
architect, will soon be called upon to make more
nature. The various methods are not primarily formal. Rather, they involve a variety of mechanisms by
which spatial meaning is controlled by the framing of
perception: they are spin.

The first of the strategies is the creation of an
apparent sustenance. By claiming a space in the
landscape to sustain something natural—by freez-
ing it out of the cycle of development—we evidence
some agreement that so doing has merit and that
the space reserved is by default natural by being
preserved. There are many examples. The National
Park system is the big one, but, on a much smaller
scale, many municipalities have instituted no development zones, usually in trade for more intense

[Fig. 4] The very small maternity
ward. (Photograph by the author)
[Fig. 5] The field guide. (Photograph by the author)

development elsewhere. While the Cockrell Butterfly Center does not preserve a noumenal environment, it nonetheless presents a phenomenal environment as a sort of necessary stand in. The rain forest may be disappearing in Central America, but an improved version is appearing here, a refugee camp for innocent orphans.

The sense of sustenance is furthered by the presence of the technology needed to stabilize and artificially regenerate the ideal environment. It is understand that such technology is no longer an option: you don't get nature by just leaving something alone! At the Butterfly Center this complex but essentially technical task is undertaken in such a clinical and expensive manner—suspended within the fine steel and glass shell (hurricane-proof, the visitor is told) is a marvelous stainless steel rainmaking device, replete with complex tracking system and catwalks—that the seriousness of the venture cannot be called into doubt. The nagging question—aren't these butterflies, for our entertainment, probably just being taken from somewhere that now has less butterflies?—withers in the face of it all.

Curiously, the presence of the evidently technical has the net effect of making the patently artificial trees and rocks seem less so. They in turn constitute another strategy—simile—that is very much at work in the broader landscape: the Scottsdale ordinance requiring the chemical aging of freshly cut rock face is a good example, one of many. At the Cockrell, simile comes in the form of the fake rain forest and sink hole. While these are exceptionally well done, people are not fooled, as they might be in instances of simile at large. Surprisingly, they do not seem to have to be. On the one hand, the extraordinary presence of the butterflies relegates the trumped up landscape to background. On the other, most visitors seek to be entertained, and they fully accept and understand the role of image therein.[5] It is not exactly reality that they seek from the natural.

Aiding the strategies of sustenance and simile is the policy of exclusivity, at work in the larger landscape in many ways, from ridge line ordinances to private conservancies to no-access zones in public lands. If once planners hoped to get people out into nature, now they seek to keep the two apart. Generally this policy is accepted by the public, which understands its necessity for the public good. While polarizing the landscape, it has the benefit of making the protected seem simultaneously more natural, and more desirable. It is founded on a marvelously weird premise: public space that the public cannot access.

Exclusivity at the Butterfly Center is based on denial and privilege. Not only are we privileged to see these creatures, and in their most intimate moments, but we are privileged to do so in a small group, at an appointed hour. The entry fee seems a paltry expense! The architectural support for this programmatic agenda is fairly straightforward. From the outside the cone is the perfect vitamin capsule, an object of desire. Through the glass we can see but not hear children laughing.

While it would seem that the policy of exclusivity is threatened by the fact that groups move through by herd control, a fine balance is achieved. The sense of something portentous taking place is heightened by the presence of many eager strangers. Being let in as groups, rather than by steady stream, fuels the expeditionary sense, which is shamelessly exploited by the architectural entry sequence described above: the group must stick together until the trails branch out above the sink hole.

One of the most startling manners by which the space of the Center is made to feel natural is by the judicious use of texts. Prior to entering the live room, the visitor passes a series of back lit panels that provide information regarding butterflies in general. Most visitors do not stop to read the panels, but one suspects that the desired effect is gained nonetheless: the live room is clearly not just entertainment! But the most effective texts are the laminated checklists that visitors carry to identify the species. Modeled on field guides—camping equipment—they keep the visitors' focus away from the conundrums of the entity at large and generate a sense of luck in what would otherwise seem an entirely controlled experience.

Along similar (postmodern) lines, photography in the live room too adds to the sense of the natural. It is not just the noted sense of the camera's presence validating an event or fact. The layout of the room is such that a maximum amount of the infrastructure is hidden by living, flowering plants. The cage is thus not in evidence, and it is rather easy to photograph

[Fig. 6] Vaucanson's Duck, 1733–34, or copy thereof. Musee du Conservatoire National des Arts et Metiers, Paris. (Image copyright by same)

the butterflies as if no cage existed. This may be like shooting ducks in a barrel, but later the photographs lead their own lives, presenting a distinct reality as concrete (perhaps more concrete) as the event itself, but determined entirely by the edited evidence of the images.

Actually, the possibility offered by the planting—a cage without bars—defines the very important agenda of the various strategies: seamlessness. Tremendous care has gone into avoiding the possibility of the visitor having a programmatic, spatial, moral, or emotional crisis of confidence in the entire undertaking. That is, one suspects, the primary reason that the death of the butterflies—a non-renewable resource (though the museum raises 20 percent of its own stock in greenhouses atop its parking garage)—is not dwelt upon. Still, what could be more natural? But that is the point. Here is more nature, and nature as it is actually wanted: safe, and pretty, without predators and prey, without crisis, guilt free; i.e.: The Garden of Eden.

Of course there is a catch. Houston's climate—its brutal heat and humidity—treats all human inventions with relentless entropic disdain. Ants have managed to breach the perfection of the Center's sealed edges. While they are kept away from the food plates, they are nonetheless attracted to the corpses of the dying butterflies. If you are really lucky you will see ants dragging one along, as they perform an environmental task to which they have precisely evolved: they are the great garbage gleaners, the recyclers, the makers of mulch. But before you rejoice in the reassertive return of Nature the Amoral, the corpse is picked up by an attendant (khaki pants, neutral polo shirt), ants clinging desperately, and whisked away to a plastic receptacle.

4 Terminators

From Daedalus to Frankenstein to *Bladerunner*, we have long been fascinated by humankind bettering nature. The invariably horrifying consequences of so doing links the various myths and stories by a common morality. Or, more precisely, it is the simultaneous presence of fascination and terror that defines a common humanity—a punishable hubris—in these stories. The terrible deed should not be done, though we know it will.

Arguably the most extraordinary examples of actual—rather than literary—attempts at mimicking nature are the automata of Jacques Vaucanson, in France, and Pierre Jacquet-Droz, in Switzerland, both working in the eighteenth century.[6] In 1738, Vaucanson exhibited, to great acclaim, three automata: a drummer, a flute-player, and—most notoriously—a duck. This last, made of gilded copper, sat on an imposing sculptural pedestal in which were hidden a system of gears and levers, the use of which made it possible for the duck to, among other things, flap its wings, splash about on water, quack, drink, eat, and digest food. Voltaire ranked Vaucanson a rival to Prometheus.

Droz, in turn, developed a series of automatons that, in the form of perfectly carved wooden dolls, performed normal human functions like making a drawing or playing the organ. The most extraordinary of these is a writing boy. "When the mechanism [fully hidden in the boy's back] is started, the boy dips his pen in the inkwell, shakes it twice, places his hand at the top of the page, and pauses. As the lever is pressed again, he begins to write, slowly and carefully, distinguishing in his characters between light and heavy strokes" (Hulten 1968, 21).

These automata were met with an overwhelming interest, characterized by a mixture of terror and pleasure. "To contemporary spectators, the great attraction was the perfect imitation of living beings and the speculations about the nature of life to which such verisimilitude gave rise . . . the little mechanical writer must have seemed almost intolerably perfect. He must have inspired feelings of curiosity, admiration, and also paralyzing inferiority. The young scholar embodies the idea of perfection—an ideal man, who never makes an error, never gets in a bad humor, and never revolts" (Hulten 1968, 20–21).

[Fig. 7] Young writer. c. 1770. Pierre Jacquet-Dros, Musee d'Art et d'Histoire, Neuchatel. (Image copyright by same)

This last could almost describe the Butterfly Center.

Stabile, constant, perfect, absent of menace—just the most beautiful things, behaving perfectly. As automaton, the addition of living creatures—like the living skin on the cyborg in Terminator—makes it far more difficult to decide where the illusion begins. What is missing—I think it has been quite consciously designed away—is the component of terror, the "speculation about the nature of life," that such an environment would seem automatically to foster.

But that is where we stand. The purpose of the Center is not metaphysical doubt, but moral certainty, packaged in pleasure. Oddly enough, the past year or two has also seen the popular acceptance of real terror in the natural landscape: a series of attacks by mountain lions on visitors to certain national parks and forests, some quite close to urban areas. Public support has by and large fallen on the side of the cougars, the resurging population of which has brought these once nearly extirpated creatures back into ranges now settled by ex-urbanites. So keep your eyes open as you walk down the driveway to your car, just now idling in the driveway, kids in the back, so excited to be off to see the butterflies!

Notes

[1] The addition is by Hoover Architects to the original building by George Pierce-Abel Pierce, architects; Staub, Rather, and Howze, associated architects. The bulk of the information regarding the museum and the butterfly center comes from two sources: on-site information gathering and an article by Gerald Moorehead, FAIA: "Butterfly House" in *Texas Architect* (Texas Society of Architects) (March/April 1995): 44–45.

[2] The issue at hand—the definition of nature—is well considered in a text by the author cited: Roderick Nash, *Wilderness and the American Mind*, revised edition (New Haven and London: Yale University Press, 1973); see especially chapters 3 and 4. Another excellent exploration of this topic is by Neil Evernden, *The Social Creation of Nature* (Baltimore and London :The Johns Hopkins University Press, 1992).

[3] Clearly there are cultures that have been so doing for a long time. A most startling example of this occurred to me while backpacking with a group of German friends in Yosemite. They found the experience of wilderness (Yosemite) a bit disheartening—scruffy—not at all the same as the experience of nature (the Black Forest). The distinction between the former—left alone and the latter—exquisitely tended—sets out nicely the problematic distinction between nature as system and nature as invention.

[4] I have written more extensively on these general strategies elsewhere: "On Making More Nature in Landscape Today," in *A Community of Diverse Interests* (Washington D.C.: ACSA Press, 1994): 480–485.

[5] This point is based on informal interviews with visitors during several visits.

[6] Information in this and the following two paragraphs is drawn from K.G. Pontus Hulten, *The Machine* (New York :The Museum of Modern Art, 1968): 20–21.

Stripscape is a dynamic urban proposal for the redevelopment of 7th Avenue, a one-mile commercial corridor in Phoenix, Arizona. In 1968, 7th Avenue was widened by the Arizona Department of Transportation to create a high volume north/south transportation corridor in excess of 60,000 cars per day. Landscape improvements typically located between the street and sidewalk were absorbed by the increased width of the street; as a result the City of Phoenix was unable to make conventional infrastructure "beautification" improvements. This condition, combined with the strip's decay caused by competition with regional malls, power centers, and strip malls called for urban action. In 1997 over sixty merchants along this one-mile commercial corridor formed the 7th Avenue Merchants Association to develop a strategy for revaluing their properties and businesses. Their objectives were three-fold: first, to establish a character for the strip that would be identifiable in the greater metropolitan area; second, to increase business by promoting renovations of existing business and new development; and third, to reduce discursive and undesirable conditions by forming a stronger pedestrian connection with the surrounding neighborhoods.

The project's clients included the 7th Avenue Merchants Association, the City of Phoenix, the Department of Planning and Economic Development, and the surrounding neighborhood organizations. Given the diverse clientele, the project required a combined process of tactical analysis based upon individual merchant improvements, with a strategic plan that the city could deploy at the end of the

Stripscape
Darren Petrucci

research. The project developed an inclusive methodology that critiques both the totalizing view of conventional master planning and the smaller tactical interventions as illustrated in contemporary theories of everyday urbanism.[1]

In order for the strip to be realized in its full potential as a dynamic urban typology, it needs to be examined with unconventional methods. Master plans with their single, fixed vision strangle the strip by limiting both its flexibility and ability to evolve dynamically. Smaller tactical interventions, such as merchant improvements, typically become incidental relative to the whole and can create mountains of paperwork in the form of permits and variances. Therefore, Stripscape employs a new system for urbanization—one that incorporates a "Kit of Ideas" that operate on the whole as a dynamic system encouraging individual improvements that complement those ideas. The Kit of Ideas manifests itself in three methods of intervention: Tactical Evaluation, Amenity Infrastructures, and Emergent Typologies. The combination of these three methods produces "urban aggregates" or localized urban environments that can develop independently and in any order. Each aggregate represents an interconnected whole, typically in the form of a city block. Together they establish a diverse network in the evolution of the strip.

[1] John Chase, et al. *Everyday Urbanism* (New York: Monacelli Press, 1999)

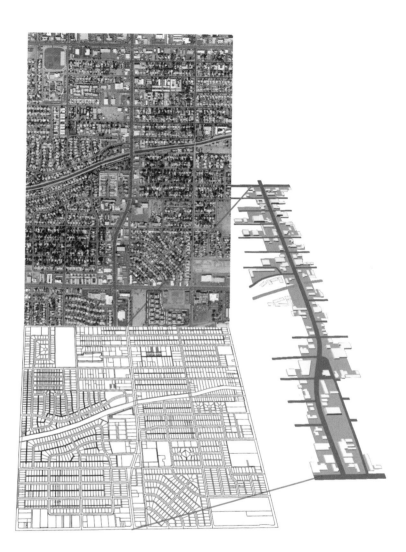

Tactical Evaluation

The point of departure for this project involved creating terminology defined by details of site situations that were recorded through photographs. These photographs were carefully framed to liberate the subject of the photograph from its immediate context; thus, the subject could be interpreted as a condition of the entire site and not just its immediate surroundings. Initial images were categorized into three types of conditions: encouraged, latent, and appropriated (or making do), for example, the "Retail Garage Sale"—a tactic by merchants to turn their store inside out by displaying merchandise on the store's exterior to draw the attention of passing motorists.

A glossary that included both existing and imagined conditions evolved through the design process. The glossary terms were used with the clients to illustrate new design concepts, as well as to promote the renovation of existing conditions. Those images and terms that described emergent typologies were diagrammed as computer models that illustrated their future development potential. The glossary represented a more passive consumptive view of the site. Existing conditions were accepted and exploited for their unique character. Those conditions categorized as "appropriated or making-do" were expanded upon in a more actively productive investigation called "Staged Public Interventions" or SPIs.

Horizontal Advertising

Product Facade

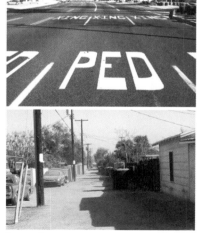

Service Boundary

Retail Garage Sale

"Everyday life invents itself by poaching in countless ways on the property of others." Michel de Certeau

Michel de Certeau's statement begins to define the tactics that illustrate the necessity of the urban dweller to "make do" in a context whose dominant economic order has intentionally not accommodated their programmatic needs and desires. These conditions are, in part, a result of modernist zoning techniques that promoted programmatic segregation, i.e., spaces defined by a particular use (work) without the possibility of other programmatic contamination (leisure). For example, typing personal correspondence at the office represents a discursive situation because of its ability to transform the dominant economic space (work) into one of leisure (personal communication). The transformative quality of "making-do" is a powerful tool in the design evolution of the commercial strip because of its ability to identify those needs and desires that are not fulfilled by the dominant order.

Billboard Theater (staged montage)   Vacant Lot Cell (staged montage)

Service Alley (montage)   Parking Lot Dining (staged)

Amenity Infrastructure

Amenity Infrastructures are public and private programmatic modifications to the existing rights-of-way, alleyways, utility easements, required setbacks along property lines, and retention areas that are perpendicular to the street, thus connecting the sidewalk to the service alley, parking lots, and the neighborhood beyond. They operate as a connective tissue of experiences composed of surfaces and landscapes that are divided into four zones: circulation, commercial, recreational, and art. Art is considered a liminal zone (or threshold) between the commercial and the recreational. This is a more abstract, less legible landscape that promotes heretofore unimagined forms of occupation.

Site

Amenity Whole

Streets Department

Merchant

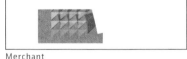

Parks Department

Arts Department

The Amenity Infrastructure is a mosaic of surfaces, landscapes, and experiences that is sponsored by public and private funding sources including the city, the merchants, the arts, and the community. The goal of establishing Amenity Infrastructures is the simultaneous qualitative contribution to the city, the merchants, and the neighborhood. These interventions are deployed by the city and maintained by the merchants. They cater to both work and leisure activities allowing both merchant appropriation (displaying wares) and neighborhood occupation (recreation and leisure activities). Amenity Infrastructures contribute to the site as both pedestrian destinations and connections.

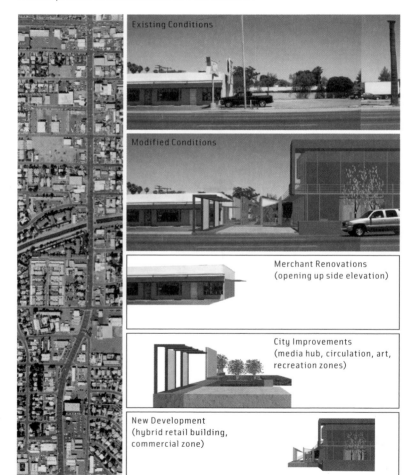

Existing Conditions

Modified Conditions

Merchant Renovations
(opening up side elevation)

City Improvements
(media hub, circulation, art, recreation zones)

New Development
(hybrid retail building, commercial zone)

Emergent Typologies

Catalyzing further development is a major impetus for the Stripscape Project. Modifications in the form of Amenity Infrastructures and individual (experience-based) merchant renovations begin to create both economic and use-value for the strip. Taking their cues from the tactical evaluations produced by the initial research, new emergent building typologies are formed and demonstrated.

The form and material quality of the proposed new building envelopes are determined not by their internal programs but by their zoning, climatic orientation, and relationship to their surrounding context. Passive environmental controls such as thermal chimneys, evaporative pools, and natural daylighting are specifically detailed as environmental infrastructures that service the programmatically indeterminate volumes. Construction materials, massing, and skins of the envelopes are developed in response to the spaces surrounding the building, promoting public/private overlaps between interior and exterior uses. One example of this is the spatial thickening of the boundary between the interior and exterior in the form of a framed volume. This creates a third space between outside and

retail garage sale

inside strengthening the relationship between the two programs and promoting public/private overlaps between interior and exterior uses. Interior volumes are provisionally surfaced (for individual modifications) or are the results of exterior responses. For example, the Garage Sale Retail condition manifests itself as a folded façade for exterior display that doubles as a solar chimney and a vertical circulation core. This hybrid construction allows its interior volume to be accessible, environmentally functional, and programmatically indeterminate.

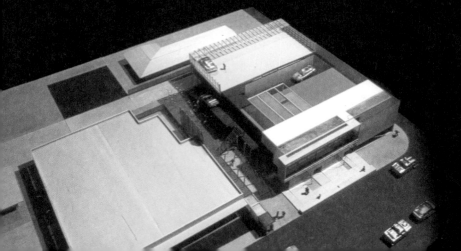

Urban Aggregates

To create an aggregate, each emergent typology is linked to an Amenity Infrastructure within its block and becomes a part of a whole or a localized-urban environment. The combination of Amenity Infrastructure, media hub (see glossary next page), merchant improvements, existing structures, and new development within each block creates an urban aggregate that is not dependent upon the development of the strip as a whole.

This urban strategy promotes incremental growth, rather than a totalizing master plan, and is perpetuated by forces of competition (each block trying to outdo the other). The inherent heterogeneous quality of the strip ensures difference and variety among aggregates. Existing infrastructures such as streets, sidewalks, and service alleys provide a connective network weaving the aggregates together.

Stripscape requires collaboration with a number of forces, the most visible being political, commercial, cultural, and institutional. Unlike large urban redevelopment strategies that begin with broad strokes (typical of urban design methodology) and work down to the details utilizing a master plan that typically results in a tabula rasa followed by instant gentrification, Stripscape proposes an alternative method that uses collaboration to develop its own universal "kit of ideas" through an in-depth exploration of the specific conditions discovered on 7th Avenue.

Throughout the process of identifying the specificities of the strip, a number of new design tools are created: a lexicon of new urban terminology, alternative methods of graphic representation, and presentation techniques that strategically engage each of the stakeholder groups (the city municipality, the merchants association, the neighborhood associations, and the developer) in a process that ultimately revitalizes the role of the designer. This process begins with a tactical evaluation by the designer, working situationally, simultaneously exploring and designing with the intention of developing methods for integration. As the process unfolds, these tactical explorations develop into an ideological strategy that allows the strip to evolve both dynamically and incrementally over time through new infrastructures without forcing a myopic master plan.

Stripscape neither erases nor blurs boundaries. Instead, it thickens them, occupying them with accommodating programs and experiences that create an Amenity Infrastructure that is permeable, while respecting the delimiting role of the boundary. These modified boundaries operate more as connectors than as separators, and promote the creation of urban aggregates—hybrid combinations of culture, commercial, work, and leisure. These localized-urban environments are the building blocks for continued urban revaluation in this generic landscape.

Stripscape is the result of work done by the Arizona State University School of Architecture's Integral Studio led by Assistant Professor Darren Petrucci. The following students assisted on the project in spring 2000: Joby Dutton, Joseph Herzog, Jeff Kershaw, Maria Pijem, Christopher Skow, Robb Smigielski, Matt Winquist, Ko Yu.

aggregate assem

contextural fac

enabling infrastru

leaseable sp

circulation

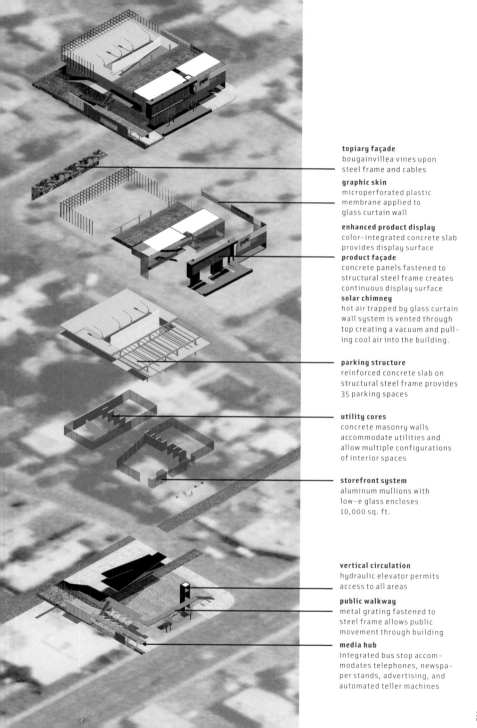

topiary façade
bougainvillea vines upon
steel frame and cables

graphic skin
microperforated plastic
membrane applied to
glass curtain wall

enhanced product display
color-integrated concrete slab
provides display surface
product façade
concrete panels fastened to
structural steel frame creates
continuous display surface
solar chimney
hot air trapped by glass curtain
wall system is vented through
top creating a vacuum and pulling cool air into the building.

parking structure
reinforced concrete slab on
structural steel frame provides
35 parking spaces

utility cores
concrete masonry walls
accommodate utilities and
allow multiple configurations
of interior spaces

storefront system
aluminum mullions with
low-e glass encloses
10,000 sq. ft.

vertical circulation
hydraulic elevator permits
access to all areas

public walkway
metal grating fastened to
steel frame allows public
movement through building

media hub
integrated bus stop accommodates telephones, newspa-
per stands, advertising, and
automated teller machines

The Return
to a Lacustrian City

Alberto Kalach

A Historic Trend to Urbanize

Since the dawn of history there has been a trend toward urban development. By the year 2005, the world will have more inhabitants in cities than in the countryside. It is natural then to question the sustainability of urban life but also to reflect upon the future development of cities and their relationship with nature to reach more harmonious and efficient patterns of habitability.

Urban development is part of economic, social, and political development; a city is the expression of the society that built it. Spatial organization reflects social organization. As the latter undergoes transformations, the city will find new ways to recreate itself as a paradigm of its time. Architects and urban planners shall ultimately bear the burden of harmonizing our spatial needs with available energy sources, ecological and demographic demands. As a city grows it uses more supplies and generates more waste. Since time immemorial cities—in essence large human concentrations—have had to import many of its energy sources, yet large cities have prospered near water. This is the case of Mexico City, originally established on a rich and fertile lacustrian basin. Today, we can hardly imagine the extension of its lakes. Accelerated and unrestricted demographic growth and inadequate water management policies have altered the basin beyond recognition. Although Mexico City's demographic growth rate and that of the country as a whole have decreased in recent years, the population keeps growing exponentially. If growth rates of the early 1990s persist, the capital's population will double by the year 2015, which would be a catastrophe not only at a local but a national level.

The City as an Organic Entity

A city is like an organic tissue that lives, grows, and evolves over time. As a city extends in size it grows in complexity. Like many creatures, a city evolves and develops ever more complex survival mechanisms. A small village requiring a simple social organization can be naturally self-sufficient in input production and waste management. City management needs complex political, social, administrative, legislative, and educational organizations. Intricate supply, sanitation, and functional infrastructure involve equally complex social and work organizations. This trend towards complexity and diversity makes planning for a future city a neuralgic question to guarantee survival. We should trust spontaneous evolution no more. We must learn to direct city growth and development.

Current Problems

Inhabitants of Mexico City know that this was once a great lake. How large was it? What did it look like? Few people have tried to recreate it. Comparing a pre-Hispanic map of the Mexico-Tenochtitlan region with a current aerial photograph is an awe-inspiring exercise. As we perceive the vast extensions occupied by the ancient lakes of Chalco, Xochimilco, Mexico, Texcoco, Xaltocan, and Zumpango, we are overwhelmed with the sensation of having lost paradise. The feeling intensifies when strong winds manage to dissipate dense air pollution, and we discover that we have lost sight of both the lakes and the mountains that surround the valley, which only appear sporadically, almost like a mirage. Resigned, we live in a city with slowly vanishing natural beauty and bounties.

Beyond yearning, this lost paradise guaranteed the subsistence of the population settled in the area. The rupture of the basin's natural balance endangers what it offered originally. Water, a vital resource, presents a dual problem: it is scarce during the spring while heavy floods occur in summer. Each year the city pollutes and drains over 3,000 million cubic meters of water into the Panuco basin. Only ten percent of water drainage (rivers) is used, while thirty percent is imported from other basins at high economic and ecological costs, and the remaining sixty percent is pumped from the aquiferous layer. This is twice as much water as infiltrates back from natural sources, thus causing an alarming sinking of the city, deep fissures in clay formations, and the imminent risk of polluting aquiferous layers. Only seven percent of the total is treated at a primary level for recycling. Our insensibility to the natural cycles of Mexico's lacustrian basin—to local topography, hydrology, and geology—has lured us into an expensive battle against nature, one that is lost before it is begun.

The hydrological retrieval of Mexico's basin would be a reencounter of the city with its geographic and historical origins, and it probably represents the only possibility to guarantee its future. It is also a fundamental step toward the comprehension and profitable use of natural and human resources throughout the country.

A Re-encounter of City and Geography

Marcus Vitruvius, a Roman architect from the first century B.C., wrote one of the most influential treatises of ancient architecture. His precepts on architecture, construction, and city planning were rigorously followed for hundreds of years, and many of them are still extraordinarily valid today. In the *Ten Books on*

Architecture, Vitruvius deals extensively with city planning. The eighth book is dedicated exclusively to water in relation to cities, to water's properties from the source onwards, to water finding methods, and to the conduction and storage of rainwater. Some of these basic notions are explained in elementary geography courses, yet they are so obvious that they have apparently been neglected by architects and engineers at the end of the twentieth century.

The basin of the valley of Mexico was originally enclosed and is now artificially drained. A broad and almost waterproof layer covers the basin's lowest level, and the area has considerable rainfall. We may assume that, except for drainage works, these natural conditions have not varied substantially since the times of the Great Tenochtitlan; so the following questions arise: What have we done to the lakes? Why does Mexico City suffer from lack of water in spring and high floods in summer? This is obviously the result of a mistaken management of the basin's hydrology compounded with a five-hundred-year inertia.

The desiccation of the lakes began in colonial times. Spanish conquerors and settlers never acquired the knowledge—which pre-Hispanic cultures possessed—to maintain a harmonious relation with the lakes, and drainage works were soon begun. The foundation of Mexico City—and of many other colonials towns in New Spain—was completely oblivious to the benefits of geography in the most pragmatic sense. The conquest's significance was literally translated into the actual superimposition of European architectures over native structures. "Ideal" cities and architectures conceived in the old continent originated many cities in Latin America that still suffer today, after a lapse of five centuries, from an initial lack of relationship with their site.

Leon Battista Alberti revived Vitruvius' ideas and he proffers the following advice in the first of his ten books: "Apparently no site is less appropriate for any construction than one that is hidden at the center of a valley; since (precluding such obvious reasons as being out of sight, which shall deprive it of honors, and denying delicious views, which shall bereave it of charm) it will inevitably suffer from ruinous rain torrents and devastating floods." Colonial cities, built by decree, extended their grid over valleys, farmlands, forests, and lakes. Most of Mexico City expanded spontaneously. Centralist policies that are still enforced today nurtured exponentially accelerated growth during the second half of the twentieth century. Five hundred years of floods and drainage works have not sufficed to make us realize the original mistake of a city that is a product of history more than geography.

A comment by colleague Axel Araño shed light on the matter. He notes, "If we were to abandon Mexico City, it would become a great lake again in a few years time. Buildings emerging from the water would become entangled in exuberant vegetation bursting cascade-like from every floor, and millions of birds would inhabit the structures built and abandoned by Man." Geography silently spans a bridge to that remote past and proves that lake formation results from millenary rain cycles that flood the enclosed basin year after year. Topography, geology, and hydrology inevitably determine the formation of lakes. Meanwhile we, the valley's inhabitants, remain blinded by the inertia of a history of drainage and desiccation works: we insist on fighting a costly and hopeless battle against nature.

A facet of the city's history concerns the desiccation of its rivers and lakes. The culminating stage began only thirty years ago with the construction of the deep drainage system. Among many other problems, the accelerated sinking of the city—due to excessive underground water extraction—caused the slope of drainage to revert, flooding the city with sewage. The drainage system guaranteed the final desiccation of the basin, since it lies deeply underground in a subsoil bed that is more stable. As the city sinks further, a system of pumping stations and regulating reservoirs must control the large rain channels that flow into the drainage system.

Before these disproportionate works began, Dr. Nabor Carrillo presented an alternate project in which he proposed the rehydration of the lakes by recycling residual waters and optimizing the use of rainwater. The proposal was more natural, ecological and economical than the construction of the deep drainage system, but it was rejected. Nevertheless, engineer Gerardo Cruickshank managed to rescue over a thousand hectares of former Lake Texcoco, relying on very limited resources and most of his life's work. He thus proved the feasibility and advantages of Carrillo's project. Thirty years later, Mexico City's population has more than doubled since the sixties, and water problems are more acute. We think perhaps this may be the last opportunity to salvage what remains of our natural environment, before an environmental collapse concludes the five-hundred-year history of the modern city.

The Return to a Lacustrian City

The fundamental thesis of this work is based on the simple idea that Mexico City not only was a great lake but potentially is still one. If we accept that the most sound solution for the city's survival is to stop fighting against nature, future urban development should be ruled by an environmental hydrological rescue plan. The plan is roughly divided into four actions that may be applied independently, yet they are all essential to achieve the final objective:

I.   Reduction of consumption: Although Mexico City does not have exaggerated water consumption rates when compared to large cities in North America, these rates could decrease without reducing life quality.
II. Optimal use of rainfall: This water resource must be "harvested" before it becomes polluted, through a system of primary and secondary dams located in peripheral areas of the city.
III. Recycling of residual waters and lake rehydration: Each lake presents different possibilities, yet all contribute to improve the environment.
IV. Rescue of rivers and canals: Once the lakes are rescued and the rainwater collectors concluded, a belt of hydraulic works will restrict urban growth.

Urban Vision for a New Lacustrian City

Urban development will be ruled by the environmental hydrological rescue plan described above. Dam construction for optimal use of water flows from the slopes on the rim of urbanized areas, as well as the rehydration of the lakes, would constitute a physical limit to contain the unchecked growth of the periphery. All future developments would contribute to the final delimitation of the city. The borders of the city would act as definite limits if we conceived them as the most important developments and if they were planned out of common sense and generosity. Once the city's expansion was completed, regeneration would be directed to central areas. I envision a city of the future capable of folding unto itself, of elevating construction density, and of liberating new green areas where necessary. Thus new parks, rivers, canals, and smaller lakes would permeate the urban area, repeating the rescue strategy begun on the periphery.

Lake Texcoco

The hydroecological rescue of Lake Texcoco is a vital project for the recovery of urban and rural areas within the valley of Mexico. The initial proposal by Dr. Nabor Carrillo in the 1960s and its successful partial implementation by engineer

Gerardo Cruickshank have shown the project's feasibility and huge environmental benefits. However, the project has not received the economic, political, and social support it deserves, and it developed in isolation through the effort and tenacity of these visionary men.

The integral planning of an urban and regional project would definitely prompt the rescue of Lake Texcoco. Once this great extension were flooded, treated water would supply water lost through evaporation of the lake, helping to improve substantially the environment of the whole city. Various activities with public and private components would shape the lakeshore, offering a significant increase in public and green areas. Dozens of rural villages on the eastern shore of the lake-to-be would retrieve their former relation with water and their foregone splendor. The pre-Hispanic city of Teotihuacan would be a few kilometers from the shore and would play a new role in the lacustrian city.

The areas of Ecatepec, Ciudad Azteca, Aragon, Nezahualcoyotl, and Chimalhuacan would shape a new urban shore, transforming the most arid and depressed zones of the city into models of development for the new lacustrian city. Almost forty kilometers of shore facing the lake and the volcanoes with generous parks, causeways, and canals, would allow for new urban expansion. Public and private investment projects would seek a harmonious development of society within a natural environment. Islands for ecological reservations, parks, cultural and sports centers, hospitals, universities, schools, stadiums, shops, workshops, industries, housing, and all metropolitan components would develop and be orchestrated around the lake, endowing the city with part of its bygone identity.

A new airport on one of the islands would help propel the lake's rescue project and would become a magnificent gateway to the future lacustrian city. The recovery of this great lake, equivalent to nine percent of the city's urban area, would bring about the following ecological, economic, and social benefits:

1. Ecological Benefits
a)   The return of the Texcoco area to its natural vocation.
b)   The rehydration of the subsoil to avoid fissures in underground clay strata.
c)   An increase in environmental humidity would promote the precipitation of airborne particles and the reduction of ozone liberation.
d)   A generation of breeze during the night and land breeze during the day creating constant air currents that favor the dispersion of atmospheric pollution.

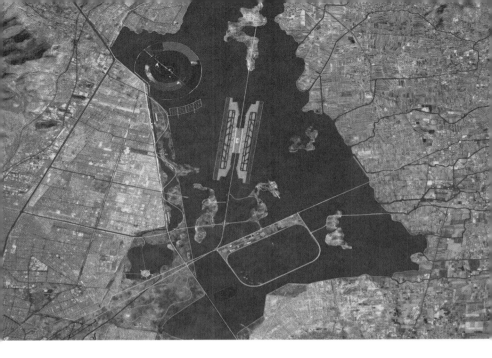

e) A natural oxygenation process produced by the lake with a capacity akin to that of a forest covering an equivalent surface.

f) A natural barrier to check urban growth to the northeast of the valley since that land is not very favorable for urban or agricultural development.

g) A gradual recovery of regional flora and fauna.

2. Economic Benefits

a) The possibility to orchestrate city growth for the next 25 years.

b) The development of shoreline (urban and rural areas) around a large lake, whose dimensions would be approximately three times the Bay of Acapulco, with magnificent views of the volcanoes and the city's skyline.

c) Ecological reservations for recreational use along the shore.

d) Future development between the reservation area and the lake. This land will be destined for uses derived from community and free market demands.

e) Construction of a new airport.

f) The economic reactivation of the construction industry and the real estate market, which will have a national impact.

3. Social Benefits

a) Beyond having a positive impact on the valley's economy and ecology, the rescue of Lake Texcoco would become the project of a city capable of providing its inhabitants with a sense of belonging to the valley.

b) Infrastructure and service improvement in the city's economically most depressed areas.

c) An improved balance between eastern and western areas of the city, giving more relevance to hitherto marginalized areas.

d) A great public space for the city and its citizens.

e) The possibility of a common project that would involve government at various municipal and state levels as well as political and social groups for the sake of a better city.

The city would embark then on a second stage in its return to lacustrian conditions, through the rescue of rivers and the creation of canals and new green areas. These will create a harmonious bond between urban development and nature, between architecture and landscape. Considering the city's constant transformations, built areas that served their lifetime and no longer need to exist will be razed to make way for new parks and architectures resulting from reflections on the future and a keen understanding of each particular site. Architectures will be more in harmony with nature and viewed as part of a global entity.

Summary

A city is an expression of society. It reflects economic, cultural, and political development as an organic entity that is capable of thought and transformation. These are not spontaneous but follow an inner intelligence produced by social organization in addition to the reflections and desires of its inhabitants. The city's historic time-frame is in relation to the basin's millenary cycles, to the work of men and nature, and to problems, mistakes, and learning. There is possibility and urgency in a reencounter between the city and its geography.

An environmental hydrological rescue plan will guarantee the city's survival, but will not exist without an urbanistic vision. In this vision, we see the future lacustrian city. Many of us already live in it.

Translation: Gabriela Lee
Illustrations: Photomontages on an
abstract north-south section running
from the Guadalupe range, showing
the proposed hydrological system.

A Vulnerable Urbanism

Nan Ellin

Grim
is the expression on our faces
Grim
are our cities and landscapes
Grim
are our lives
When soul is purged.

Prometheus was bound to a rock for stealing fire from the gods and giving it to people. Adam and Eve were banished from the Garden of Eden for eating fruit from the Tree of Knowledge. And the Babylonians were forced to speak mutually unintelligible languages and scattered across the earth for attempting to build a tower to heaven and to achieve notoriety. These cautionary tales describe punishments inflicted and suffered for the crime of wanting to know, to explain, to create, and to obtain recognition. As allegories about our desire for control and self-determination, they advocate against rationality and for wonder, awe, mystery, and sanctity. They advocate against hubris and for humility. They serve as reminders to acknowledge and celebrate our human qualities in contrast to the dual temptation to become god-like or machine-like.

This dual temptation is endemic to architects and planners. The last century particularly was dominated by attempts to plan cities and design buildings that would be "machines for living" (*machines à habiter*, Le Corbusier) through the omnipotent application of master planning and zoning and by adhering to Louis Sullivan's tenet of "form follows function."[1] Master planning and modern urbanism failed, however,

"Cool Connectors," Dan Hoffman
with the Integral Studio at ASU.

because they are too inclusive and utopian to be realized fully. And realized only partially, they produce fragments of cities that do not congeal into an urban fabric. In addition, the segregation and rigidity of master planning and modern urbanism run counter to the integration and dynamism of the life lived in them. Widespread dissatisfaction with these efforts has been inspiring alternative approaches that do not forgo technological advances but relinquish nonetheless some of the control that twentieth-century planning and architecture presupposed. Emphasizing process rather than product, relationships (or context) rather than isolated objects, and complementarity rather than opposition, these approaches and the landscapes they generate might be considered a vulnerable urbanism.

From Pretense of Permanence to Permeability (Process)

With the acceleration of change, we can no longer sustain our pretense of permanence. With time more integral to space than ever before, the process becomes as important as the product. In fact, it becomes part of a product that is never completed. As novelist John Barth declared in his ode to minimalist literature *Tidewater Tales*, "The key to the treasure may be the treasure itself" (1986). The journey and the destination become inseparable. As do the means and the ends. Therefore, it can no longer even be a question of the end justifying the means, itself a modernist notion.

This has implications for how we think about design, what we design, the role of clients/users, and how we teach design. Regarding process as paramount, rather than the finished product, a vulnerable urbanism veers away from master planning's focus on inclusivity and control, aiming to master everything including nature.[2] Instead, it proposes more punctual interventions that contribute to activating places through the creation of thresholds or places of intensity.[3] It emphasizes infrastructures and flows as opposed to typologies and formal concerns (Wall 1999).

A vulnerable urbanism allows things to happen, things that may be unforeseen. Gilles Deleuze and Felix Guattari might describe this process as liberating the natural flows of desire (which perpetually seek connections and syntheses) from the repressive and hierarchical modern city (1988). This approach might also be regarded as a form of "urban acupuncture" that liberates chi, or the life force.[4] Applied to existing built environments as well as new development, these interventions may have a tentacular (Wiscombe) or domino effect by catalyzing other transformations. A vulnerable urbanism highlights the role of users since the process of building continues with inhabitation and appropriation. Users become collaborators rather than passive recipients as design becomes more interactive. This emphasis on process rather than product suggests that education for environmental design be context-based and self-reflective rather than object-centered.[5]

From Objects to Context (Relationships)

Connections missed
Connections made
Connections illusive
Longed for and imagined.

Connections lost
Found
Severed
Invented
Disconnected
And secured.

Nothing exists in isolation, only in relation (or context), whether it is a building, a city, or a person. It is only in the ideal realm of mathematics that things may exist in isolation. The twentieth century is characterized, however, by numerous struggles to achieve this ideal. The western notion of the self as autonomous and free-willed, reflected and reinforced by the notion of "ego boundaries" in psychology, has contributed to numbing our empathy with others and with the rest of nature (Spretnak 1977). Countering the alienation aroused by this understanding of self, more recent understandings of self recognize more permeable boundaries between self, others, and the rest of nature. Cultural anthropology has undergone similar transformations from its earlier interpretation of cultures as monolithic and functioning like machines to current views that regard cultures as inextricably intertwined and leading to studies of "multiple subjectivities," "hybrid cultures," and "border cultures."[6] Parallel transformations have been occurring in the sciences over the last several decades. As Arthur Erickson contends, "By ceaselessly bombarding particles of matter to get at the core of things, science has found that, as Einstein inferred, relationship is the only reality" (1980, 23). The concurrent shift in architecture and urban planning has been from the earlier emphasis on objects and the separation of functions to context and programmatic hybridity. In sum, the essentialism and purism characterizing earlier twentieth-century pursuits is being supplanted by an acknowledgment of diversity, complexity, embeddedness, and unpredictability.

In the environmental design fields, this recent shift in attitude must contend with the longstanding privileging of objects and the "ideal" that still predominate our professions, our academic curricula, and our landscape. Just as the modern city separated functions in its quest for machine-like efficiency, so modern practice divided and subdivided over the last century into architecture, planning, landscape architecture, interior design, industrial design, and graphic design, each with its circumscribed responsibilities, professional organizations, journals, and academic departments. Productive collaborations among them have been all too rare and the precious talents and energy wasted over turf skirmishes is a tragedy and embarrassment, going a long way toward explaining the sorry state of our built environment as well as the crises suffered by the design professions.[7]

Our current task, then, becomes that of mending the seams in our disciplines, professions, and urban fabrics that have been torn asunder. Rather than presume an opposition between people and nature, buildings and landscape, and architecture and landscape architecture, a vulnerable urbanism regards these as complementary or contiguous. Rather than generate perfect objects and separate programs and functions, a vulnerable urbanism aims to build relationships. Our attention thus shifts from objects and centers to the border, boundary, edge, periphery, margin, interstices, and in-between space.

In contrast to the modern attempt to eliminate boundaries and the postmodern tendency to ignore or alternatively fortify them, a vulnerable urbanism seeks to generate porous membranes or thresholds. By allowing for diversity (of people, programs, construction technologies, and so on) to thrive, this approach seeks to reintegrate (or integrate anew) without obliterating differences, in fact, preserving and celebrating them. This approach and the landscape it generates reflect the complementary human urges to merge (connect) and to separate (distinction, individuation) with the resultant ongoing tension and dynamism. It recalls Martin Heidegger's contention that "a boundary is not that at which something stops but, as the Greeks recognized, the boundary is that from which something begins its essential unfolding. That is why the concept is of *horismos*, that is, the horizon, the boundary" (1954, 356).

Paralleling the shift from "ego boundaries" in understanding ourselves, this concept of the urban boundary as connector rather than divider, as the place where relationships take place, is variously articulated. As James Corner explains, "rather than separating boundaries, borders are dynamic membranes through which interactions and diverse transformations occur. In ecological terms, the edge is always the most lively and rich place because it is where the occupants and forces of one system meet and interact with those from another" (1999a, 54). Corner's method of "field operations," his alternative to the master plan, provides "ways in which borders (and differences) may be respected and sustained, while potentially productive forces on either side may be brought together into newly created relationships. Thus, we shift from a world of stable geometric boundaries and distinctions to one of multidimensional transference and network effects" (1999a, 54).

According to Linda Pollak, the boundary should be understood "as a space of communication rather than a line of sharp division" (1999, 54). Demonstrating this in her work (e.g., Petrosino Park project for New York City), Pollak bridges layers of "infrastructural relationships," natural layers, transportation infrastructures, and virtual layers. She also points out that projects can operate "at a theoretically unlimited number of scales" if the designer can construct such interdependencies (1999, 51). Pollak maintains: "Conceiving of landscape as layers rather than an unbroken surface supports the construction of an urban landscape as an overlay of scales, that is understood in section as well as plan and in time as well as space. Cutting through multiple layers of urban information supports a project whose formal result is not a stylistic signature, but an intersection of concerns, intensities and modes of inhabitiation." (1999, 51). Alex Wall suggests that the designer's role become that of providing "flexible, multifunctional surfaces," creating connective tissue between city fragments and programs to support the diversity of uses and users over time (1999, 234). In contrast to the distillation implied by modern urbanism, Marc Angélil and Anna Klingmann advocate a "hybrid morphology [that] unfolds a system of relations between different, sometimes contradictory forces, no longer as an absolute but in reference to other structures," in a process that is "unceasingly renegotiated" (1999, 24). [See also Darren Petrucci's project for Seventh Avenue in Phoenix "Stripscape," this volume.]

Not only are the various components of urbanism reintegrated, so are design practices and professions.[8] Rem Koolhaas suggests the term "SCAPE©" to encompass town-scape and land-scape, echoing midcentury sentiments of Hans Scharoun who spoke of "urban-land-scape" comprised of natural forms, built forms, and communities of people (Angélil and Klingmann 1999, 21–22) and Victor Gruen (1955) who called upon architects to design landscape as well as "cityscape" (Wall 1999, 235). While these earlier critiques were lone voices that went largely unheeded, the current one falls upon much more sympathetic ears prepared to challenge distinctions between figure and ground, inside and outside, and center and periphery, as well as between architecture, landscape, and infrastructure.

From Opposition to Synergy (Complementarity)

This movement toward re-envisioning practice as well as product suggests a paradigm shift (or return) away from binary logic and towards the principle of complementarity. Complementarity presumes that light requires darkness and shadows. That there would be no sound or music without silence. No fullness without emptiness. No slowness without velocity. No self without other. No exaltation without lamentation. No inhaling without exhaling. No harvest without cultivation. No pleasure without pain and suffering. No strength without weakness. No ease without difficulty. No health without illness. No life without death.

Complementarity departs from modernist binary logic, because it does not regard the pair as oppositional nor does it seek a synthesis or resolution. Rather, it understands each as not only allowing the other but embracing or embodying the other. Prometheus's punishment of having his liver eaten each day by vultures and healed each night suggests the importance of the darkness for becoming whole or healing, even if the harm will inevitably come again. Adam and Eve's banishment from the Garden allowed for agriculture and childbearing, not to mention the first fashion design. And although the Tower of Babel faltered, it allowed for the diaspora and cultural diversity. While these risks may have opened the door to suffering, they were also acts of heroism that permitted creative opportunities otherwise denied.

The goal of intervention, then, is not to resolve conflict or to produce clearly intelligible landscapes but to generate places of intensity with the lovely tensions they embody. The goal is not to produce cities that are entirely in flow or places that are consistently in flow over time. This is because, as the principle of complementarity maintains, flows require ebbs. From the designer's perspective, these interventions may resist analysis, recalling Isadora Duncan's remark to a reporter: "If I could tell you what it meant, I wouldn't have to dance it." Form follows function once again, but function is defined more holistically now to include emotional, symbolic, and spiritual "functions." As a result, the users' experience may not be merely instrumental but also interesting, surprising, luminous, even sublime.

This approach brings our subjective, transactive, qualitative, and intuitive ways of knowing back to complement the objective, autonomous, quantitative, and rational ways of knowing valued by the modern project. Produced by people for people, these interventions are inspired by the physical context (site) as well as social, historical, and virtual contexts. Accordingly, they may not be developed or represented primarily in plan and section. For example, Dan Hoffman's abstract imagery for Cool Connectors in Phoenix suggests the latent experiential quality that these interventions could activate (chapter frontispiece). In another instance, Paul Lewis, Marc Tsurmaki, and David Lewis's hybrid drawing forms (combining hand drawing with computer rendering) "produce multiple and simultaneous readings not available in typical drawing formats" (12–13).

The shift from the machine and utopia as models to ecological models (webs, networks, thresholds, ecotones, tentacles, and rhizomes) is indicative of this paradigm shift. In contrast to the earlier models that bespoke aspirations for control and perfection, these current models suggest connectedness and dynamism as well as the principle of complementarity. On the ecological threshold, for instance, there is competition and conflict (Corner 1999a, 54) but also synergy and harmony. There is fear but also adventure and excitement. It is not about good or bad, safety or danger, pleasure or pain, winners or losers. All of these occur on the threshold if it is thriving.

In psychology, the notion of the "integrated personality" was applied by Carl Jung to suggest the blending of both light and dark components of personality.

If we suppress our shadows, rather than acknowledge and accept them, they may emerge deviously in other guises such as projection and self-sabotage. The same might apply to the city. Rather than neglect or abandon "in-between" and peripheral spaces ("no-man's lands"), then, we turn our attention toward them, care for and nurture them. In contrast to the modern fear of change, we surrender to it. Rather than ignore or seek to overcome fear, we embrace it. (Perhaps this principle is illustrated by the vaccine that protects us from contracting an illness by introducing it into our system. Or by relaxation, which is best achieved through prior tension.) In contrast to the modern clean-it up, fix-it-up mentality, we accept the dirt, the broken, the imperfect. Such integration of the urban shadow might be described as an "integrated" or "integral" urbanism.[9]

This paradigm shift is not limited to the world of design. Charlene Spretnak explains:

Just as modern scientists discounted and ignored perturbations observed outside of the accepted model, so modern economists ignored the effects of unqualified economic growth on the "fragment" of the whole that is nature. Modern states-manship proceeded by ignoring the sovereignty of native people, a "fragment" that was clearly outside the accepted model, and modern rationalists denied any spiritual perceptions as anomalous quirks not to be mentioned. [Now], however, scientists engaged in chaos research . . . try to absorb into their conclusions everything they observe through their measurements; ecological economists consider the total costs of production, including the depletion of our primary "capital," the biosphere; advocates of a postmodern world order defend the precious diversity of cultures that comprise the planetary whole; and people no longer boxed in by the tight constraints of highly selective modern rationalism now allow themselves subtle perceptions of the grand unity, the ground of the sacred (1997, 19–20).

Conclusion

Listening to the minute differences noticed by my six-year-old daughter Theo-dora between her Star Wars Legos® and the characters from the movie, I remarked that she remembered many more details from the movie than I did. Theodora responded, "Children who found the beauty of being a child when they were a child remember these things. I guess you didn't find the beauty of being a child when you were a child. Or you lost it." Struck by the painful recognition of my innocence lost, I asked, "Is there any way I could get it back?" She thought for a moment and replied, "If you lose the beauty of the child, it's very hard to get it back. You get it by playing a lot. Maybe if you have lots of fun as a grown-up, you can get it back. Once you've got your child back, there's nothing that can stop you from doing anything" (Theodora Ellin Ballew 1/4/00).

Just as the "beauty of the child" (vitality, awareness, and spontaneous joy) can get buried beneath the responsibilities of adulthood, so the vitality of a city—its soul and character—can disappear if squeezed into a rational and overly prescribed master plan. Rather than throw any discipline or planning to the wind, perhaps we might rethink how and when to apply them. Keeping a place's "child" alive, or bringing it back to life, would not mean zero intervention but instead a gentle guidance that is responsive, flexible, playful, and nurturing, permitting self-realization.

A vulnerable urbanism, then, combines system with serendipity.[10] It also combines intellect (spirit) with qualities of soul such as "subtlety, complexity, ripening, worldliness, incompleteness, ambiguity, wonder" (Moore 1992, 247). Psychologist Thomas Moore describes intellect and soul:

The intellect wants a summary meaning . . . but the soul craves depth of reflection, many layers of meaning, nuances without end, references and allusions and prefigurations. (235) The intellect often demands proof that it is on solid ground. The thought of the soul finds its grounding in a different way. It likes persuasion, subtle analysis, an inner logic, and elegance. It enjoys the kind of discussion that is never complete, that ends with a desire for further talk or reading. It is content with uncertainty and wonder. Especially in ethical matters, it probes and questions and continues to reflect even after decisions have been made. (246–47) Soul yearns for attachment, for variety in personality, for intimacy and particularity. So it is these qualities in community that the soul seeks out, and not likemindedness and uniformity. (92) Relatedness is a signal of soul. By allowing the sometimes vulnerable feelings of relatedness, soul pours into life. (94) Truth is not really a soul word; soul is after insight more than truth. Truth is a stopping point asking for commitment and defense. Insight is a fragment of awareness that invites further exploration. Intellect tends to enshrine its truth, while soul hopes that insights will keep coming until some degree of wisdom is achieved. Wisdom is the marriage of intellect's longing for truth and soul's acceptance of the labyrinthine nature of the human condition. (246–47)

In sum, the approaches and products of a vulnerable urbanism emphasize reintegration (functional, social, disciplinary, and professional), porous membranes or permeable boundaries (rather than the modernist attempt to dismantle them or postmodernist fortification), and design with movement in mind, both movement through space (circulation) and through time (access to the past as well as dynamism and flexibility). From attempting to deny or control change, an attitude characterizing most of the twentieth century, we are now witnessing an acceptance or even embracing of change. A vulnerable urbanism is about:

Networks not boundaries
Relationships and connections not isolated objects
Interdependence not independence or dependence
Natural and social communities not just individuals
Transparency or translucency not opacity
Flux or flow not stasis
Permeability not walls
Mobility not permanence
Relinquishing control, not dominating nature
Catalysts, armatures, frameworks, punctuation marks,
Not final products, master plans, or utopias.

We are passing through a rare moment when environmental design theory is not bucking political, economic, and social trends. Many of the qualities described above that designers are embracing are being realized only because concurrent developments fortuitously support them. In other cases, these qualities are being realized without the input of designers at all. The political trends that support a vulnerable urbanism include widespread opposition to urban sprawl, interest in conserving the environment and preserving historic urban fabrics, the rise of regional governments, the renaissance of central cities, the exponential growth of neighborhood associations and community gardens, and the establishment of community land trusts. Our political philosophy of universalism (or abstract rights) has been yielding to a politics of difference or recognition (Charles Taylor, cited by Jencks 1993, 10) whereby decision making depends on context rather than on modernist binary logic. Economic trends include mixed-use development and transformations brought on by the new economy (e-commerce, partnering, and technological convergences). Social trends reflect and coincide with these, expressing a frustration with the fragmented landscapes produced by conventional urban development and a craving for the excitement, spontaneity, and sense of flow characteristic of truly urban places. Some implications of these trends for urban design include the building of transit-oriented developments, the creation of quality public spaces and transit systems, urban infill, and alternative typologies and morphologies that respond to current needs and tastes. In the best-case scenarios, the efficiencies allowed by these trends conserve energy and other resources while decreasing social isolation thereby empowering people to envision and implement their own community designs.

After centuries of technological innovations serving as prosthetic devices that have combated the natural environment while alienating us from it, we have reached a point where technology is corroborating and elaborating upon holistic world views. Computer technology is providing a means of representing the "higher level order" that has long been integral to the divergent world views of Buddhism, Taoism, and the Romantics, as well as to cosmologies proposed by Albert Einstein (quantum mechanics, 1905), Arthur Koestler (the holonic), Alfred North Whitehead, and others. This may itself illustrate the proposition that our universe is self-organizing on ever higher levels. Perhaps we have reached a place where the question of whether to continue or abandon the modern project has become moot.[11] Our hyperrational embrace of computer technologies along with the simultaneous revalorization of process, relationships, and complementarity may be conspiring to eradicate the either/or proposition of continuing or abandoning. We are now doing both simultaneously, each providing feedback for and adjusting the other accordingly, holding potential for achieving integration at another level.

Vulnerability does not denote weakness, indifference, or anarchy. Rather, it bespeaks an openness toward and acceptance of our human qualities along with a certain relinquishing of control, an embracing of our shadows (personal, collective, and urban), and recognizing change as the only constant. For designers, it translates into an enhanced receptivity towards conditions such as site, client, budget, culture, and political considerations. Rather than constraints, these become opportunities and sources of inspiration. The stories of Prometheus, Genesis, and the Tower of Babel all tell about an initiation into complementarity: good and evil, joy and suffering, success and defeat, pride and shame, harmony and conflict, knowledge and ignorance, as well as vulnerability and control. If we truly wish to heal our landscapes and the design professions while improving our quality of life, to forge proactive solutions to contemporary problems, we must not forsake our vulnerability.

References

Marc Angélil and Anna Klingmann, "Hybrid Morphologies: Infrastructure, Architecture, Landscape," *Daidalos* 73 (1999): 16-25.

John Barth, *Tidewater Tales* (New York: Putnam, 1986).

Katherine Benzel, *The Room in Context: Design without Boundaries* (New York: Mc Graw-Hill, 1997).

Ernest L. Boyer and Lee D. Mitgang, *Building Community: A New Future for Architecture and Practice* (The Carnegie Foundation for the Advancement of Teaching, 1996).

Anita Berrizbeitia and Linda Pollak, *Inside/Outside: Between Architecture and Landscape* (Gloucester, Mass.: Rockport, 1999).

James Corner, "Field Operations," in *Architecture of the Borderlands* (New York: John Wiley & Sons, 1999a).

James Corner, ed. *Recovering Landscape* (New York: Princeton Architectural Press, 1999b).

Gilles Deleuze and Felix Guattari, *A Thousand Plateaus: Capitalism and Schizophrenia* (London: Athlone, 1988).

Nan Ellin, *Postmodern Urbanism*, rev. ed. (New York: Princeton Architectural Press, 1999).

Arthur Erickson, "Shaping," in James Hillman, William H. Whyte, and Arthur Erickson, *The City as Dwelling* (Dallas: The Dallas Institute of Humanities and Culture, 1983).

Kenneth Frampton, "Seven Points for the Millenium: An Untimely Manifesto," 1999 UIA Conference in Beijing, *Architectural Reccord* (August 1999): 15.

Martin Heidegger, "Building Dwelling Thinking," in *Basic Writings* (San Francisco: Harper, 1954): 347-363

Charles Jencks, *Heteropolis* (London: Academy Editions, 1993).

Rem Koolhaas, "Pearl River Delta: The City of Exacerbated Difference," in *Politics, Poetics: Documenta X, the book* (Ostlildern: Hatje Cantz Verlag, 1997).

Paul Lewis, Marc Tsurumaki, and David J. Lewis, *Situation Normal. Pamphlet Architecture 21* (New York: Princeton Architectural Press, 1998).

Thomas Moore, *Care of the Soul* (New York: HarperCollins, 1992).

Linda Pollak, "City-Architecture-Landscape: Strategies for Building City Landscape," *Daidalos* 73 (1999): 48-59.

Richard Sennett, "The Powers of the Eye," in *Urban Revisions: Current Projects for the Public Realm* (catalogue compiled by Elizabeth A.T. Smith. Cambridge, Mass: MIT, 1994).

Charlene Spretnak, *Resurgence of the Real: Body, Nature, and Place in a Hypermodern World* (New York: HarperCollins, 1997).

Alex Wall, "Programming the Urban Surface," in *Recovering Landscape* (New York: Princeton Architectural Press, 1999).

Tom Wiscombe, "The Haptic Morphology of Tentacles," in *BorderLine*, edited by Lebbeus Woods and Ekkehard Rehfelds (Vienna; New York: Springer Verlag, 1998).

Notes

[1] There were exceptions such as the work of Aldo Van Eyck, Constantinos Doxiadis, Shadrach Woods, and the Situationists. See for instance, Liane Lefaivre and Alexander Tzonis, Aldo Van Eyck, *Humanist Rebel: Inbetweening in a Postwar World*, Lefaivre and Tzonis; "Beyond Monuments, Beyond Zip-a-ton" in *Le Carré Bleu* no.3-4, 1999: 4–44, Alex Tzonis "Pikionis and the Transvisibility" in *Thresholds* 19, 1999: 15–21.

[2] Earlier rejections of the master plan include Cedric Price's "Non-Plan" (1969) and Christopher Alexander's "pattern language" (1977 and 1987).

[3] The ecological threshold as metaphor for urban interventions has been suggested by Sennett (1994, 69), Berrizbeitia and Pollak, and Corner, among others.

[4] Ignasi de Solà-Morales defined "urban acupuncture" as catalytic small-scale interventions that are realizable within a relatively short period of time and capable of achieving maximum impact on immediate surroundings (Frampton 1999).

[5] There have been earlier versions of this discussion. Paul Klee maintained that art should be experienced as a process of creation, not just a product (1944). Hans Scharoun considered open systems or the "unfinished" essential in designing cities that should be responsive to prevalent tendencies (Angélil and Klingmann, 21–22). Charles Eames' asserted that "Art is not a product. It is a quality" (1977). Millenia prior, Heraclitus contended that reality is ever-changing while Parmenades argued that all change is illusory.

[6] See Ellin 1999, Chapter 8, Nestor Garcia Canclini and Silvia Lopez, "Hybrid Cultures" (1995), Robert J.C. Young, *Colonial Desire: Hybridity in Theory, Culture and Race* (1995). Ruth Behar and Deborah Gordon, eds. *Women Writing Culture* (1995). and Anna Lowenhaupt Tsing, *In the Realm of the Diamond Queen* (1992).

[7] See Ellin 1999 Chapter 7 "Crisis in the Architectural Profession."

[8] This holistic approach has been described as "designing without boundaries" (Benzel 1997). The widely hailed Carnegie Foundation report on architecture education (Mitgang and Boyer, 1996) supports such an approach, calling for more interdisciplinarity as well a greater symbiosis between school curricula and professional practice.

[9] I am currently developing this theme in my book *Integral Urbanism* (forthcoming), which describes four other qualities in addition to vulnerability: hybridity, connectivity, porosity, and authenticity.

[10] This distinction resembles those made by Deleuze and Guattari between "striated" and "smooth" or "molar" and "molecular" lines (1988).

[11] See Ellin 1999, Chapter 6 "The Modern Project: Continued or Abandoned?".

Testing Homes for America
Alessandra Ponte

"A considerable amount of information on the blast response of residential structures of several different kinds was obtained in the studies made at the Nevada Test Site in 1953 and, especially, in 1955. The Nuclear device employed in the test of March 17, 1953, was detonated at the top of a 300-foot tower and the yield was about 16 kilotons. In the test of May 5, 1955, the explosion took place on a 500-foot tower and the yield was close to 29 kilotons. In each case, air pressure measurements made possible a correlation, where it was justified, between the blast damage and the peak overpressure.

The main objective of the tests on residential structures were as follows: (1) to determine the elements most susceptible to blast damage and consequently to devise methods for strengthening structures of various types; (2) to provide information concerning the amount of damage to residences that may be expected as a result of a nuclear explosion and to what extent these structures could be subsequently rendered habitable without major repairs; and (3) to determine how persons remaining in their houses during a nuclear attack may be protected from the effects of blast radiations."

Samuel Gladstone ed., *The Effects of Nuclear Weapons*, prepared by the United States Department of Defense, Published by the United States Atomic Energy Commission, revised edition 1962 (first edition 1957).

Wood-frame house before a nuclear explosion (above)
Wood-frame house after a nuclear explosion (5 psi overpressure) (below)

Unreinforced brick house before a nuclear explosion (above)
Unreinforced brick house after a nuclear explosion (5 psi overpressure) (below)

Ramber–type house before a nuclear explosion (above)
Ramber–type house after a nuclear explosion (5 psi overpressure) (below)

Reinforced precast concrete house before a nuclear explosion (above)

Reinforced precast concrete house after a nuclear explosion (5 psi overpressure). The LP-gas tank, sheltered by the house, is essentially undamaged (below)

Reinforced masonry-block house before a nuclear explosion (above)

Reinforced masonry-block house after a nuclear explosion (5 psi overpressure) (below)

The American Outdoor Theater:

A Voice for the Landscape in the Collaboration of Site and Structure

Linda Jewell

[Fig. 1] Denver's Red Rocks
Theater (1937–41) remains one of
the country's most popular outdoor
venues for musical performance.
Photo by Anton Grassl

*Through the spoken work, the rendition of music,
through song and dance the outdoor theater can
contribute to mental, physical, and spiritual
growth. If it is healthful to exercise, work, play,
and sleep in the open, it should be even more
beneficial to have our finer sensibilities unfolded
in the same favorable atmosphere.*

*Emerson Knight, "Landscape Architect,"
in* Architect and Engineer, *1924*

Contemporary outdoor theaters, like so many of today's public structures, are typically erected by entrepreneurs and institutions who view the landscape as real estate. In fact, today, the primary motivation for building a theater outdoors is that it costs only a fraction of a comparably sized interior theater. As a land-scape architect, I find this attitude deplorable.

During the early decades of the twentieth century, a group of theatrical profes-sionals, naturalists, wealthy patrons, and designers spawned a movement that created outdoor performances as antidotes to the commercialism and technical emphasis of interior theaters. Influenced by Greek artistic and democratic ideals, these drama enthusiasts built outdoor theaters to "contribute to mental, physi-cal, and spiritual growth" of the American public. The only two books written on American outdoor theaters: Outdoor Theaters (1917) by the landscape architect Frank Waugh and The Open-Air Theatre (1918) by theater critic Sheldon Cheney, were published during this period. Significantly, both publications focused less on architectural style and programmatic concerns than they did on the impor-tance of a creating a meaningful landscape experience. This concern for the landscape continued into the early 1940s with the numerous outdoor theaters built by Roosevelt's New Deal programs in federal, state, and local parks.

After World War II, priorities in outdoor theater design shifted to concerns for large seating capacity, audience comfort, commercial concessions, and the accommodation of sound and lighting technology. Although these issues still dominate new theater designs, the public continues to support performances in numerous pre–World War II theaters that lack these amenities. For example, Denver's Red Rocks Theater [fig.1], built between 1937 and 1941, remains a prestigious location for major performers despite its relatively small seating capacity, box office receipts, and less technical support than newer theaters. In fact, Red Rock's spectacular rock formations and dramatic vistas have insured its continued top position in Pollstar magazine's annual survey of "best outdoor concert venue."[1]

The post-war tendency to ignore the landscape has by no means been limited to the building of outdoor theaters; it has dominated the construction of all built environments. While it is easy to blame this situation on the commercial demands of clients and ever increasing code requirements, the influence of modernist architecture also explains the devaluation of the landscape. Elizabeth Meyer discusses the tendency of modern architecture to separate architecture and nature: "When architectural historian Sigfried Giedion writes about 'the juxta-position of nature and human dwelling' as a constituent fact of architecture, he defines architecture and nature in binary terms that are juxtaposed as opposite. Architecture is the positive object and nature is opposed to it, negative."[2]

This binary thinking has identified the landscape as either wild and untouched or a neutral counterpart to the architectural object. For architects, the result has often been to locate and design all buildings, roads, and other structures first and then assign a shapeless, undifferentiated landscape to the "leftover" spaces. On the other hand, many landscape architects joined forces with the environmental movement to create a milieu—as well as legislation—mobilized around what not to do or where not to build. Both positions supported the land developers' view of the landscape as a locational commodity while neither exam-ined the opportunities that landscapes offer. Consequently, the landscape has often been overlooked as a positive contributor to the complicated equation of designing contemporary environments.

My own education, first in architecture and later in landscape architecture, has reflected these separate roles of the two disciplines. As an architecture student, my studio assignments emphasized the creation of architectural objects, usu-ally with little regard for the landscape as anything other than an amorphous background for the sculptural building. Later, studying landscape architecture during the height of the 1970s environmental planning movement, I frequently saw buildings and other structures presented as a menace or disturbance to a pristine landscape that was to be preserved rather than changed.

Yet I continued to be fascinated by designed places where structures and land-scapes were not separate, but parts of a common effort. My view of outdoor the-aters as equally site and structure made them important references for teaching and practice. Although I was intrigued by the classic Greek and Roman theaters, American theaters, especially those constructed by Roosevelt's New Deal, were accessible models. I therefore began collecting images and measurements of these terraced structures.

Eight years ago I began a more comprehensive study of American outdoor the-aters by visiting more than seventy theaters and producing measured drawings and histories of twenty-four theaters as case studies for an exhibition and book. To my delight, I discovered numerous outdoor theaters that became memorable spaces through the interdependency of landscape and architecture.

Although most such theaters were built before World War II, many still host
scheduled performances. Moreover, they attract people for weddings, picnics,
and impromptu events as well as for quiet contemplation of the landscape. So the
question arises: can early outdoor theaters help us design new theaters and other
built environments that reveal the positive attributes of the landscape? I believe
they can if we examine the following strategies that were used to create them.

1 Spend time at the site to understand its changing physical characteristics
Frequently designers are so intrigued with the effects they wish to create with
their proposed new elements they forget to identify and take advantage of the
drama inherent in a site. Landscapes are not a mere background; they are complex
and dynamic. Even the smallest site has distinctive variations. To understand the
nuances of a landscape's natural systems and aesthetic components, a designer
must spend considerable time on the site at different times of day and under
different climatic conditions. The designers of many early theaters, including
the Hollywood Bowl and Red Rocks, had the advantage of seeing performances
on the unimproved sites before permanent facilities were built. They observed
various seating layouts, stage arrangements, and circulation schemes that they

[Fig. 2] At the Mount Tamalpais
Mountain Theater, the stone seats
undulate with the topography to
accommodate native oaks and rock
outcrops. Photo by Anton Grassl

evaluated and adjusted to avoid unnecessary disruption to the site's natural patterns.

Before producing a schematic design for the California's Mountain Theater, landscape architect Emerson Knight saw many performances on the Mount Tamalpais site. He learned its variations in sunlight, breezes, views, and natural acoustics and observed vegetation growth and drainage patterns. Although his scheme was inspired by classical Greek theaters, it warps the traditional semicircular seating plan towards the site's partially filled drainage way, creating an axis around the old ravine. The stone seats, constructed by the Civilian Conservation Corps under Knight's direction, undulate up and down with the topography, accommodating native oaks and protruding rock formations [fig.2].

On the other hand, landscape architect Thomas Sears proposed a regularized circular geometry of stone seats at Swarthmore College's Scott Theater. The bowl-shaped land form, already used for student gatherings, was carefully regraded to

maintain the existing soil around most of the tall tulip poplars that cast dappled sunlight across the site. A few poplars were left protruding from the low walls while several others were removed, but young poplars were planted in random patterns to reestablish the original density and verticality of the grove [fig.3].

2 Accentuate a memorable site feature

Unusual rock formations and topographic configurations, soil or vegetation colors, the sounds of a nearby stream, or a spectacular vista are a designer's tools to make a theater experience more memorable. But respecting a natural feature does not mean the landscape cannot be changed. Landscape manipulation, inherent in the building of any structure, can enhance the original site if the change intensifies the audience's perception of its unusual aspect while still respecting the site's ecological functions. For example, a thirty-foot deep cut of soil adjacent to Red Rock's monumental Creation Rock not only provided a usable platform for seating, but it exposed formerly buried portions of this extraordinary sandstone ledge, reinforcing its role as an enclosing wall for the theater. Yet this grandiose earth movement accommodated the site's natural drainage pattern by collecting run-off in open swales and tilting the entire auditorium floor towards

[Fig. 3] At Scott Theater, new tulip
poplars were planted to supplement
ones saved. Photo by Anton Grassl

its original low point. To emphasize the majestic rock formations rather than the
new construction, architect Burnham Hoyt created a simple sloped plane for the
seating from which the rugged stones ascend. Avoiding the visual clutter of individual seats or the distraction of feeder aisles, this simple surface is articulated
only by a series of long, gently curving backless benches.

*3 Evaluate whether or not architectural features will contrast or merge with the
surrounding landscape*
Structures that blend with the surrounding landscape are easily identified
as respectful of nature, but those with contrasting forms can also respond
appropriately to a site's ecological systems and aesthetic character. Although
followers of the early drama movement were motivated by the desire to
experience nature, they did not have a bias for theaters that merged with
the landscape over those that had forms and colors that contrasted with it. In

From left to right:

[Fig. 4] The intact Theosophical Society Greek Theater (1901), an example of Cheney's "architectural theater" was sited for its view from the theater and relies on its contrasting color and geometry to draw attention to the adjacent ravine. Photograph courtesy of San Diego Historical Society, Photograph Collection

[Fig. 5] By locating Berkeley's semicircular Greek Theater (1903) on a naturally concave site, topographic manipulation was minimized. Photograph courtesy of Bancroft Library

[Fig. 6] The Bohemian Grove Theater (c. 1890), an example of Cheney's "nature theater" treats the performers a part of a redwood covered slope. Photograph reprinted from Cheney, Open Air Theaters, 8. Photograph by Gabriel Moulin.

[Fig. 7] At Los Angeles's intact Anson Ford Theater (1931), the seating was designed to be architecturally distinct from the surrounding landscape while the stage merges into the mountainside. Photograph courtesy of Security Pacific National Bank Photograph Collection/ Los Angeles Public Library

[Fig. 8] The stage and landscape merge into one at the Anson Ford Theater where the mountainside was utilized for stage processions in 1930s Pilgrimage Plays. Photograph courtesy of Security Pacific National Bank Photograph Collection/Los Angeles Public Library

his 1918 book, Sheldon Cheney described both "nature theaters" that visually became a part of the landscape and "architectural theaters" that contrasted with the landscape. Two examples of architectural theaters, the Point Loma, California Theosophical Society Greek Theater [fig.4] and Berkeley's Greek Theater [fig.5], required minimal reconfiguration of the topography because the original concave land forms were specifically selected for the circular shapes of the theaters. Like its classical Greek precedents, the Point Loma theater was sited for its view from the theater rather than the view to the theater. Nevertheless, its contrasting white geometric form draws attention to the adjacent rugged ravine.

The stage of Bohemian Grove Theater [fig.6], illustrated in Cheney's book as an example of a "nature theater," intertwines with a redwood covered hillside to make the structures, performers, and audience a part of the scenery. Similarly, at the Mountain Theater, indigenous stone seats merge into the original topography rather than terminate in the end-walls typical of classical theaters. However, the different elements of some theaters relate to the landscape in different ways. At Los Angeles's Anson Ford Theater, the seating area is architecturally distinct from the surrounding landscape [fig.7] while the stage, once used to depict the descent of Christ from a mountain top in pilgrimage plays [fig.8], disappears into the mountainside.

4 Design a spatial sequence based on the visitor's movements

With rare exceptions, the aesthetic benefits of landscapes can only be understood by moving through them, rather than from a few well-chosen views. Through the subtle manipulation of views, reshaping of topography, modification of vegetation, and the careful introduction of architectural elements, early theaters created sequential experiences that enhanced the rituals of arriving and gathering. They not only moved people gracefully through the theater spaces, but they often engaged the landscape beyond to connect both performers and patrons to a world larger than the one on-stage.

At Boulder's Flagstaff Sunrise Circle [fig.9], Mount Helix Nature Theater east of San Diego [fig.10], Red Rocks, and the Mountain Theater, the distant vistas provide stunning backdrops to events on stage. But at other theaters, including Berkeley's Hearst Theater and Manteo, North Carolina's Waterside Theater [fig.11], distant landscapes can only be seen when entering from the top rows of seating. At Waterside, visitors arrive over a sand dune and then descend into an enclosed "fort" that is a part of the stage set. The elevated arrival point provides a glimpse of water beyond the stage backdrop, making the later appearance of distant sailing ships all the more believable.

[Fig. 9] The Flagstaff Sunrise
Circle (1933–34), built by the Civilian Conservation Corps, captures
a stunning vista. Photograph by
Anton Grassl

[Fig. 10] The Mount Helix Nature
Theater (1924) relies on a spectac-
ular vista as a backdrop to events.
Photograph courtesy of San Diego
Historical Society, Photograph
Collection

[Fig. 11] At Manteo's Waterside
Theater (1937), a distant view of the
water is captured as patrons enter
the theater over a sand dune. Photograph courtesy of North Carolina
Division of Archives and History

5 Modify the parti to accommodate landscape features, including those that are revealed during the construction process

Most historically significant gardens and parks did not take their finished form from a set of construction drawings but evolved over time in response to site conditions. Although the initial designs of many theaters began as a simple symmetrical geometry, these "perfect" forms were modified to address the particulars of the site. Some of these site-determined adjustments were made in drawings, but significant changes were often made during construction when schemes were refined to reflect newly exposed stones, vistas revealed by cleared vegetation, or the reality of accurate tree locations.

Landscape architect Emerson Knight and architect Richard Requa initially proposed a symmetrical, fan-shaped plan for the Mt. Helix Nature Theater atop a mesa with a spectacular view. Their auditorium design was long and narrow to minimize the amount of fill required to counter the conical shape of the mesa. But the design of the upper seating was changed substantially when they discovered that the survey had inaccurately located rock outcroppings, and the construction revealed bedrock just below the surface. Requa visited the site several times a week, overseeing field adjustments to these unexpected conditions. The original design's consistent 1:3 slope was steepened in the upper tiers to avoid bedrock, thus giving the theater's profile a distinctive bend. The central aisles were diverted around rock outcroppings which were made into picturesque box seats. These "distortions" of the original symmetrical proposal highlight the rugged, spiritual character of the site while avoiding any compromise to its usefulness as a theater.

6 Celebrate the unpredictability of landscapes

Outdoor theaters, like all landscapes can be noisy, messy, cold, hot, windy, or buggy. Still, members of an audience often treasure their memories of dramatic clouds, colorful sunsets, or the unexpected appearance of a bird or a plane. Rather than capitalize on these natural spectacles, contemporary theater builders go to considerable effort and expense to transform outdoor sites into the controlled, predictable environments of interior theaters. Bugs are eradicated, walls are built to deflect wind, canopies hide the sky, and sometimes mechanically cooled air is even pumped into the open air. The provision of such amenities often results in the obliteration of vistas, the destruction of native topography, and the removal of significant vegetation and natural drainage ways. Designers of early outdoor theaters never attempted to match the controlled environments of interior theaters. Instead, they allowed the unexpected to be a part of the outdoor experience. At the Mountain Theater, the south facing seats can some-times become quite hot during June performances. But rather than adding a cov-ered canopy, Mountain Play Association volunteers circulate through the seats spraying patrons with cooling water. At San Diego's Starlight Theater, the airport directed flights directly over the 1930s theater. Undeterred, the production com-pany has developed a system of lights that signals performers to "freeze" just before a plane passes overhead. At the nearby New Globe Theater, Shakespeare is often accompanied by a background of animal screeches from the San Diego Zoo. At other theaters, patrons watch fireflies, listen to crickets, and accept cooling summer showers as a part of being outdoors.

7 Evaluate the impact of minor programmatic requests on the landscape
Influenced by television sound bites, computer generated images and cinematic special effects, audiences today expect every entertainment event to provide an audiovisual spectacle as well as the comfort of their own living room. Although the contemporary audience's desires cannot be ignored, the designer can make clear to clients the potential impact of each decision on the health and aesthet-ics of the landscape. The color of seating, the type of lighting, or the placement of equipment structures can either enhance or destabilize the fragile aesthetics and natural patterns of a landscape. In nearly half of the theater case studies I examined, the thoughtless additions of canopies, lighting structures, service parking, accessible ramps, and other "updating" have compromised the original serenity of the older theater landscapes. Although many of these improvements were necessary for the theater to function successfully today, they have been added without regard to their impact on drainage, vegetation, views, or other amenities. Even at Red Rocks, the necessity of providing a canopy to protect valuable musical instruments from rain and sun was met with a strictly functional solution—a clumsily proportioned metal roof that cuts unceremoniously across the view of Stage Rock [fig.1].

Summary

Modernism's 50-year legacy of separating architecture and the landscape still haunts much of contemporary design. A resurgent interest in the landscape by writers, theorists, and historians has created an encouraging trend for artists and architects to look to the landscape for conceptual inspiration when proposing innovative structures. But most such projects respond to the landscape symbolically rather than to a site's particular aesthetic attributes or its biological functions. On the other hand, landscape architects still struggle with finding ways to creatively intervene in a landscape without compromising their ecological commitment. Consequently, there are few projects designed by either discipline that respond to the particulars of a landscape while also creating a memorable place.

These early outdoor theaters are evidence of a time when landscapes and architecture routinely worked together to create inspirational settings that reflected the specifics of a site. However, landscapes with the spectacular natural features of Red Rocks are seldom available today, and it is a mistake to base contemporary designs on these theaters. Designers can, however, use the strategies listed above to make the landscape's voice more effective in any new project, whether it is located in a national park, an urban center, or a derelict brownfield.

The landscape is more than a place to put buildings; it is where intimate contact with earth, sky, and vegetation remind us of our own connection to nature. Each landscape has positive attributes; if we build projects that both respect and enhance these attributes, we shall foster public and entrepreneurial support for a landscape that contributes more to our daily lives than its value as real estate.

The tree which moves some to tears of joy is in the eyes of others only a green thing that stands in the way.[3] William Blake

The above essay is an excerpt from a forthcoming book on American Outdoor Theaters. Partial funding for the exhibition and book was provided by the National Endowment for the Arts, The Graham Foundation, the Hubbard Fund and by the University of California Committee on Research and the Department of Landscape Architecture's Farrand Fund.

Notes

[1] "1990 Concert Industry Award Winners," *Pollstar, The Concert Hotwire* (February 4, 1991): 2.

[2] Elizabeth K. Meyer, "The Expanded Field of Landscape Architecture," in *Ecological Design and Planning,* ed. George F. Thompson and Frederick R. Steiner (New York: John Wiley & Sons, Inc., 1997): 45–79.

[3] Blake to Dr. John Trusler, Lambeth, 23 August 1799, *The Letters of William Blake,* ed. Geoffrey Keynes (London: Rupert Hart-Davis, 1968): 29–30. This quote was used on a T-shirt designed by the Berkeley student ASLA chapter in 1996. The T-shirt designers were participants in a joint architecture/landscape architecture studio.

References

"1990 Concert Industry Award Winners," *Pollstar, The Concert Hotwire* (February 4,1991):2.

William Blake, "Letter to Dr. John Trusler. Lambeth, 23 August 1799," in *The Letters of William Blake,* edited by Geoffrey Keynes (London: Rupert Hart-Davis, 1968): 29-30.

Sheldon Cheney, *The Open Air Theater* (New York: M. Kennerly, 1918).

Emerson Knight, "The Mountain Theater on Mt. Tamalpais," *Landscape Architecture Quarterly* 40, no. 1 (October 1949): 5–9.

– – – – . "Outdoor Theaters and Stadiums in the West," *The Architect and Engineer* 78, no. 2 (August 1924): 53–91.

– – – – . "The Mount Helix Nature Theater," in *A Book of Memories for the Ages* (Dedication Publication, 1925).

Elizabeth K. Meyer, "The Expanded Field of Landscape Architecture," in *Ecological Design and Planning,* edited by George F. Thompson and Frederick R. Steiner (New York: John Wiley & Sons, Inc., 1997): 45–79.

Richard Requa, "My Greatest Opportunity," in *A Book of Memories for the Ages* (Dedication Publication, 1925).

Frank Waugh, *Outdoor Theaters* (Boston: R.G. Badger, 1917).

The Magic of a Place Discovered

Will Bruder

The integral kinship of architecture and landscape is at the center of the finest architectural works of our time. This random sampling of commentaries on modern architectural icons from my travels is presented to communicate the significance of this union, albeit as an exemplary manifestation of the creative human instinct. In this essay, I will examine the magic of places I have discovered, generating an architecture of the landscape. These projects not only convey the palpable fascination with specific landscapes, but they also demonstrate a rare ability to skillfully reinterpret notions of residential imagery. These houses are eclectic yet resonant reminders of the fluidity of the modernist impulse—as a simple confluence of site and structure, technology and beauty.

Any discussion of the quintessentially modern American house inevitably must reference the Kaufmann residence in Mill Run, Pennsylvania, better known as Fallingwater, the touchstone in Frank Lloyd Wright's oeuvre. The significance of this building, relative to this essay, remains its graceful opposition to the European modernist notion of a house as a "machine for living"—set on the land rather than embedded within the landscape. Unlike some of his peers, Wright not only understood the fundamental relationship between utility and form, structure and tectonics, but also the importance of integrating architecture into the natural landscape to great dramatic and humanistic effect. His genius lay in his radical reinterpretation of material and structural possibility, skillfully oriented to compliment and amplify natural site features, logical paths of approach, and careful insertions into the topography of every site. His became a modernism not as mere repetitious standard module, but as a startling tour de force of surprise and delight. In the instance of Fallingwater, built between 1934–37, Wright proposed a daring, syncopated rhythm of horizontal planes. He simultaneously realized intimate interior spaces finely tuned to senses of touch and sight while establishing one of the most dramatic sculptural images of human occupation integral to the landscape conceived in the twentieth century. In his use of the stream as the conceptual and visual anchor of this house, Wright underscores an innate humanism that enables his passion for landscape to empower the architectural idea.

In his own summer cottage, built in a forested site on a lake in central Finland, Alvar Aalto makes architecture and site one in a most casual manner. Meant to be approached from two directions, by either land or water, the home, built between 1952–54, sits both gently on the site—using natural rocks and logs as a foundation system for the frame elements with no reshaping of contours—and grows from it with strength as the brick walls of the building's outdoor room seem to effortlessly extrude up out of the rock, again with no site disturbance. Finding the small, informal forest paths that lead to the house, make the experience of the architecture sculptural as well as unassuming, vernacular and humble. With the formality of the square "solar" courtyard open south to the lake view and sky, and its highly textured unpainted brick and tile interior walls, this experimental house blurs all normal expectations of architectural and landscape space. Aalto's lifelong understanding of natural place is masterfully evidenced in this modest study from which we can all learn important lessons of how to create buildings and landscapes whose unified wholeness is greater than its parts.

The Bavinger residence of 1950 in Norman, Oklahoma, by the American architect Bruce Goff, took the idea of organic site integration to new levels of meaning. Located at the northern edge of a rural stone quarry, the south-facing, wildly original helical plan of the scheme virtually coils out of the site. The main flagstone floor of the house, built for a painter and his family, takes the form of a landscape terrace bathed in the warm winter sun, and the private living spaces float above this interior landscape, suspended lightly from the roof. In keeping with the owner's desire of living in a garden, the stone walls and floors are perforated with planters and the landscape stone effortlessly moves between

the interior and exterior spaces. The cleaning of the floor and the watering of the garden occurs quite simply with a hose. The fanciful form, unique use of glass, cullet and stone cobbles, and spiderweb-like structure, demonstrate Goff's concern for creating an architecture of total oneness with the landscape

and inspire us to think creatively as we address a new site.

The Villa Ottolenghi, a later house by Carlo Scarpa built in 1974, gives us a built reality of his life-long concern for the organic integration of landscape and architecture. An architect of the Veneto region of Italy, Scarpa was a man of history, a Venetian, and a man of his place and time. He was as well an architect with a great knowledge and respect of the work of Frank Lloyd Wright. In the case of this commission, the combination of all of his experiences and interests and a unique set of bureaucratic site restraints, resulted in a masterful landscape intervention.

With a rural site overlooking Lake Garda near Bardolino, Italy, and adjacent to the local tennis club, the community imposed a restriction on the house, preventing any visual access into the privacy of the club from any buildings on his client's site. With the challenging grade changes of the site's slope, Scarpa proposed a radical conceptual idea, resulting in one of the finest houses of the late twentieth century. Upon arrival to the home on a simple dirt road, one is greeted by a front gate with doorbell and the ambiguous view, not of a house but of a mysterious, faceted brick piazza floating almost as a ruin with the vista of the lake beyond, magically abstracting the experience. A lushly enhanced natural landscape is beautifully cleared open beyond the gate as one descends into a twisting concrete canyon—a subterranean, vine-covered pathway, open to the sky. With a concrete retaining wall holding back the site on one side, the house forms the opposite edge of the path. Filled with daylight, this metaphoric geologic event choreographs all one's senses as the experience finally penetrates the architecture into a sunlit meadow space filled with plants, a reflecting pool, and a simple sod staircase to the front door. The variety of the landscape textures remains entirely complimentary to the variegated surfaces and details of the architecture. This important work speaks to our time and the ages as we think about the meaning of the timeless. It shows how a building conceived of the landscape can easily blur all perceptions of the real and the surreal.

Moving to the desert I have called home for the past three decades, I am drawn to comment on two very important but very different examples of landscape-driven architecture. First, the gardens, courtyards, and buildings of Paolo Soleri's Cosanti studios in Paradise Valley, Arizona, created between 1954–74. Having been a student of Wright, this Italian visionary created a unique sequence of small houses, studios, and gardens, approximately six feet below the level of the desert, with significant—real and perceptual—thermal reduction in the heat of the natural desert floor.

Beginning with the creation of a ceramics and drafting studio adjacent to an existing house and then the construction of the "Earth House" in 1958, the compound grew loosely about a central axis. With the Earth House, having a concrete roof cast over the earth as its formwork and then excavated (a technique now common for the construction of freeway bridges) out to two adjacent sunken courtyards—north and south—a new prototype of architecture and landscape for desert living was posited. A simple earth-covered structure of minimal visual presence, the idea of a house at one with the land has never been more resonant.

On a mountaintop outside of Sedona, Arizona, Paul Schweikher designed a very different variation of a marriage between architecture and landscape. This second-generation modernist from the midwest, Schweikher designed the residence in 1970 for his wife and himself. This house, Schweikher's last, became in a way, my graduate school experience to my art. From my first visit to the home upon its completion, I visited the Schweikhers for almost two decades until the unfortunate demise of the house. Set literally on top of a rocky mountain overlooking the red rock of Oak Creek Canyon, the home was a contemporary temple, a beautifully proportioned and simple homage to the Japanese living pavilion. With the site barely altered, a flat datum was established and a cleft carved to create the auto/arrival court, setting the house and garage at the eastern end of the composition. Exercising an astute economy, the auto court was used only by the owners with guest parking at the adjacent road's end. Carefully raked red gravel covered the ramped path of the driveway, framed by the rock of the mountain to the left and the massive dry stone walls on the right. At the arrival court, a hard turn north moved one onto a floating wood deck, through a boulder gridded field, to a breezeway-covered vertical passage. With a series of ninety-degree twists and turns from wood deck to modest pedestal, one moved through this outdoor passage of more than eight feet of vertical change under the structure's massive roof with a constant awareness of the site and its spectacular vistas. Arriving at the datum of the living level, one was drawn not to the door, but to the landscape as the axis of entry and its simple wood deck projected ahead to apparent infinity. At the end of this procession, a lean wood gazebo, an apparent remnant of the main roof of the house, hovered with its shadow—the perfect specter to view and understand the site and the setting. Finally, after a pause to contemplate the day, the rocks, the wildflowers, and the architecture, the barely enclosed, totally transcendent interior experience was made accessible. As an original invention of stark elegance, this house was one

of my most important lessons in the weaving of architecture and landscape. A quiet masterpiece, it redefined my world.

In starting my own practice, my earliest commissions all revolved around a series of backyard gardens, landscape, and shade structures. Not surprisingly therefore, the Rothermel Pavilion, in 1975, was conceived to complete a garden. A work/play program found this leftover corner of a tract house cul-de-sac lot as its site. Carefully crafted of circles, concrete, glass, water, and landscape, the little building strives to disappear in the oasis. A mere three feet to the two property lines, the finished floor is three feet below natural grade, the concrete roof is covered with earth and plants, and the entry sequence through the large glazed walls allows you to walk on water. This strong architectural idea is completely intertwined in the beauty and power of the landscape.

With this as an early evidence of my concerns with site and architecture, all of my work, large or small, has continued this evolution. The project in a rural desert setting for the Cox residence in 1988 carefully created a shelf for a rusticated masonry and glass structure, from which its occupants could view the flora and fauna of the surroundings. On its eastern end, a circular, sunken east walled courtyard, redefines one's perception of the sky.

The overlooked urban-suburban site of the Hill/ Sheppard residence in Phoenix revolves around a simple and subtle checkerboard of outdoor courtyards and gardens in opposition to the interior living zones. Tied together by an inside-outside three-story staircase of stone, wood, and industrial steel grating on the northern edge of the property, the arrival sequence from the street directs one through a gate into a "canyon" of masonry, metal, and sky. This space reveals the cool energy of a spring-fed seep leading to a glowing lush garden enclosed by bright yellow walls and richly textured groundscape. Outdoor living zones focused on the east and west of the living room reveal a walled swim garden with the Squaw Peak view, and a more intimate but dynamic garden with the shear rock face of the site thrusting up to the sky. A quiet north-edge garden and a small rooftop courtyard,

minimally framed in yellow walls, allows for a quiet contemplation of the entire place—a house of strength deferring to the landscape.

More recently, the Byrne residence in north Scottsdale reflects my continued interest and pursuit of an architecture at one with the landscape and nature— physically and visually. This scheme, growing on a desert ridge, choreographs a sequence of movements that celebrate and reveal the topographic contouring of the site. Arrival by automobile is down a sculpted concrete plain to a walled courtyard, which prevents any view of the vista. Entering parallel to the contour, the sloped and leaning concrete masonry walls convey an impression of a natural geologic shift, at once dynamic and unsettling. Moving through this skylit zone, one is constantly drawn to views of the undisturbed site and distant vistas. To the east, a master bedroom deck is defined by perforated metal scrim to filter the view and imply privacy and limit, and to the west a low masonry wall reaches out into the desert to establish an abstract boundary of habitation. Again, I have sought to create an architectural event in union with the landscape.

While my architecture assumes its place within its age, it seeks a union with illustrious predecessors and maintains a responsibility for the evolution of a creative design approach to the character of a site. My buildings seek to embody a fundamental human engagement with landscape, inserting themselves into the land with a unique sense of materiality, transparency, and form. I choose to participate in the task of reading a site and translating its nuances. My archi- tecture celebrates the perpetual wonder of habitation, the cerebral journey of human imagination, and the enormous responsibility of living beautifully and carefully upon the land.

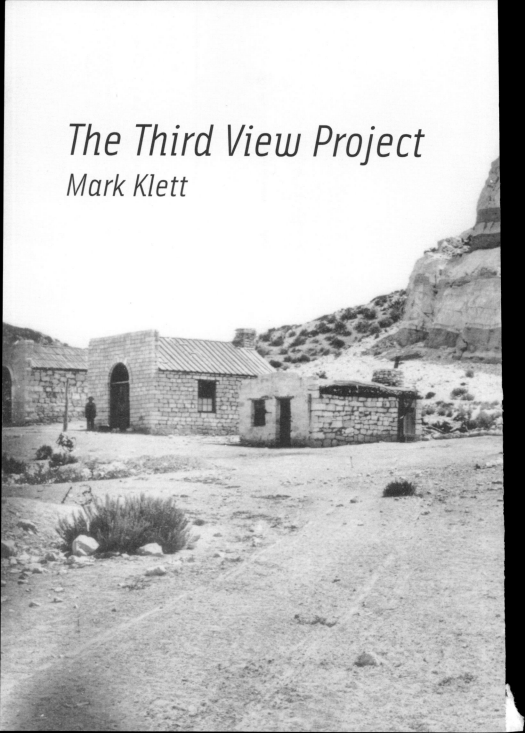

The Third View Project

Mark Klett

The Third View Project was formed in 1997 to create the documents needed to gain perspectives on time and change in the American West. Third View rephotographs historic landscape views from the 1860s and 1870s and then makes new photographs, video, sound recordings, and collects other information about the land, its people, and their stories. The resulting work is combined in a multimedia format linking the past to the present.

Seeing change at work presents a difficult, interdisciplinary problem for the visual artist. The premise of Third View is that without a way of comparing visions of the land over time, knowledge of the past is easily lost, outlook on the present is hard to form, and future objectives remain unclear. The project accepts the idea that photography is the best medium for visualizing changing landforms. When made properly, photographs allow us to see through time. Photographs become the common connection between past and present needed to understand dynamic processes, and the images themselves become both documents and artifacts, useful in understanding history and forecasting trends.

The project draws upon the impressive heritage of photographs that make the American West unique among landscapes. Initial groundwork for Third View was laid by the Rephotographic Survey Project (RSP) between 1977–79. The RSP first rephotographed the nineteenth-century geological survey photographs taken by William Henry Jackson, Timothy O'Sullivan, William Bell, and others from the exact same vantage points and at the same time of day and year. The Third View field team was formed from an interest in revisiting the sites of the RSP photographs after twenty years. Some of the questions that guide this new effort are: Is there more change in the last twenty years than in the first one hundred? Can three points be used to project a future view? Do changes in technology mean we must see or visualize the West differently from the past? What other kinds of information can be collected now that could not have been considered twenty years ago? If we tell new stories about the West, will that change our interaction with the land?

Conceptually, the Third View team attempts to move away from older models of landscape photography based on single photographers searching for beautiful images of pristine wilderness or manifest cultural abuses of the land. The project redefines the practice of contemporary landscape photography with a new and interdisciplinary approach to the medium. The team combines perspectives from fine art photography, history, literature, and the natural and social sciences.

The focus of the project's fieldwork is in collecting a wide range of materials about landscape locations and the many stories associated with the changes in the land. Third View is an updated version of the traditional western geographical survey. Rather than exploring unknown territory, the field team re-explores the once open spaces of the West as it has become home to millions of inhabitants.

The project's methodology has several components. Beginning with the nineteenth-century photographs and those from the RSP, Third View relocates the vantage points and adds new photographs to continue the series. Sound files and oral history interviews are recorded with people connected to sites. Other made-for-computer visual recordings place scenes in a contemporary context. In addition, artifacts (contemporary and not of antique or archaeological value) are collected at significant locations. Later, the many components gathered in the field are edited and combined into interactive presentations.

As of July 1999, eighty-eight sites have been revisited by the Third View field team, and of these approximately twelve are new and not first revisited by the RSP project. The types of changes encountered range from natural catastrophic episodes and large-scale human interventions to subtle erosional shifts in terrain and variations in plant cover.

As example illustrations, two contrasting scenes are offered: Salt Lake City, Utah, and Logan, Nevada. Originally this material was presented as a multimedia presentation combining photography, sound, and video. Only the rephotographs are shown here, but the results should illustrate the connections between past and the present.

Salt Lake City was first photographed in 1867 by Timothy O'Sullivan for Clarence King's Survey West of the One Hundredth Meridian. The original image shows what was then called "Camp Douglas" to the north and east of the present day city center. Small structures dot the distant planes and lead the viewer to the edge of the Wasatch Mountains. When revisited in 1978 for the Rephotographic Survey Project, rephotographer Gordon Bushaw found he was standing near the edge of urban growth. The exact location of the O'Sullivan vantage point was difficult to pinpoint due to changes in the drainages and the lack of clear foreground information in the original. But the site was determined to be located just north of the state capitol building on a grassy hillside, which at that time had remained undeveloped. The second view at this location shows the city growth moving toward the camera. The houses in the middle ground are at the edge of the drainages and

a slope, which to that time presented the boundary of urban growth.

Revisiting the site again in 1997, the Third View team found that the earlier boundary was under transition. Using the second view as the guide to finding the site, the foreground of the new view shows a mound of dirt on the right hand side and on the left, the front end of road building machinery. The site had become part of a housing project called Dorchester Pointe, a gated community which had only recently broken ground.

Ironically, a National Public Radio Talk of the Nation broadcast on the date we visited this site, August 1, 1997, carried a story on housing developments like the one now unfolding before O'Sullivan's view. The audio track includes the following quote: "Gates are going up all across America, some old neighborhoods are closing themselves in, and many new subdivisions are walled-off from the traffic, and they hope, the crime of the world at large. More than three-million houses are already behind closed gates."

While the third view was being made of this site, the project team met a man who had purchased a neighboring lot and was awaiting construction of his own home. An interview was recorded and is included with the site photos made at this location: "Yeah, we started looking for a lot . . . and found out there just weren't many left. And then we found out they were opening this up, so all these lots sold in the first few weeks. It's hard to find property; it's going really fast." Looking at the photographs one might assume with some justification that the next view will be the front façade of a house.

The example of Salt Lake City should meet with the expectations of most observers of the contemporary western scene. Any place located near an urban center visited by Third View will show similar patterns. At the turn of a new century the West is experiencing perhaps its greatest period of population growth. The photograph made by O'Sullivan over one hundred and thirty years ago seems the disconnected product of an age known now only in a shared mythology; a period, which due to dynamic change, is becoming more and more difficult to imagine. For those connected with life in Salt Lake City it is difficult to believe that this period of rapid growth will ever end and even harder yet to conceive that it would reverse itself.

The second, but I think related site, should offer an alternate perspective on the West of the late twentieth century. Several hours north of Las Vegas on a dirt road in early July 1998, the project team found the site of a budding western

town once labeled in a picture caption "Logan City." At the site of the O'Sullivan photograph the buildings had disappeared, and only a few more contemporary, and abandoned, structures remained. The following is excerpted from Bill Fox's field notes of the journey:

We have no idea why Logan is here, although we surmise mining as the logical reason. A small town with no pits, tunnels, quarries, or industrial machinery discernible in the immediate vicinity, it remains a mystery that the stone structure only compounds. Looking as if it sits in the same site as the building nearest O'Sullivan in his photo, [the new house] also appears if the stones were taken apart and reconfigured. Inside the ceiling is taking a slow entropic dive onto a floor of decaying shag carpet squares of mixed colors .

The abandoned house became a focus point for the Third View team. There were other small dwellings at Logan, also abandoned. Yet the reason why these houses were constructed in such a remote location, and for whom, was a mystery. The collected artifacts provide some clues, and from them we determined it was a Mormon family who occupied the large house. Evidence indicated that the last occupation was sometime in the early 1970s. The real mystery of Logan is in its dual abandonment, exoduses that span almost exactly one hundred years. We don't know why the inhabitants of the original Logan chose to build in this location, what they did, or why they disappeared. The occupants of the later era, in one case inhabiting a dwelling made from the ruins of the earlier time, once again left a ghost town.

In fact, the fate of Logan runs contrary to the conventional belief that development and progress are paired in an unbroken continuum of successful settlement. It's an example contrary to that of Salt Lake City, but unlike the former not altogether a unique occurrence in the changing western scene. Could it be that the fate of other western locations will follow the lead of Logan rather than that of Salt Lake? Will Salt Lake City itself one day also see a reversal of growth? The photographs can only raise the questions, but the realization that ghost towns are not just figments of the distant past, indicates how much the present is connected to the past, implying questions about the future.

References
Mark Klett, Ellen Manchester, and JoAnn Verburg, *Second View: The Rephotographic Survey Project* (Albuquerque: University of New Mexico Press, 1984).

Environment Shifted

Götz Stöckmann
and Achim Wollscheid

sound

noise noise noise noise noise noise noise noise noise noise noise noise noise noise noise noise

Living Room is the name given to a new house in the medieval center of Gelnhausen, near Frankfurt, designed by architects, artists, and a poet. The project unites art, architecture, and landscape but not in the sense of a self-contained total artwork. The art created here is integral to the house but also autonomous. It encompasses different mediums: painting, installation, photography, poetry, sculpture, light, and noise.

Götz Stöckmann—together with his work partner Gabriela Seifert—has initiated the idea of the Living Room House. They have designed the house and landscaped its rocky interior. The house negates the usual distinction between inside and outside, public and private. Roof and wall, interior and exterior—all are covered with the same smooth, unifying material. A rigorous grid of windows punctures the building shell. Passersby can look inside and see what they would normally expect to find outside: the landscape. The private spaces, a sleeping cell and a deck, are suspended five meters above the "landscape" in a box.

Achim Wollscheid is working in the Living Room House with noise: the right, front, and left walls of the building each contain an integrated transformation system, which consists of two microphones, a sound-computer, and two loudspeakers. Environmental noise is recorded, transformed via programmed composition—preset and emitted in real time. A control unit in the house enables the degree and direction of the transformation to be adjusted: from soft to strong, from inside to outside, or from outside to inside.

Götz Stöckmann interviewed by Achim Wollscheid

<u>Achim</u>: *Götz, how do you see the term landscape?*
<u>Götz</u>: The word landscape is most appropriate when talking about the genesis of our planetary environment. I prefer a singular definition of the word landscape: an absolute, a continuity. The exploitational, the rural, the pastoral, the garden-esque, the urban are temporary installations into its context: intermezzi.

My interest in landscape is earthy, rocky, green. I am in love with humans' interventions read as conscious attempts of separation and differentiation in all forms of expression, which artists, designers, farmers, architects, or other exploiters of landscape perform. I do not care for any kind of moral that sees landscape as something that needs healing as soon as we dare to work it. I see landscape as the always superior entity to be used with a sane amount of common sense and respect.

<u>Achim</u>: *Götz, can you name some of those interventions, perhaps in the architectural field, which picture your view?*
<u>Götz</u>: Fallingwater by Frank Lloyd Wright and the Landhaus by Mies van der Rohe. They stand for the modern architectural relation toward the natural. They celebrate the issue of horizontality—horizontality as the major expression of its setting into the natural environment. Seen that way, they are occupational, in a sublime, almost mythological way.

Fallingwater, built upon a creek—could a building merge more dramatically with the most essential element—water? The waters flow, the building is static. The extreme cantilevers reach out. The cantilevers seem to pause before flowing from rest of the building at any time, almost an oscillation between building and nature. If the waters stopped, would the building move?

Mies' Landhaus shares the open plan of Fallingwater. Its horizontality is indicated less symbolically but more rationally, more radically: the environment *(to page 284)*

Achim Wollscheid interviewed by Götz Stöckmann

<u>Götz</u>: I guess your interest in landscape as an exclusive issue is limited. Nevertheless I'd interpret your work as related, because the models you deal with can be applied to such topics as environment, ecology, and so on.

<u>Achim</u>: *My reservation toward the term landscape stems from the fact that the state of culturation here in central Europe is the domination of the urbanist paradigm. Landscape cannot serve an alternative blueprint or as counterprinciple to the conceptual might of this domination; it is comparable to the minimal success of establishing the concept of nature as a recoding principle during the Romanticism period at the beginning of the nineteenth century. Even*

if our view is directed to landscape as embracing contradicting phenomena like cities, infrastructure, and nature, the predominant apparatus is governed by an architecture of concepts that were developed along with the development of reason—which runs parallel to the technological reason that inflicted and still inflicts our thinking and perception. So I have some doubts whether terms can be developed to deal with the subject. Reading the respective recent literature on landscape, the different examples to illustrate the term serve as a base to grasp and discuss complexity—centerless agglomerations in which a multitude of organizing principles interact on changing levels. I find ceasing to focus on entities like individuals or buildings and proceeding to interdependent forms like groups or conglomerates very challenging. For artistic work this means to swoop from the symbolic (which in dualist opposition of the one thing denoting the other, remains in the realm of "entities") to the transitory—meaning to conceive the artwork as one of several elements in a context that actively influence each other. The artwork thus becomes a function that enables the recoding of context rather than just another version of the pars pro toto.

(to page 285)

literally flows through its structure. The plan is open to all sides; walls gather within the landscape. Space is rather a densification than enclosure. Both of these houses engage the immediate location and address the peripheral terrain horizontality, making connection to the adjacent. No verticality, no connection to the godly, no cosmic dust.

Achim: Götz, besides architecture, can you think of artifacts that relate to landscape even more directly?

Götz: When land art is set in the wilderness, art can radically act as quasi-universal, removed from human possession, handed over to the forces of the environment. If you think of Michel Heizer's Double Negative or Christo's Isolated Mass, there is the aspect of (non) materializing by simply manipulating the given. The biological material itself is employed as the very substance of the art piece—sand, soil, grass—natural material restructured as the messenger of an artifact, the brittleness of the pieces, the strangeness of their scale, their lostness yet environmental presence.

But neither art nor architecture has changed humans' relation to the environment as drastically as the new media. Besides the known biological environment and the geometric environment new media have introduced a third category: the virtual environment. This virtual environment forces us to make our perception of the natural (and geometric) relative to our idea of time and reality. Its potential omnipresence dissolves the conflict of natural distance and time. I refer to a banality but doesn't the visual presence of the most distant, the most removed, the most dangerous biological environment dilute our sometimes respectful attitude toward landscape? If you are zapping the TV, any type of landscape becomes available. Did you read this, Achim?

"Crazy Nature: Ver-rückte Natur." An article in the FAZ, (9/19/99, no. 21/2: 11) reads: [Zürich] One hour earlier as planned and with minor injuries only four alpinists have completed their two days tour of the Eigernordwand, which was televised live (continuously without interruptions, author). They were welcomed
(to page 286)

<u>Götz</u>: Could you describe your method to think about and produce artworks as processes of amalgamation and rediscovery, and what is the actual result you want to achieve?

<u>Achim</u>: *My artistic measures could be titled "deviations through abstraction." Usually the nervous system and the connected "reasoning apparatus" is understood as a means to adopt and process environmental information. The multiplicity and complexity of such information and the given limits of our time-based means to understand and store it could well describe this system as a rather complex set of filters that actually prevents us from perceiving and processing most of the environmental heterodoxies. According to this reversed view, I would describe most of our human activities, including the use of symbols, as a trial and error method to reinclude abstracted "information" into our environment. The process could be imagined as a "recording" of a certain selection of environmental stimuli (or information), an ordering process both on the vertical (between "subconscious" and "conscious") and the horizontal level (somehow language/time-based), and according to exterior*

stimuli a likewise selected "implanting" of actions and/or symbolic utterances.

Needless to say that these processes will run in synchronicity most of the time and that the underlying differentiation between a so-called individual and his/her environment is an idealized one. Moreover does the term "information" not refer to the common interpretation of "sense" or certain concepts of "transport." It rather describes a formal measure, the sheer fact of something being differentiated from a multiplicity of other things.

I read any artistic activity as a paraphrase of such "abstraction" processes, following the model of a filtering (selection of matter and method), ordering (ranging from "pictures" to programmed structures), and output (selected "implanting" or distribution)—the difference to the individual perception process lies in both the fine-tuning of the selection and the extended time frame given for each of the steps or levels. I regard an artwork not as an object but as a stimulus for the transformation of activities including perception and reception and the specific (to page 287) by a Swiss camera team at the peak. The mountain guide Evelyne Binsack and her Swiss colleagues Hansruedi Gertsch and Stephan Sigrist and the mountain guide Ralf Dujmovits from the German Black Wood Forest started their tour on Thursday, in order to climb the most dangerous 1800m wall of the Alps. The alpinists carried helmet mounted cameras, mics, and five kilogram transmitters in their rucksacks, such that every sound and movement of the climbers got broadcasted.

Achim, if we come to believe that humankind has crossed over all deserts, peered into all forests, walked through the great savannahs, dived into all seas, stormed every peak, our illusions are not misled and such conquests grow together like a total experiment for us all. Any space now gets scanned by our sense organs. By the way, where has Armstrong been? On the moon or in our living rooms?

Landscape transforms from the very natural, from the distant wilderness toward something available, right in front of us—our living rooms. Landscape as an virtual image has almost paradoxically established itself as an available source material to picture our (western) possessive relation to this matter.

Achim: So here the rock moves in?

Götz: The solidity of the rock did build up our confidence, how to actually negotiate the paradox of landscape into the living room. Now, as we build the Living Room house its ground floor plane is missing. There is gravel, egg-shaped

rubble, flats, basalt columns, boulders—kind of a dry riverbed governed by a 42-tonner, quarried around Trier: Udelfanger Sandstone. Dense, no soft layers anywhere, solid, tough, yellow. Some superficial insertions, small shellfish. Life and shallow tiny wave traces on recently opened flanks. He was sand before standing still and solid stone before being liquidized. Ever sedimented before, 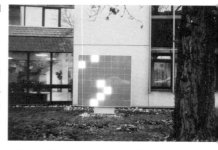 now extracted to 10/18 feet, four-feet-thick, cubical. Most even across the top. Not made for our living room. Quarried, lorried, and layed into it. As a ground condition. Horizontality. Around and above this the house—a shelter, an osmotic membrane. Verticality.

Our original initiative—the inverted landscape, landscape as an interior—for a long time never positively transforming our idea of turning the natural into an

(to page 288)

social rules that guide or channel behavior. Because (contemporary) artworks only exist in communication with social background—the emphasis in my case is on the calibration of the artistic abstraction (or transformation) process with common chronology—creates feedback loops. The source for the artistic "material" is the given data of this environment that are, in most cases, selected and processed in real time, meaning in synchronicity with the sonic or visual events that they are taken from and which they at the same time accompany. Thus I hope to achieve an "unfolding" or enrichment of reality, an unveiling of the fact that reality is not just a set of facts but a combination of possibilities.

Götz: While you tend to describe your work in quite abstract terms, the practical results very often develop a strong sensual impact. How do you agree and get along with such a paradox?

Achim: I don't see it as a paradox. I have my difficulties with the common prejudice that sensual results (or results causing empathy or sympathy) can only be achieved through sensual or "spontaneous" measures. On the contrary (as we have to deal with a world of growing complexity), I find that careful and analytical reflection can produce a base on which artistic action can flourish. Of course, the use and function of language has always to be seen in connection with the specific features of the subject matter: if (like in my case) artistic work includes a good deal of collaboration with coworkers based on technical procedures, I have to care for a certain clarity of my methods, and this again I try to reach through a reflection on terms and their use.

Götz: In regard to the Kuhgasse-house, how would you describe the scope of your artistic intervention, including the points mentioned above and their possible connection to the term "landscape," affirmatively or controversially?

Achim: Put simply, I refrain from differentiating between an "inside" and an "outside," be it the case of your house or texts or so-called systems. Of course (to page 289) artifact, not quite an impossibility (the mountain and the pyramid or Double Negative). The dominant green, the powerful vegetative, the smallness of the location, the concretion, made all our such structured concepts and design attempts look picturesque. Slowly we felt suspicious of our idea, frustrated, trapped by romanticism. We wanted to do away with the distinction between the natural and the illustrative versus the abstract. We wanted to exclude nature as the instance of morality. Neither were we interested in the traditional gardening, horticulture, the oriental oasis, the perspective to the horizon, the natural flow.

We found the outdoors as artistically workable as the indoors and at that very moment we banned almost every form of growth, life, and liquidity from the living room's interior. We choose the most static representation: stone. Gravity. This natural material for buildings, for the arts. Now the limitations of dealing with landscape within the house were liberated from counteractive properties. All of a sudden, the question of the relation between the natural and geometrical environment lost its interdependency: the natural insertion could act equally within the architecture and the art works, the natural sharing the free assembly, or the conglomerate, as you call it, Achim. The whole thing, a rigorously man-made environment.

The discipline, content, and chosen medium of the artworks in the Living Room House derive from the artist's own sensibilities as a collection of individual positions. The artworks have no overriding  content. They have only the place and the house in common—the parallel circumstances of their conception. So does the rock. It just delivers the context of its compositional assembly, positioning it into the new location. Sand and shells sedimented create a fulminant ground floor to live on.

Perhaps this combination of rock, lyrics, painting, sculpture, architecture, prose, traces of the old house, sound, and light will create a work with its own context. An open station for different artistic, architectural, poetic, and landscape positions. Everything is oriented indoors as well as outdoors but not in a representative way. The whole thing stands for itself and awaits response.

there is "surface" and "structure" and like terms that help us define one position in respect to another (and/or others). Still, I see the most rewarding possibilities to both the development of new terminologies and a new grammar of building (and, of course, artistic work) in overcoming centralist models of seeing or perceiving.

In the case of the Kuhgasse-house, your partial reversion of the interior/exterior scheme suggests measures that emphasize the resulting openness. The decision to "open" the walls of the house through electronic "filters" largely depends on the notion that a border or a separation set up by a wall is superficial; even in commonly built structures there is a permanent exchange that crosses these borders. Of course the openness created through my intervention is by no means a thorough one; on the contrary, it's an openness reached through limitation. The real-time sound-transformation taking place scans the sound-profiles, selects according to a preprogrammed structure, transforms (this can happen as accompaniment via sine-wave sound but can also take shape in complex alterations), and emits. The degree of abstraction imposed by the system changes due to programmed presets and the choice of the "inhabitant." Of course the system can also be switched off; it works like a stereo, although I'd prefer it to appear more like an acoustic background. The openness is not just a sonic one (the ubiquitous diffusion of sound) but spatial: the source, meaning the person or happening creating the sound and its transformation, can be perceived within a situational unit. Sometimes this can appear as a superimposition (a car passing generating some sort of melody), sometimes as a subtraction (a bird's song vanishing in a polyphonic veil), still these alterations happen in a (visually, situationally) perceivable space, which I hesitate to call "unit."

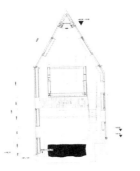

sound   noise   sound

M. Christine Boyer is Professor of Architectural Theory and History at Princeton University. She is the author of several books including *City of Collective Memory: Its Historical Imagery and Architectural Entertainments*.

Will Bruder is an architect in Phoenix, Arizona. His work is internationally published. He has been a visiting critic at numerous schools of architecture including Massachusetts Institute of Technology, Washington University, and Arizona State University.

Nan Ellin is an Associate Professor at Arizona State University. She has also taught at University of Cincinnati, SCI-ARC, and New York University. She holds a Phd from Columbia University an is the author of *Postmodern Urbanism* and editor of *Architectures of Fear*.

David Heymann is an architect in Austin, Texas and Associate Professor at University of Texas, Austin. He is a graduate of Cooper Union and Harvard University. He has written numerous essays on the landscape, urbanism, and architecture.

Coy Howard is an architect in Los Angeles. He has taught and lectured extensively at many institutions in the United States including Southern California Institute of Architecture, California College of Art and Architecture, and University of California, Los Angeles.

Linda Jewell is a landscape architect and Professor of Landscape Architecture at University of California, Berkeley. She holds degrees from North Carolina State University and University of Pennsylvania. She is currently writing a book on the American outdoor theatre.

Alberto Kalach is an architect in Mexico City. He has exhibited and lectured extensively and has been a visiting critic at several institutions in the United States, including Harvard University. His architectural work has been widely published.

Mark Klett is a photographer and Associate Professor of Photography at Arizona State University in Tempe, Arizona. He has published several books on his work,

Martha LaGess is a Professor at University of Texas, Arlington. She has taught for several years at the Architectural Association, London, and is in architectural practice with Michael MacNamara in London.

Bruce Lindsey is Associate Professor of Architecture at Carnegie Melon University, where he is the director of the beginning design program. He has a design practice that includes furniture, architecture, and urban projects.

Robert Mangurian is a principle of Studio Works along with Mary-Ann Ray. He teaches at the Southern California Institute of Architecture and holds degrees from Stanford University and University of California, Berkeley.

Laurel McSherry is Associate Professor in the School of Landscape Architecture and Planning at Arizona State University. Her writings focus on issues of memory and reading of the cultural landscape. She is a recipient of the Rome Prize 1999-2000 for landscape architecture.

Charles Menefee is Associate Professor of Architecture at University of Virginia. He is a principal in the practice of Clark and Menefee in Charleston, South Carolina. Their work has received recognition for its sensitivity to place and attention to detail.

Darren Petrucci is an Assistant Professor at Arizona State University. He holds degrees in architecture and urbanism from Harvard University, and is the founder and principle in A-I-R, (Architecture, Infrastructure, Research).

Alessandra Ponte has taught architectural history and theory at Princeton University and Cornell University. She has written extensively on topics of the American landscape including "The American Desert: Genre, Gender, and Myth."

Albert Pope is an architect in Houston, Texas. He is the author of *Ladders* and is Wortham Professor at the Rice University School of Architecture. He holds degrees from the SCI-ARC and Princeton University.

Mary-Ann Ray is a principal of Studio Works in Los Angeles along with Robert Mangurian. She holds degrees from the University of Washington and Princeton University, and currently teaches at the SCI-ARC. She is the author of *Seven Partly Underground Rooms* and *Buildings for Water, Ice, and Midgets*.

Michael Rotondi is the principle of RoTo Architects in Los Angeles. His work is widely published and exhibited internationally. For over a decade he was the director of SCI-ARC and is now Professor at Arizona State University.

Peter Smithson (1923-2003) with his wife and partner Alison Smithson (1928-1993) practiced architecture for over 60 years. Together they authored numerous books on architecture and urbanism including, *Heroic Period of Modern Architecture, Ordinariness and Light: Urban Theories 1952-1960 and Without Rhetoric; an Architectural Aesthetic 1955-1972.*

Catherine Spellman is an Associate Professor at Arizona State University. She holds degrees from Rice University and University of California, Los Angeles. From 1992-1994 she was Assistant to Enric Miralles at the Städelschule, Frankfurt and taught with Peter Cook at the Bartlett, University College London. She has a practice in Phoenix.

Götz Stöckmann is a principle of Seifert-Stöckmann Architekten, in Frankfurt. Together with Gabriela Seifert and Ottmar Hörl he founded the art/architecture group Formalhaut. He has been Assistant to Peter Cook at the Städelschule für Bildende Kunst, and is currently teaching at the AA in London.

Peter Waldman is an architect in Charlottesville, Virginia and a Professor of Architecture at University of Virginia. He has also taught at Rice University and Princeton University. His work is widely published in the United States and abroad. He is a recipient of the Rome Prize in 1999-2000.

Achim Wollscheid is an artist, writer, and teacher living in Frankfurt. He has created both recorded and installation work since the early 1980s. His work in sound has led him to an interest in the relation between sound, light, and architectural space.

My special thanks go to the late Enric Miralles (1955-2000) who set me off in the direction of this book, my colleagues at Arizona State University who encouraged and supported the project, in particular, Nan Ellin, Mary Kihl, Ron McCoy, Laurel McSherry, Scott Murff, Darren Petrucci, and Fredrick Steiner, my savior Julie Russ who took on the tedious job of copy-editor, the family at ACTAR, especially Albert Ferré who started this ball rolling, my life-long friends Kathy Basil and Kurt Eggert who are always behind me in spirit, and of course, Michael Groves who makes everything possible.

Catherine Spellman, ed.

Re-envisioning Landscape/Architecture

Editor
Catherine Spellman

Published by
Actar   .
with the support of the Herberger Center for Design Excellence,
the Schools of Architecture and Planning and Landscape Architecture
at Arizona State University
and the Graham Foundation for Advanced Studies in the Fine Arts

Copy-Editor
Julie Russ

Graphic Design
David Lorente

Production
Actar Pro

Printing
Ingoprint S.A.

Distribution
Actar
Roca i Batlle, 2
08023 Barcelona
Tel. +34 93 418 77 59
Fax +34 93 417 67 07
info@actar-mail.com
www.actar.es

ISBN 84-95273-99-3
DL: B-41471-2003

Cover photograph by Michael Groves

Printed and bound in the European Union

Barcelona, 2003